£5.95

Contents

* S = silver; G = gold; P = platinum; ( ) = the line must be played but cannot be assessed for a Medal.

Song for Guy

Elton John
arr. Alan Haughton

8 beat ♩ = c.100

INTRO

gold 1 piano

silver 2 flute

C G B♭ F C G B♭ F FILL C F C FILL B♭ Dm G E F E♭ G7 C STOP

Music by Elton John

Boho Blues

Sarah Walker

Swing waltz ♩ = c.112 (♪♪ = ♩♪ triplet)

INTRO Am Em Am Dm

gold 1 — flute

(gold) 2 — '60s organ

6 E7 Am F Em

11 D B♭ Am G F

16 E7 FILL Am Em Am

21 Dm E7 Am F

26 Em D B♭ Am STOP

I Predict a Riot

Kaiser Chiefs
arr. Anthony Marks

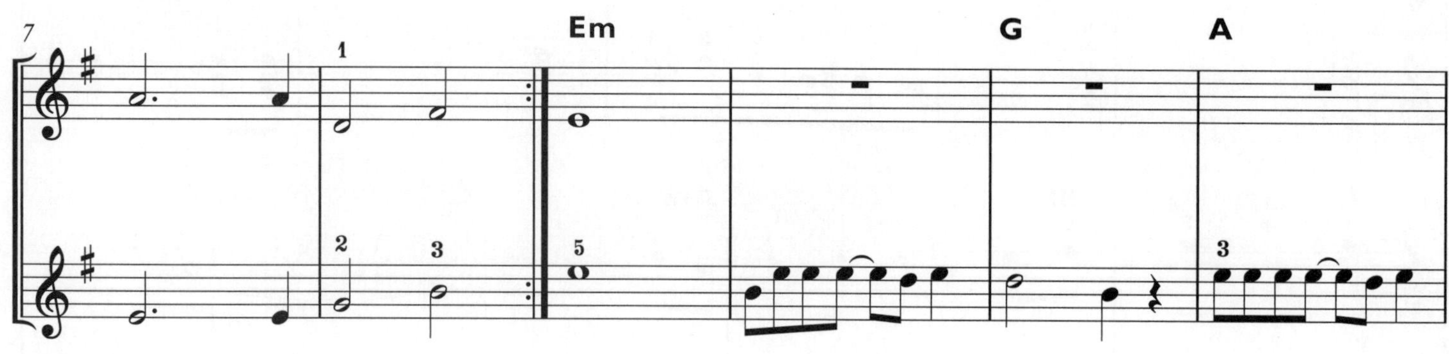

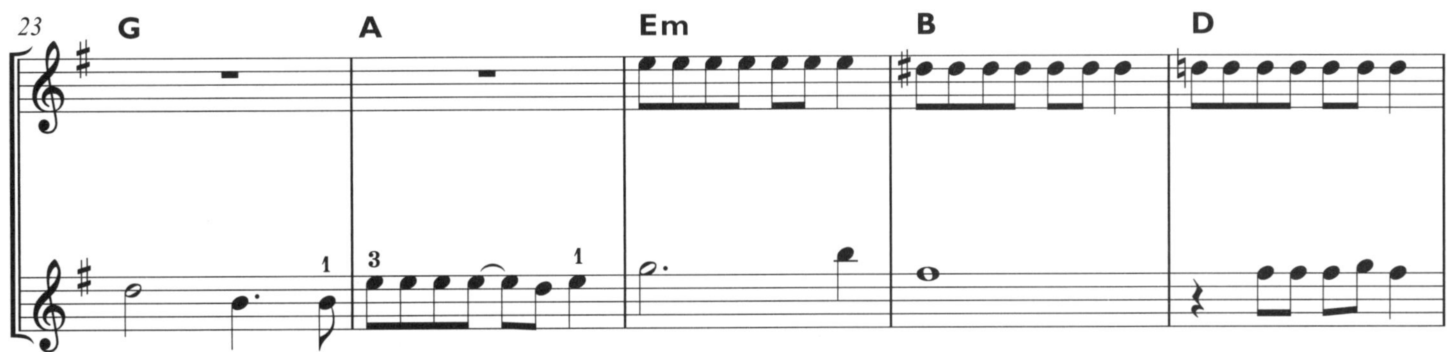
23
G
A
Em
B
D
3
1
1

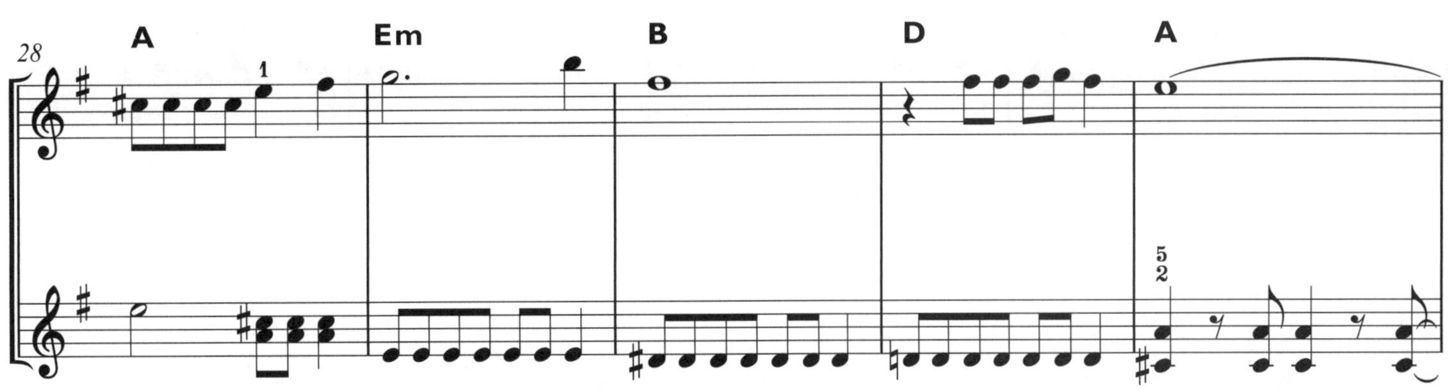
28
A
Em
B
D
A
1
5
2

33
C
F
C
5
1
5
1

38
C
F
C
Em
STOP

Don't Stop Movin'

Simon Ellis, Sheppard Solomon & S Club 7
arr. Tom Horton

Club dance style ♩ = c.120

RHYTHM ONLY

FILL

gold 1 — synth lead

(gold) 2 — strings

5 Gm7 Gm

9 Cm7 Gm FILL D7

13 Gm Gm7

17 Cm Cm7 Gm FILL

N.C. = no chord; rhythm only.

I'm Beginning to See the Light

Duke Ellington, Don George, Johnny Hodges & Harry James
arr. Alan Haughton

Big band ♩ = c.100

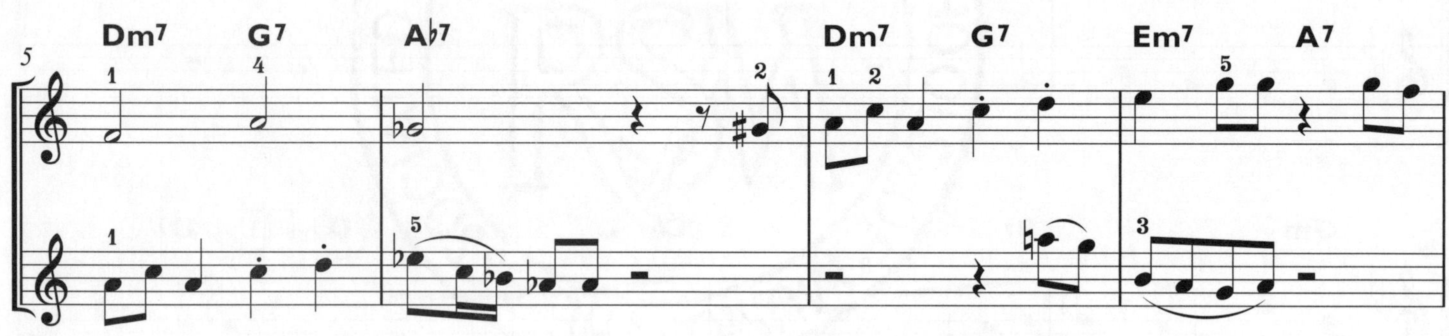

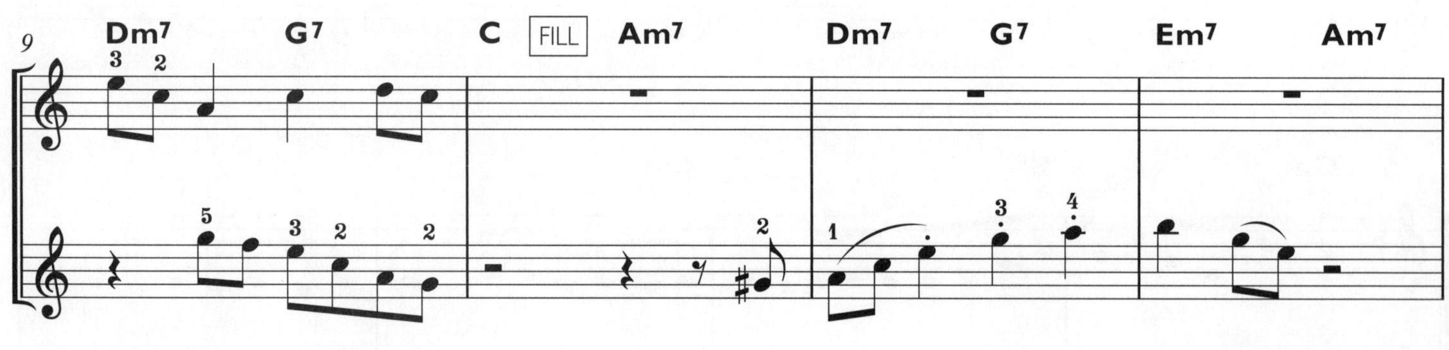

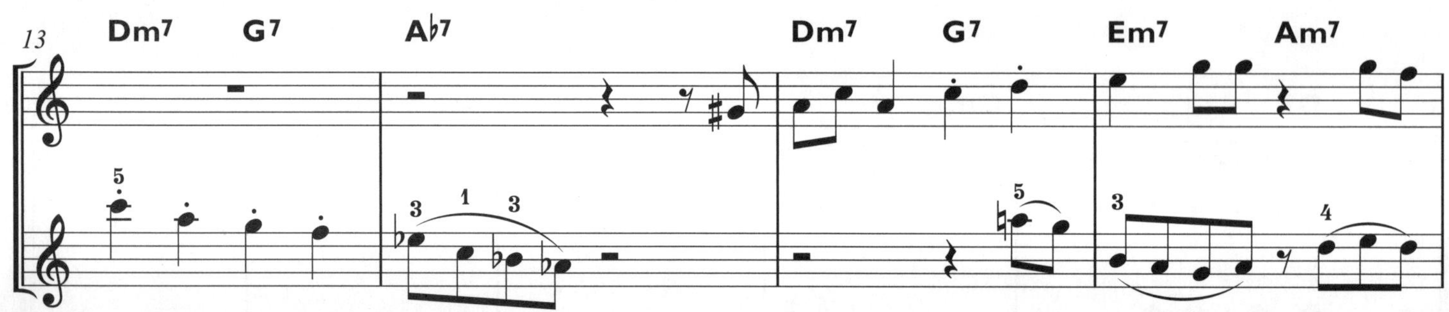

17
Dm7
G7
C
FILL
E
F♯m
E
E♭
Fm
flute
clarinet

22
E♭
D
Em
D
E♭
A♭7

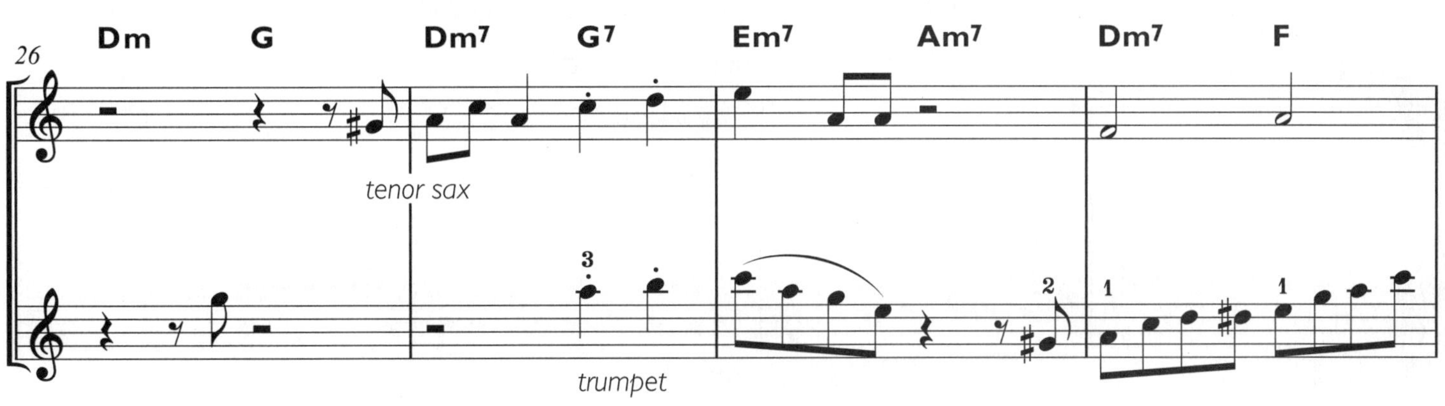
26
Dm
G
Dm7
G7
Em7
Am7
Dm7
F
tenor sax
trumpet

30
A♭7
Dm7
G7
Em7
Am7
Dm7
G7
C
FILL
ENDING

Out and About

Mike Cornick

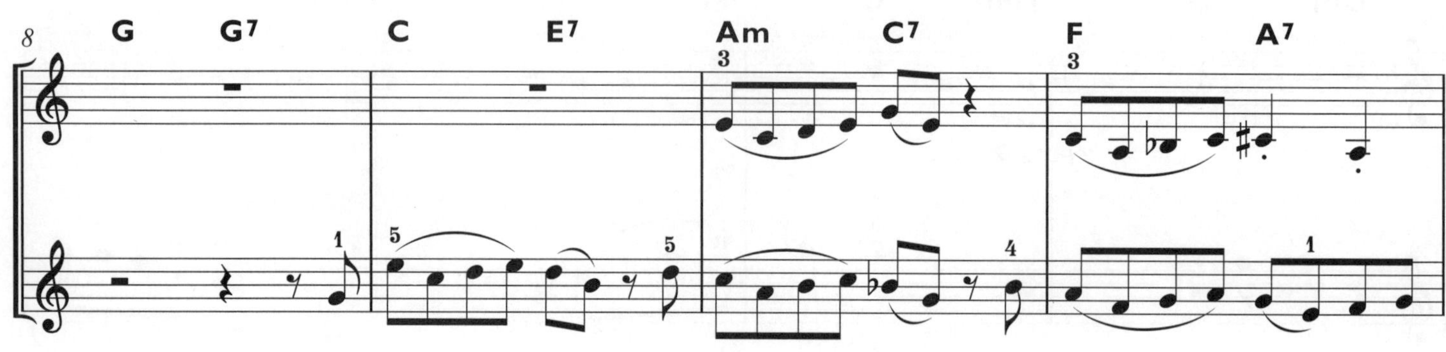

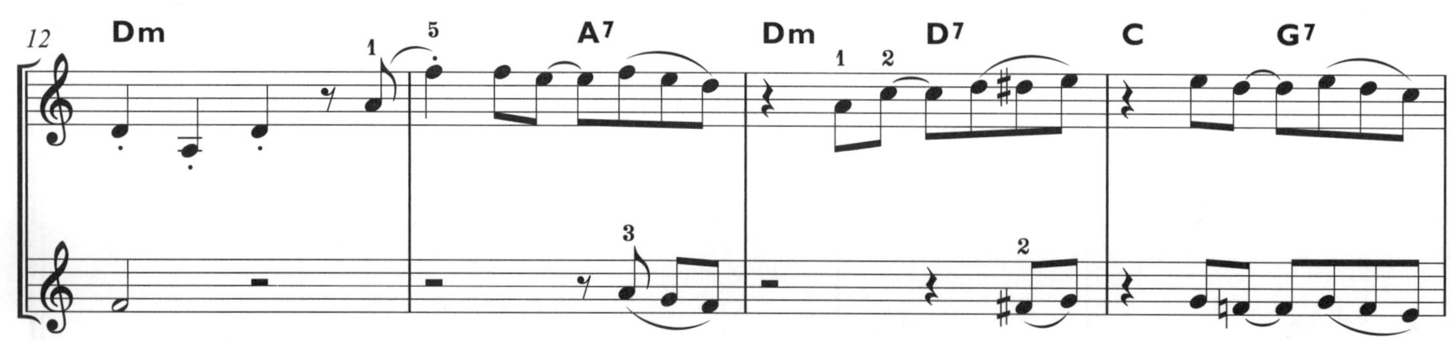

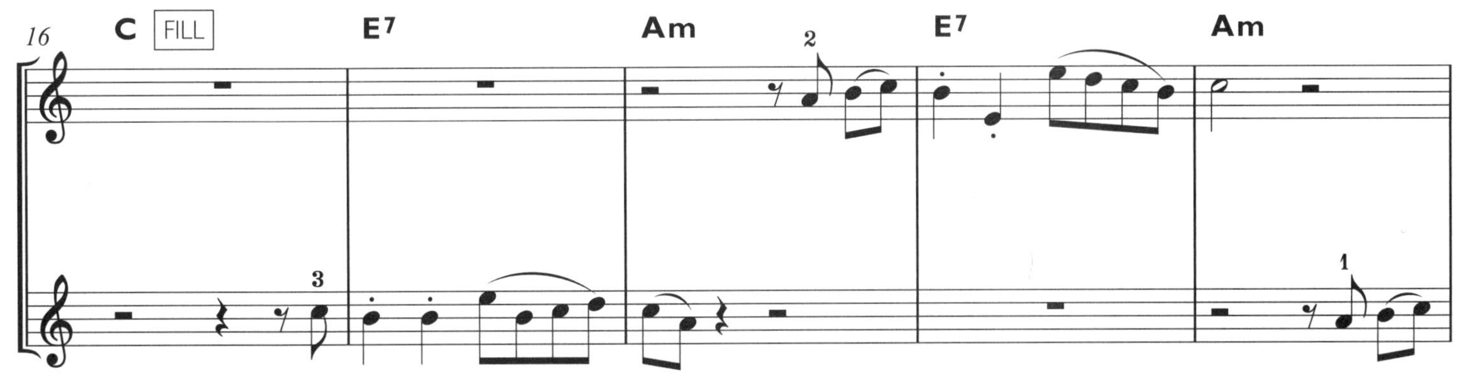
16
C
FILL
E7
Am
E7
Am
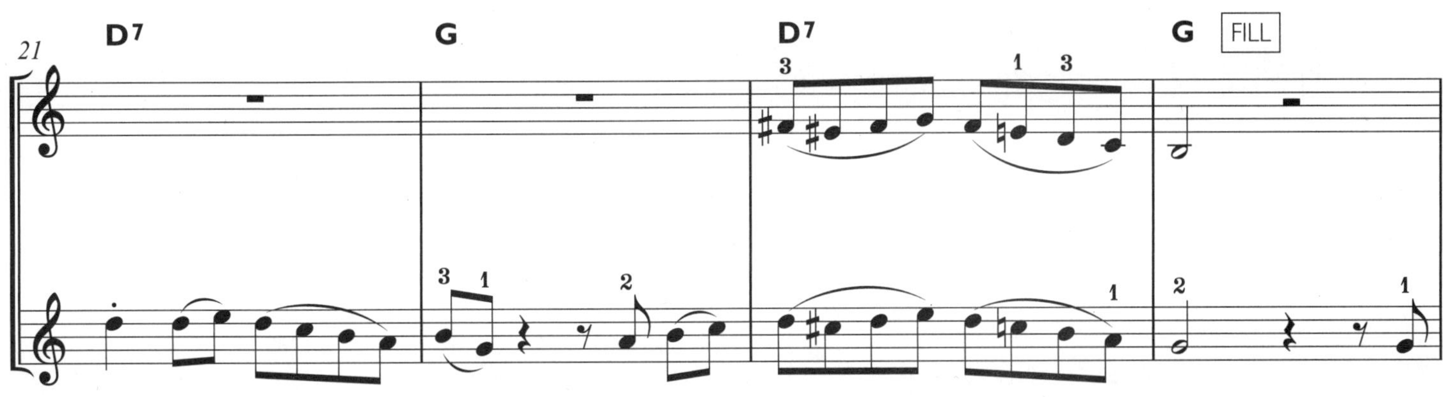
21
D7
G
D7
G
FILL
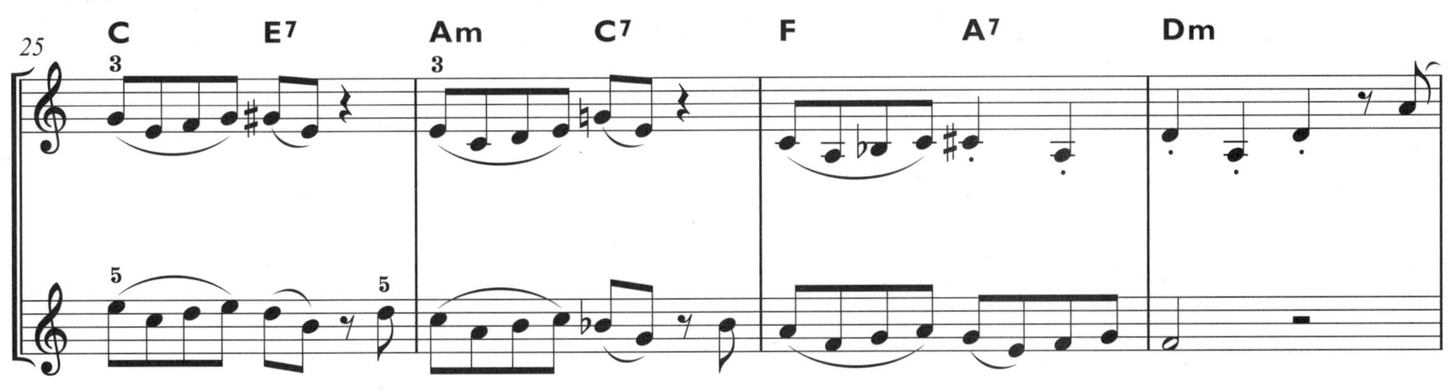
25
C
E7
Am
C7
F
A7
Dm
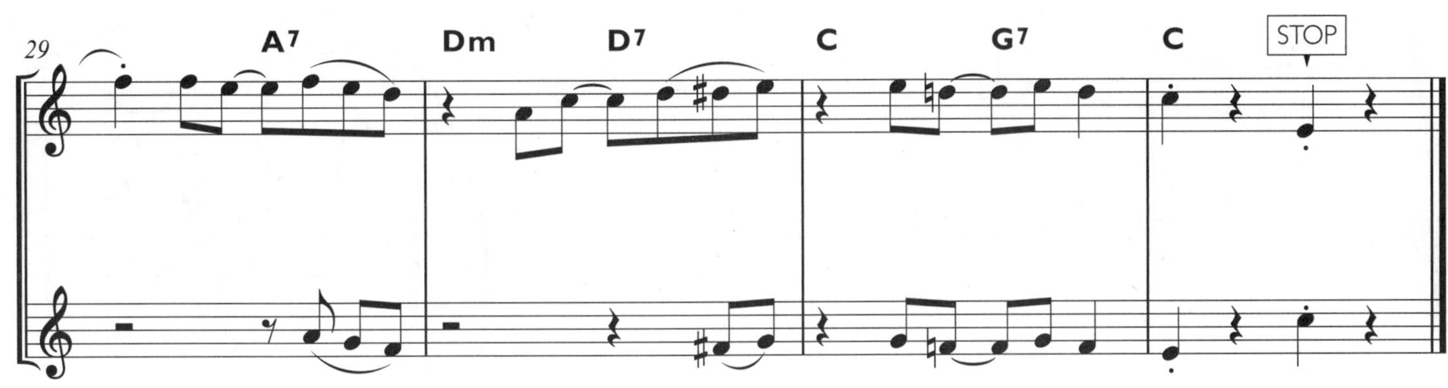
29
A7
Dm
D7
C
G7
C
STOP

Orbit of Orion

Derek Hobbs

Pop techno ♩ = c.128

INTRO

A D A D A D E7 A D

gold 1

trumpet

platinum 2

brass ensemble

A D A D E G7 FILL C F C F

C F E7 FILL A F

strings

B♭
Gm
E♭
Cm
D
E7
FILL
A
D
brass ensemble
B♭
STOP

What the world needs now (is love, sweet love)

Burt Bacharach
arr. Anthony Marks

Jazz waltz ♩ = c.112

RHYTHM ONLY

gold 1 vibraphone

platinum 2 electric piano

7 Am7 Dm7 Am7 Dm7 Gm7

13 Am7 C Am7 Dm7 Am7

18 Dm7 Gm7 to Coda A7 FILL

Dm7
Cm7
F7
B♭
Cm7
F7
B♭
Dm
G7
C
FILL
D.S. al Coda
CODA
Am7
Dm
Gm7
B♭
F
STOP

Gold Leaf Rag

Mike Cornick

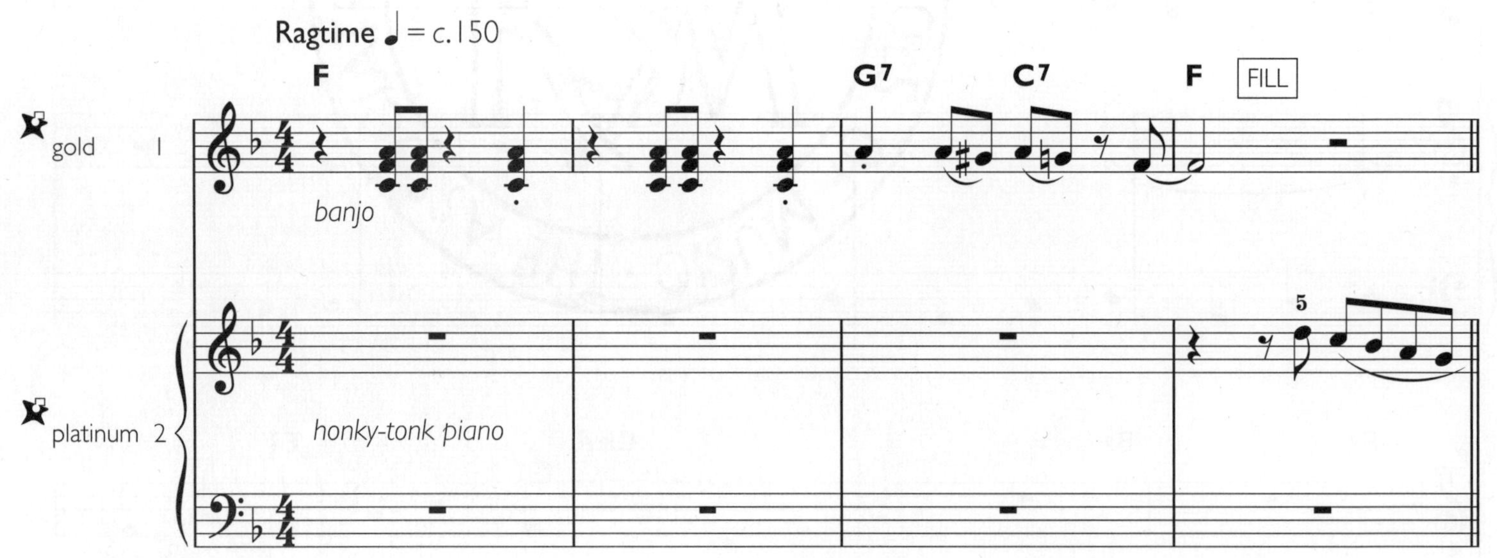

C
G7
C
F
B♭
A7
B♭
F
D7
G7
C7
F
FILL
F
STOP
1.
2.

Live and Let Die

Paul & Linda McCartney
arr. Martin Lawrie

Hard rock ♩ = c.150

NO ACCOMPANIMENT UNTIL BAR 10

gold 1

distortion guitar

platinum 2

electric piano + strings

SYNC START

Gm

brass section

FILL

C
G7
D7
Em
F
FILL
Gm
STOP

Autumn Leaves

Joseph Kosma
arr. Nigel Scaife

Swing ♩ = c.112

SYNC START

gold 1 flute

silver 2 solo trumpet

silver 3 jazz electric piano

Am D7 G C

Am B7 Em FILL

Am D7 G C

Am B7 Em FILL

B7
Em
Em7
Am7
D
G
FILL
Am
B7
Em
B7
Em
Am
B7
Em
ENDING

Life is Just Too Short

Andrew Eales

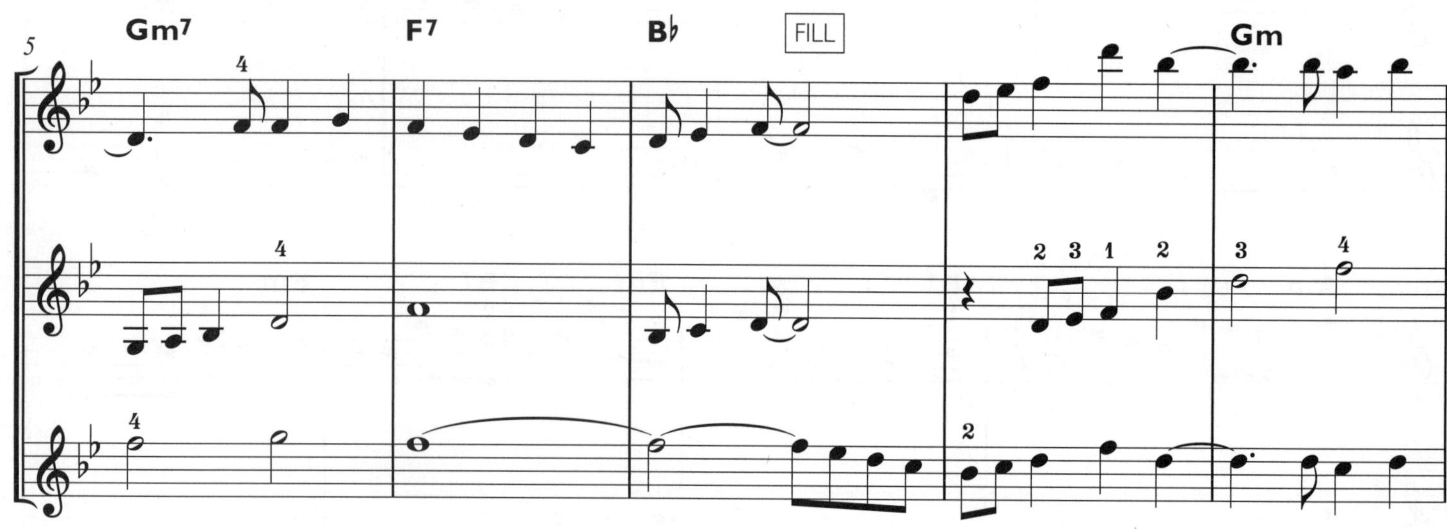

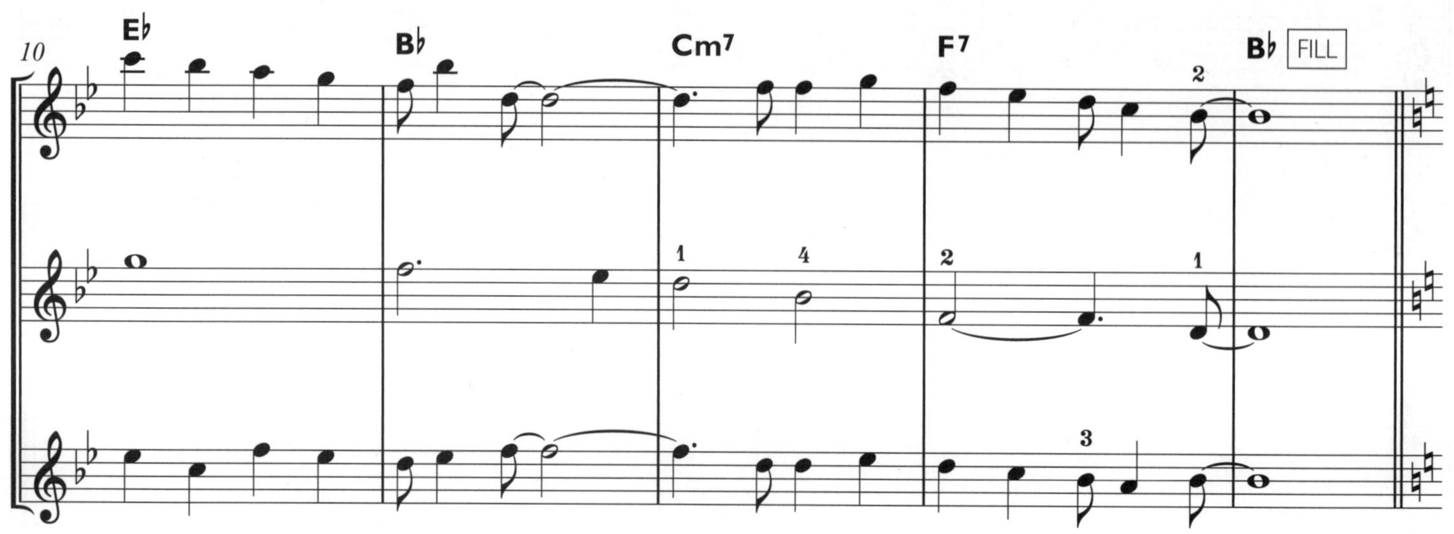

15
C
Am
F
C
Am7

20
G7
C
FILL
Am

24
F
C
Dm7
G7
C
ENDING

Liszt Goes Latin

Nancy Litten after Franz Liszt

Tango ♩ = c.120

RHYTHYM ONLY

gold 1 trumpet

(gold) 2 alto sax

(gold) 3 clarinet

Am

Dm G7

C Dm Am

E7
Am
FILL
A7
Dm
G7
C
FILL
A7
Dm
E7
Am
ENDING

A Very Blue Danube

Peter Gritton after Johann Strauss II

Jazz waltz ♩ = c.216

SYNC START

gold 1 — vibes
(gold) 2 — strings
(gold) 3 — saxophone

F C7 F C7 F C7 F B♭ F C7 F C7 F B♭ C F

to Coda

G7
Dm7
G7
RHYTHM ONLY
G7
Dm7
G7
Am
Dm7
C
G7
C
RHYTHM ONLY
FILL
F
CODA
C
F
STOP
D.S. al Coda

You Might Need Somebody

Tom Snow & Nan O'Byrne
arr. Peter Gritton

Slow hip hop ♩ = c.80

SYNC START

gold 1 — tenor saxophone

(platinum) 2 — trumpet or brass section

platinum 3 — electric piano

Em7 A D A

5 Em A D A

9 Em7 FILL Bm Em7 Am7 Em7 Am7 Em7

13
B
Bm7
Em7
Am7
Em7
Am7
Em7
17
D
G
D
FILL
Am7
21
Bm7
A
Em7
Am7

Bm7
A
Em7
Bm
Em7
Am7
Em7
Am7
Em7
B
Bm
Em7
Am7
Em7
Am7
Em7
D
G
D
Em
STOP
on 3rd beat

Can't Get You Out of My Head

Cathy Dennis & Robert Davis
arr. Anthony Marks

Electro-pop ♩ = c.124

RHYTHM ONLY

Dm7 | Am7

gold 1 — *electric organ*
silver 2 — *square lead*
silver 3 — *saw lead*
silver 4 — *clavinet*

1. | 2. FILL

6 | Dm7

10 Am7 | Dm7

14 Am7 FILL B♭ A

18 E Dm A Gm

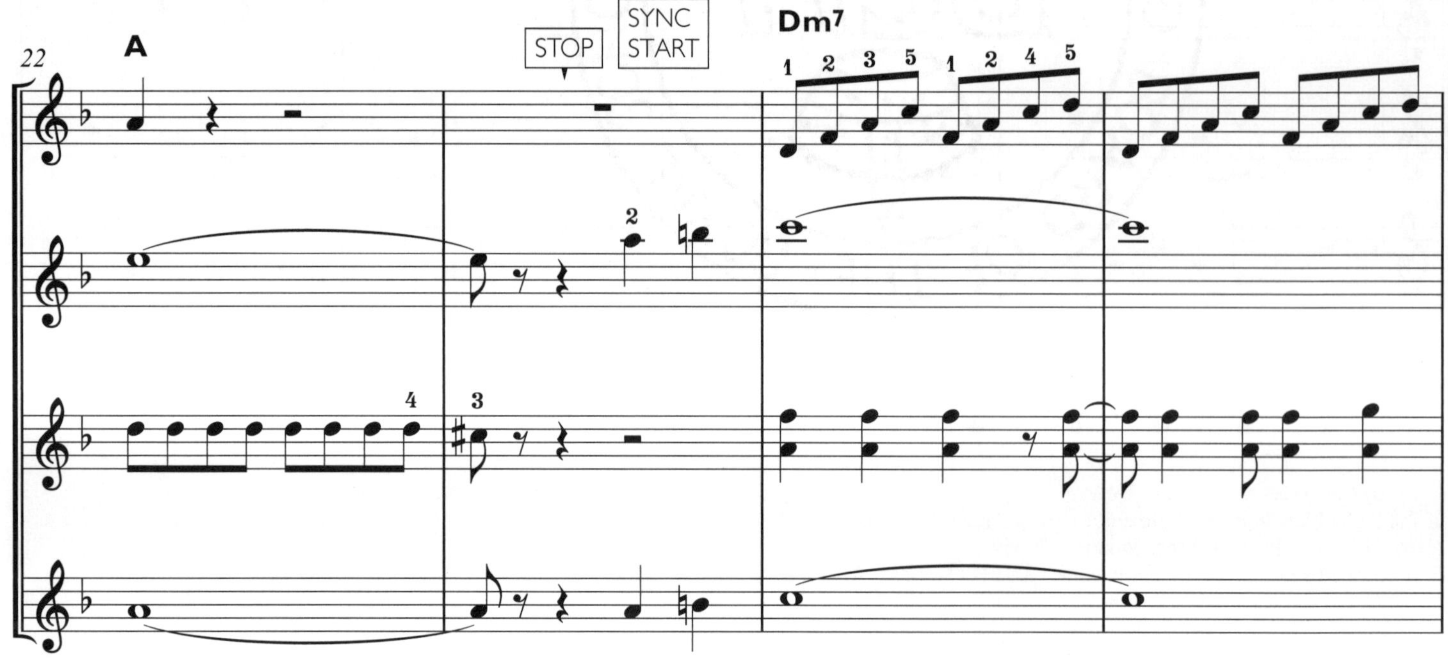

26
Am7
1 2 3 5 1 2 4 5
Dm7
30
Am7
FILL
3
5
1
B♭
2
34
STOP
SYNC START
1
Dm
STOP

Gold Star

Andrew Eales

Cha cha ♩ = c.116

RHYTHM ONLY (1st time)

C (2nd time)

gold 1 strings

(gold) 2 clarinet

(gold) 3 vibes

silver 4 trumpet

5 C A

9 Dm G7 C FILL

C7
F
FILL
C
G7
C
FILL
F
C
G7
C
ENDING
(2nd time only)

AUTHENTIC TRANSCRIPTIONS WITH NOTES AND TABLATURE

ISBN 978-0-7935-0990-4

7777 W. Bluemound Rd. P.O. Box 13819 Milwaukee, WI 53213

Visit Hal Leonard Online at
www.halleonard.com

CONTENTS

INTRODUCTION

It's only natural that instrumentals were hits at the dawn of rock history. Rock was always dance music, and the musical styles it drew upon—blues, R&B, country, and swing—had strong beats and engendered danceable instrumentals themselves.

Because rock is eclectic, many instruments can take their place in the spotlight. Saxophone players, those heroes of jazz and swing, were the stars of many early rock instrumentals ("Raunchy" and "Tequila," for example). Organists and drummers were leaders of some combos (check out "Red River Rock" and "Green Onions"). However, guitar players were important soloists in country, blues, and R&B, so it didn't take long for rock to create a new pop hero: the electric guitar player.

Into rock came guitar heroes from an R&B background, like Chuck Berry and Bo Diddley, country influenced stars, like Carl Perkins and Duane Eddy, and mavericks who bridged the gaps between styles, like Lonnie Mack. Then at the beginning of the sixties there were the Ventures, a guitar instrumental band that spawned countless guitar/bar bands all over the country. A few years later, Dick Dale, the Beach Boys, and other Southern California groups turned the country on to surf music, which instrumentally, was just like the Ventures—a combination of pop influences with guitar in the forefront and pounding drums behind.

Some of the early rock instrumentals were recorded by groups who were thrown together by a studio pro or producer ("Tequila" and "Raunchy" were two examples). A few were the product of teen high school bands like the Chantays and Johnny and the Hurricanes. Others came from powerhouse innovators like Duane Eddy and Lonnie Mack whose playing would inspire future generations of guitarists. Together they established a rock tradition, and their instrumentals continue to live on to this day.

It's interesting that many of the classic instrumentals in this collection didn't come from Hollywood or New York City, but from places like Toledo, Cincinnati, and Seattle. They came from anywhere folks danced to rock 'n' roll in clubs! Many classic hits ("Tequila," "Wipe Out," and "Hide Away") were first considered throwaways, B-sides recorded hastily in one or two takes. The success of these tunes was as big a surprise to the recording artist as it was to the public—which only proves that the public likes a simple, unpretentious groove tune!

I hope you enjoy this collection of *Classic Guitar Instrumentals*. The tradition of rock instrumentals is alive and well, and includes a wide range of guitar styles as this book proves. It also includes essential knowledge for you rock guitar addicts; your musical education is far from complete if you can't play "Wipe Out," "Rebel 'Rouser," "Walk Don't Run," or "Pipeline!"

Good luck,

Fred Sokolow

Fred Sokolow

SONG NOTES

APACHE

Inspired by the 1954 Hollywood western, *Apache*, British songwriter Jerry Lordan wrote an instrumental with the same name. In 1960, he played it on the ukulele for British pop group the Shadows, with whom he was touring, and taught it to their guitarist Hank Marvin. It became a #1 hit in England for the Shadows, and a year later Danish jazz guitarist Jorgen Ingmann scored a #2 hit with "Apache" in the US. It became a standard among surf-rock bands, and was recorded by the Ventures, Chet Atkins and many other guitarists. Oddly enough, a 1973 version by the Incredible Bongo Band has been sampled by so many rap and hip hop artists, "Apache" has also become a hip-hop anthem.

The Shadows' version, recorded at Abbey Road in London, is transcribed here. It has four sections, and nearly all of it is played on the first few frets in the key of A minor. Marvin enhanced the sound of his Fender Strat with a unique echo chamber given to him by British singer-guitarist Joe Brown, and used his tremolo bar on the tune as well.

BECK'S BOLERO

In the late sixties, fledgling "underground" FM radio stations offered a bold, new format: they played rock album cuts rather than Top 40 singles. The psychedelic sound of Jeff Beck's guitar and the unusual (for rock) bolero rhythm made "Beck's Bolero," from his 1968 *Truth* record, an often played favorite.

Listening to Beck's guitar tone—his screaming, blues infected solo at the end of the song, and the riffs in the rock section—one hears the seeds of heavy metal and hard rock being sown.

DEE

Fiery guitarist Randy Rhoads, co-founder of the 1975 proto-metal group Quiet Riot, wrote and performed the classic guitar piece "Dee" in 1980 when he was playing with Ozzy Osbourne. Rhoads' career was ended by a fatal airplane accident in 1982. The song is dedicated to Rhoads' mother, who ran a music school in North Hollywood, California.

ERUPTION

Van Halen's eponymous 1978 debut album included this brief instrumental which Eddie Van Halen used to perform live in clubs. (It was only included on the album because producer Ted Templeman heard Eddie rehearsing it for an upcoming gig at Los Angeles' famous Whiskey a Go Go.) Often cited as one of the greatest guitar solos of all time, "Eruption" featured some ground-breaking tapping that popularized a new rock guitar technique and made tapping a permanent part of the rock guitar lexicon. The tapping section of the piece is said to be based on one of Rodolphe Kreutzer's etudes, and the introductory section roughly imitates the intro to Cactus' "Let Me Swim," played by former Detroit Wheels guitarist Jim McCarty; but the overall effect of "Eruption" is original and revolutionary.

Van Halen played the tune on his hybrid Strat-and-other-parts Frankenstrat guitar. The non-tapping sections of the tune are blues-based in the key of A♭, because Van Halen played in A but tuned down a half-step to A♭.

FRANKENSTEIN

Keyboard rocker/synth pioneer Edgar Winter topped the charts in 1973 with this instrumental from his album *They Only Come Out at Night*. It's basically a two-chord tune, though it features several orchestrated riffs that venture momentarily off the one and four chords. Various portions of a much longer version of the song were spliced together to create the single, hence the name "Frankenstein." The guitarist on the track was Ronnie Montrose, who was a sideman for Winter, Boz Scaggs, Van Morrison, and others before embarking on a solo career that began with the group Montrose in 1973. He plays some dazzling riffs in "Frankenstein"—mostly blues-based riffs in the key of G—in addition to doubling Edgar's synth lines. Note the classic, string-bend-to-unison ascending lick in section J, which has since been widely imitated by other guitarists.

GREEN ONIONS

In 1962, Booker T. & the MGs' instrumental, "Green Onions," was a hit on the pop and soul charts. The tune has been used in many popular films and TV shows. It's a minor key, 12-bar blues in F featuring a blues riff that has become iconic, and it includes a taut Telecaster solo from the legendary Steve Cropper.

Booker T.'s band, which was probably named after producer Chips Moman's car, is synonymous with sixties Memphis soul. They were the Stax house band that backed up all the label's artists on countless hits by Otis Redding, Sam & Dave, Wilson Pickett, and many more. They were also the first racially integrated soul band. When the Blues Brothers, who began as a comedy act mimicking Sam & Dave on TV's "Saturday Night Live," became a touring act, they hired several members of the MGs to gain a more authentic sound!

Steve Cropper's backup guitar licks, heard in countless soul tunes have been widely imitated, and he co-wrote many soul standards as well ("Knock on Wood," "In the Midnight Hour," "Dock of the Bay"). Cropper's solo in "Green Onions" goes twice around the 12-bar form of the tune. The second twelve bars consists of a blues lick, based on the first fret F chord formation, Cropper moves that lick to the sixth fret and the eighth fret, following the song's chord progression.

GUITAR BOOGIE SHUFFLE

Frank Virtuoso created the Virtues in 1946, modeling the group after the then-popular Nat "King" Cole Trio. It was thirteen years before they had their first and only hit, the "Guitar Boogie Shuffle." Virtuoso embellished a boogie lick that his old Navy buddy Arthur Smith taught him and soloed in a very swingy vein. The tune went to #5 on the pop charts in 1959.

HAWAII FIVE-O THEME

Recorded in 1968 as the theme song for the TV police show, this song went to #4 the following year and sparked new interest in the Ventures. Nokie Edwards had been replaced by session guitarist Jerry McGee who had played on the first two Monkees albums. His lead guitar part was surrounded by twenty-eight musicians besides the other Ventures including brass and kettle drums. The record is as ornate as the Ventures ever produced; a full orchestral treatment with several key changes.

HIDE AWAY

In 1960, inspired by Hound Dog Taylor's "Taylor's Boogie," Freddy* King and Magic Sam put the instrumental 12-bar blues, "Hide Away," together and played it as a break tune in Mel's Hideaway Lounge, where west-side blues players performed. King's 1961 recording of the tune crossed over to the pop charts. He went on to record other charting instrumentals (see "San-Ho-Zay," transcribed in this book) and became a blues legend, playing and singing on the "Chitlin' Circuit." King's vocals and guitar style were much admired and imitated by 1960s British rockers like Eric Clapton, Peter Green, and Mick Taylor. In 1970, rock legend Leon Russell signed King to his label, Shelter Records, and toured with him introducing him to white audiences all over the world, revitalizing his career. King continued to perform and record until his untimely death in 1976.

"Hide Away" has four themes or sections. King said he got the tempo change from pianist Jimmie McCracklin's "The Walk," added a stop-time figure that featured a jazz chord Robert Junior Lockwood showed him, and followed that with a variation on the "Peter Gunn" theme (also transcribed in this book). The song has been recorded by Eric Clapton, Stevie Ray Vaughan, King Curtis, Jeff Healey and others.

*He recorded under the name "Freddy" early in his career. In later releases, the spelling of his name was changed to "Freddie."

JESSICA

The Allman Brothers Band scored their first hit single, "Ramblin' Man" (#2 in 1973) after Duane Allman, already a legendary guitar hero, was gone, killed in a motorcycle accident in '71 at the age of twenty-four. Dickey Betts, the other guitar player in the famous twin-lead solos, stepped into the forefront of the band and "Jessica," the flip side of the "Ramblin' Man" single was his tour de force. The song includes the twin-lead sound, an ever-changing musical head with many different sections, and a high-energy Betts solo.

JUST LIKE A WOMAN

This track is vintage B.B. King (early sixties), although it has been reissued many times over the years in compilation albums and has a jazzier flavor than much of his later work. The 12-bar blues shuffle is B.B.'s tribute to Louis Jordan's 1946 hit, "Ain't That Just Like a Woman." B.B. kicks off the instrumental with a solo that mimics the introductory solo by Carl Hogan (Louis Jordan's guitarist), then proceeds to jam over the band

and make the tune his own. The only other vestige of the Jordan hit is B.B.'s band shouting out, "Just like a woman!" in the same rhythmic spot where Jordan's lyrics lie. Chuck Berry also copied Carl Hogan's intro when he kicked off "Johnny B. Goode," so that lick has been heard around the world!

MISIRLOU

Dick Dale's family was Lebanese and the young Dale often played an Arabic drum while his uncle played "Misirlou" and other Arabic folk tunes on an oud, plucking the strings with a turkey quill. At times they could be found accompanying a belly dancer. In the early sixties, thousands of teens did their version of the belly dance to Dale's electrified "Misirlou." He was billed as the King of the Surf Guitar and this tune, along with his earlier "Let's Go Trippin'" (the song that allegedly kicked off the surf music craze), were later covered by the Beach Boys.

Dale's guitar style in "Misirlou" resembles oud playing: he plays the melody in tremolo or sixteenth notes, moving up and down the neck on a single string.

PETER GUNN

"Peter Gunn," a popular late-fifties TV detective show, featured a jazzy soundtrack by Henry Mancini (Gunn, the noir private eye, was a jazz fan in the story line). The show's theme song, a one-chord sax solo supported by a one-bar, endlessly repeated boogie bass line, is better remembered than the show. Duane Eddy's twangy bass figure provides the platform for steamy sax improvisation by Steve Douglas, one of several members of Eddy's band who later became part of the legendary "Wrecking Crew," the Los Angeles studio team that played on countless hits in the 1960s. The boogie bass riff was quoted by Freddie King in his hit instrumental, "Hide Away."

PIPELINE

One of the few surf instrumentals to reach the top 10 (#4 in 1963), "Pipeline" was written by two teenage guitar players who were classmates at Santa Ana High School: Bob Spickard (lead) and Brian Carman (rhythm). Three more students at this Southern California high school rounded out the Chantays—a bassist, pianist, and drummer. The tune, named after a surf flick about the famous Hawaiian pipeline waves, was a national hit, but being full-time students, the Chantays could only tour during summers and the group disbanded after a few years.

Like most surf instrumentals, "Pipeline" is played in first position on the first few frets. The trademark glissando on the 5th string is not played exactly the same way twice. Play sixteenth notes with your pick while smoothly sliding down on the 5th string starting at the 14th fret.

RAMROD

Duane Eddy's "Ramrod" hit #27 on the charts just two months after his "Rebel 'Rouser" in 1958. It's a much higher-energy record with a rockabilly, almost swamp-rock feel. The capoed guitar churns out first-position boogie riffs, and the E7–D7 turnaround lick is played in a down-home fingerpicking style.

RAUNCHY

Sax player Bill Justis, born in Birmingham, was a music director and arranger at various universities before coming to Memphis where he performed the same duties at Sun Records. He led the bands that recorded at Sun, a veritable roster of rock and country giants. In 1957, he and guitarist Sid Manker wrote "Raunchy" (originally called "Backwoods") and recorded it with rockabilly artist Billy Riley on bass and Manker on guitar. Justis played sax at the last minute when the session player didn't show, and his rusty chops resulted in the funky sax sound that helped propel "Raunchy" to #2 in 1957.

RAWHIDE

"Rawhide" was Link Wray's second charting hit, going to #23 in 1959. Unlike the ominous sounding "Rumble," this is a rambunctious rockabilly piece with a swamp-rock, first-position head and Chuck Berry-like solos. As in many surf tunes, Wray often moved the F formation around with the chord changes instead of playing it as a blues position at the 5th fret. (See "Red River Rock" and "Wipe Out" for more examples of this technique.) Notice his amazing one-note solo toward the end of the song when he plays nine bars of just a high A! As in "Rumble," excitement builds and the pace quickens as the tune nears a climax.

REBEL 'ROUSER

Often called rock's #1 instrumentalist, Duane Eddy was one of the first to play melody on a rock instrument, thus helping the electric guitar as a lead instrument. "Rebel 'Rouser," his first hit (#6 in 1958), became his signature tune. He later called his band The Rebels.

Eddy had fifteen instrumental hits over a five-year period, including several TV and movie theme songs. The "Peter Gunn Theme," "Because They're Young," and "Have Gun, Will Travel" themes are a few examples. He played melodies simply on the bass strings of his Gretsch guitar using a lot of echo. (His producer, Lee Hazelwood, wouldn't let him improvise solos!) The echo on "Rebel 'Rouser" consisted of an empty water tank with an amp at one end and a microphone at the other.

RED RIVER ROCK

Sax player John Paris led the teenage instrumental quintet called Johnny and the Hurricanes. The Toledo, Ohio group charted several times and was mentioned in the lyrics of a Kinks' song called "One of the Survivors." "Red River Rock," a rocked-up folk standard, went to #5 in 1959 and got the group touring all over the States, in Britain, and Hamburg, Germany where they played with the Beatles.

Guitarist Dave Yorko's solo is in the Chuck Berry, double-stop blues vein. He plays from an 8th fret, F-formation base and often changes positions with the tune (unlike blues players who tend to stay on one position through the chord changes). "Wipe Out" (also in the key of C) uses similar F-formation chords.

(GHOST) RIDERS IN THE SKY (A COWBOY LEGEND)

Stan Jones' song was already a classic when the Ramrods, an instrumental quartet from Connecticut, brought it back to the charts (#30) in 1961. Lead guitarist Vinnie Lee's performance was Duane Eddy inspired; he played the melody in a low register with no frills and lots of echo. The record brought instrumentals to a new height of gimmickry with overdubbed cowboy whoops, mooing cattle, and a high falsetto Theremin-like voice that was popular during this period.

RUMBLE

Like Duane Eddy, Link Wray's late-fifties groundbreaking instrumentals established him as one of the first rock guitar heroes. Born in North Carolina, Wray's guitar style was rawer than Eddy's, and his legend was larger in England than in the States, where Pete Townshend, Jeff Beck, and others have cited him as a major influence.

"Rumble," Wray's biggest hit went to #16 on the charts in 1958, though he claimed to have recorded it in '54. The song's rhythmic feel was suited to a popular, late-fifties, slow group dance called "The Stroll." Wray's guitar was drenched in reverb and tremolo, which he increased in intensity toward the end of the tune, just as the drummer sped up the tempo a bit. To further darken his sound, Wray punched pencil holes in his amp speaker. This gave his guitar a ragged, primitive fuzz sound that won a permanent place in guitar history as a precursor to heavy metal!

SAN-HO-ZAY

Born in Texas, Freddie King moved to Chicago in 1950 where he honed his blues guitar playing with Magic Sam, Hound Dog Taylor, Robert Junior Lockwood, and Jimmy Rogers. His 1961 hit, "Hide Away," led to an album of instrumentals that had a big effect on both British blues-revival bands and California surf music. "Hide Away," "San-Ho-Zay," and "The Stumble" were club-band standards throughout the sixties.

King recorded his instrumental pieces on a gold-top Les Paul, wearing a plastic thumbpick and metal fingerpick—a style he learned in Texas from players like Lightnin' Hopkins.

SCUTTLE BUTTIN'

Unlike other guitar heroes of the eighties, Texas born-and-raised Stevie Ray Vaughan stayed within the blues tradition and paid homage with his music to Hendrix, Clapton, T-Bone Walker, Freddie King, Otis Rush and the other great bluesmen of the century.

"Scuttle Buttin'," a twelve-bar blues instrumental from Vaughan's 1984 album, *Couldn't Stand the Weather*, sounds like Freddie King in overdrive. Like King's "Hide Away," the tune's head and some of the soloing is in first-position E and includes lots of slides and pull-offs. In the second solo, Vaughan plays in the basic first, moveable blues position on the 12th fret (as Freddie King does in "San-Ho-Zay," but in the key of C on the 8th fret).

SLEEPWALK

Brooklyn's Farina brothers, Santo & Johnny, co-wrote this sleepy tune with their sister Ann. It went to #1 in 1959, a year in which twenty-seven other instrumentals charted. In the eighties, it became a favorite in Los Lobos' repertoire and many others have covered it since.

Johnny played rhythm guitar and Santo played lead on a triple-necked lap steel. The lead part has been arranged for electric guitar in this transcription using an open C6 tuning, a fairly common tuning for lap-steel players.

TEQUILA

In 1958, songwriter/A&R man/guitarist Dave Burgess assembled a group of Southern California bar-band and studio musicians to record his song "Train to Nowhere." The hastily recorded B-side, written by sax player Chuck Rio, a.k.a. Danny Flores (who utters the word "tequila" during the tune), went to #1 and became an all-time favorite instrumental. Burgess and Buddy Bruce played guitars, and later incarnations of The Champs included guitarists Seals and Crofts, Glen Campbell, and Jerry Cole.

WALK DON'T RUN

The Ventures are the most successful and longest-lasting instrumental guitar group in pop history. Their metallic guitar sound and pounding drums set the standard for sixties guitar bands. Bob Bogle and Don Wilson, two guitar-playing hod carriers in Seattle, organized the band. Nokie Edwards (lead guitar) and Howie Johnson (drums) were the two other members. They were fans of Duane Eddy and Chet Atkins, and a Chet Atkins version of jazz guitarist Johnny Smith's "Walk Don't Run" brought the tune to their attention.

Their demo version of "Walk Don't Run" was rejected by so many record companies that Wilson's mother created a label and released the single. It went to #2 in 1960 and began a decade-long string of hits for the Ventures who, after a few personnel changes, are still touring to this day.

Johnny Smith got the title for this song from a New York subway sign.

WHAM

Indiana-born Lonnie Mack was a link between the guitar styles of the fifties and sixties; between fifties rockabilly and Chuck Berry styles, and between blues-rock and country-rock of the sixties. Noted for his speedy "chicken pickin'," bluesy note bending, and swamp-rock licks, Mack's blend of blues and country had a big impact on Jimmy and Stevie Ray Vaughan, Clapton, and many other guitarists.

When "Wham" reached #24 on the charts in 1963, Mack was just twenty-two. However, he had already been honing his chops since the age of five and was a veteran of the clubs and studios of Cincinnati. He cut "Wham" and "Memphis" (his other hit) during twenty minutes of studio time leftover from another artist's session. Mack played a heavily-strung Gibson V with a Bigsby bar through a Magnatone amp.

All the above mentioned blues and country techniques are evident in "Wham." The head is a swamp-rock lick in first-position E (though his guitar is tuned down a whole step and capoed at the 3rd fret) and most of the up-the-neck licks are played in the moveable blues position on the 12th fret (respective to the capo).

WIPE OUT

A *wipe out* is what happens when a wave knocks a surfer off a board. It's also the only hit scored by the Surfaris, a five-man surf band from Glendora, California that featured Jim Fuller on lead guitar and Bob Berryhill on rhythm guitar. The tune was an afterthought, the B-side of "Surfer Joe," a song written by drummer Ron Wilson and was essentially an instrumental version of "Surfer Joe." Manager Dale Smallin supplied the maniacal laugh in the intro. The tune included rock's first and most imitated drum solo by unsung hero Ron Wilson, who once set an endurance record by drumming non-stop for 104 and a half hours. "Wipe Out" went to #2 in 1963 and charted again three years later; it has always been a bar-band favorite.

Apache

By Jerry Lordan

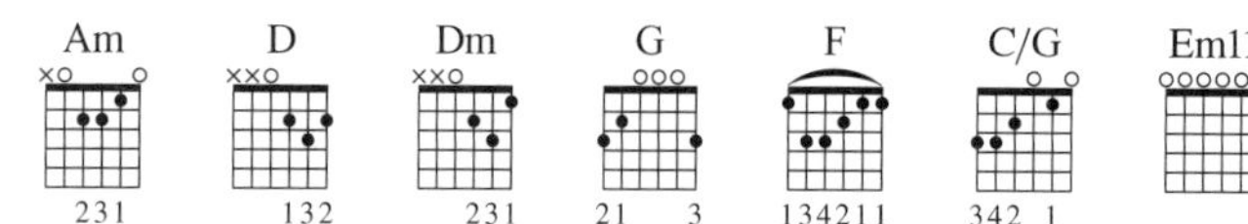

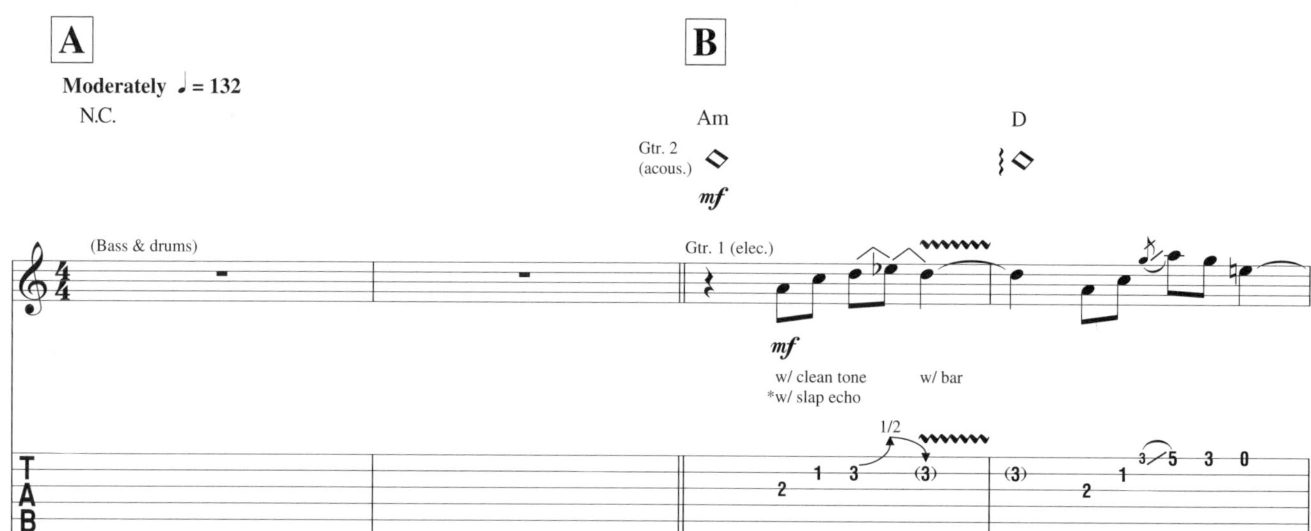

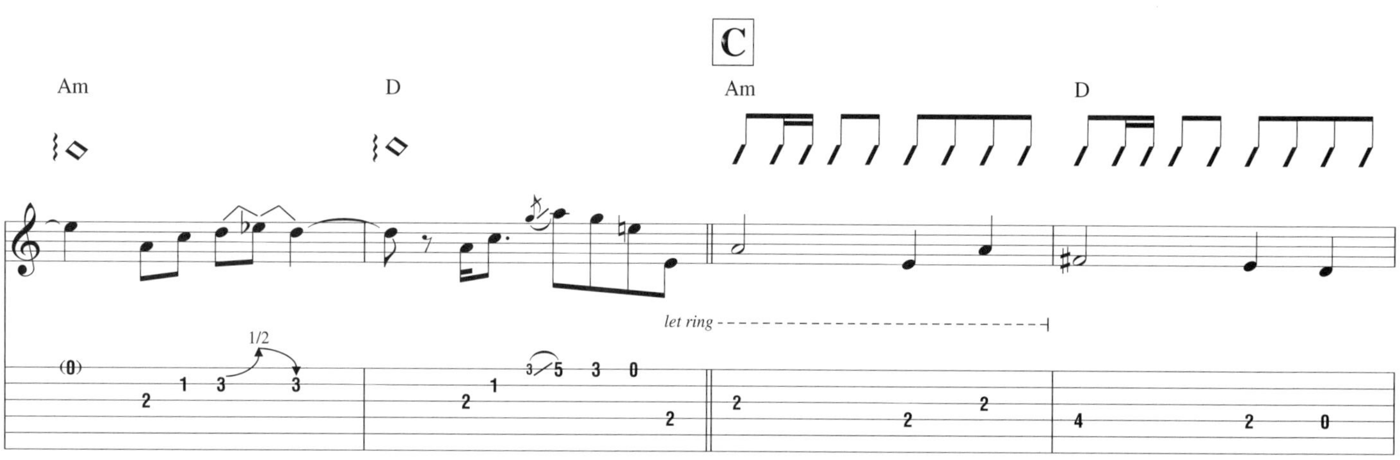

Am
Dm
G
let ring

Dm
Am
D
let ring

D
Am
F
P.M.

Am
F
P.M.
P.M.

To Coda

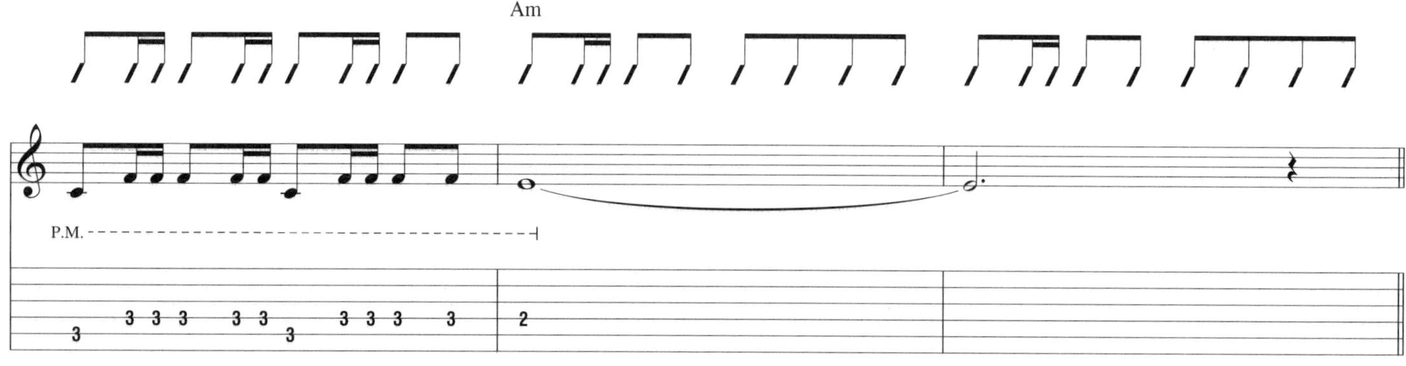
Am
P.M.
3 3 3 3 3 3 3 3 3 3 3 3
2

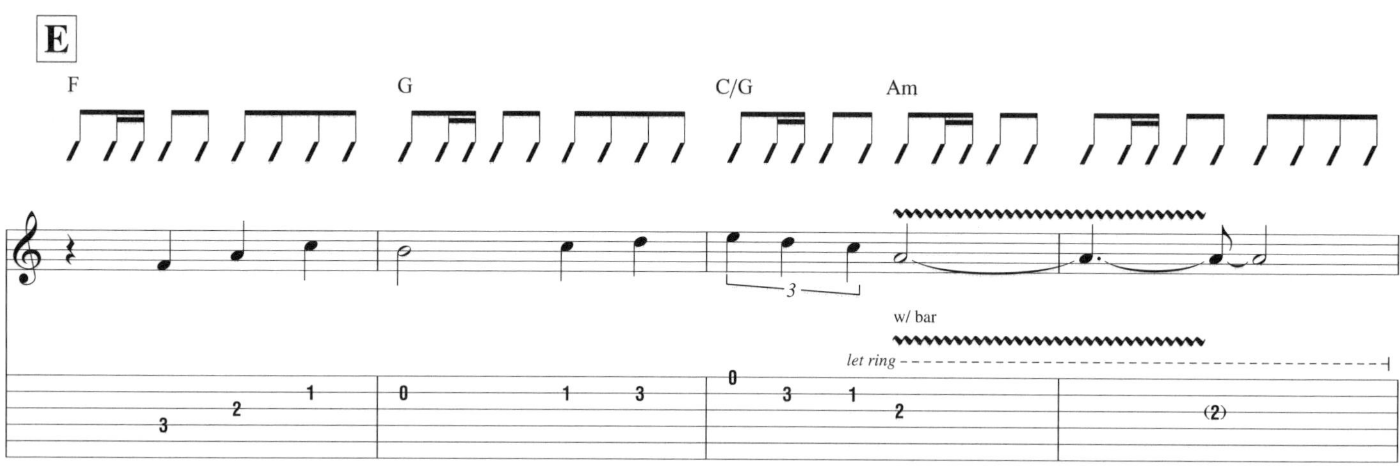
E
F
G
C/G
Am
w/ bar
let ring
3 2 1
0 1 3
0 3 1 2
(2)

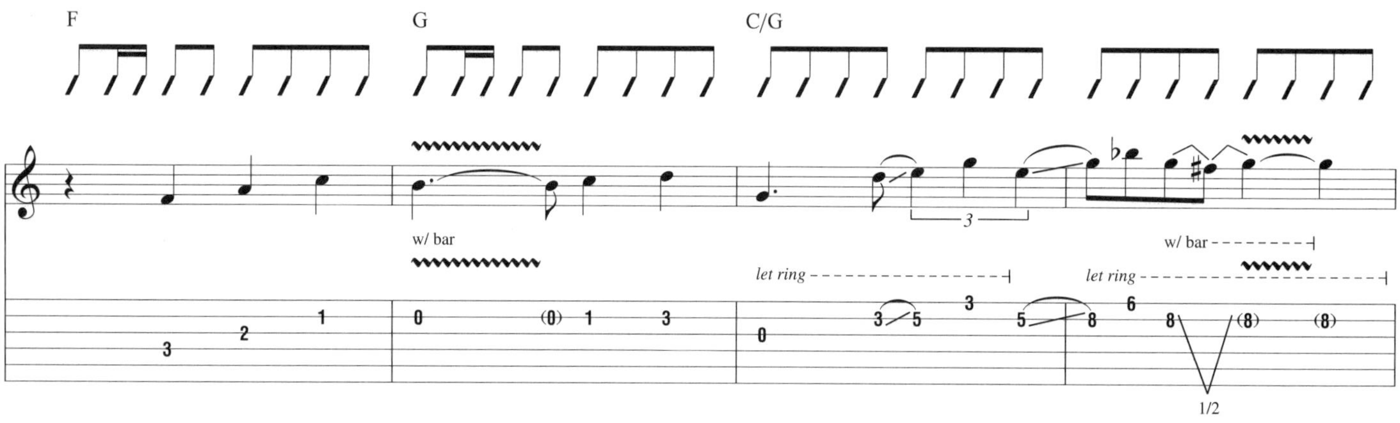
F
G
C/G
w/ bar
let ring
let ring
w/ bar
3 2 1
0 (0) 1 3
0 3 5 3 5
8 6 8 (8) (8)
1/2

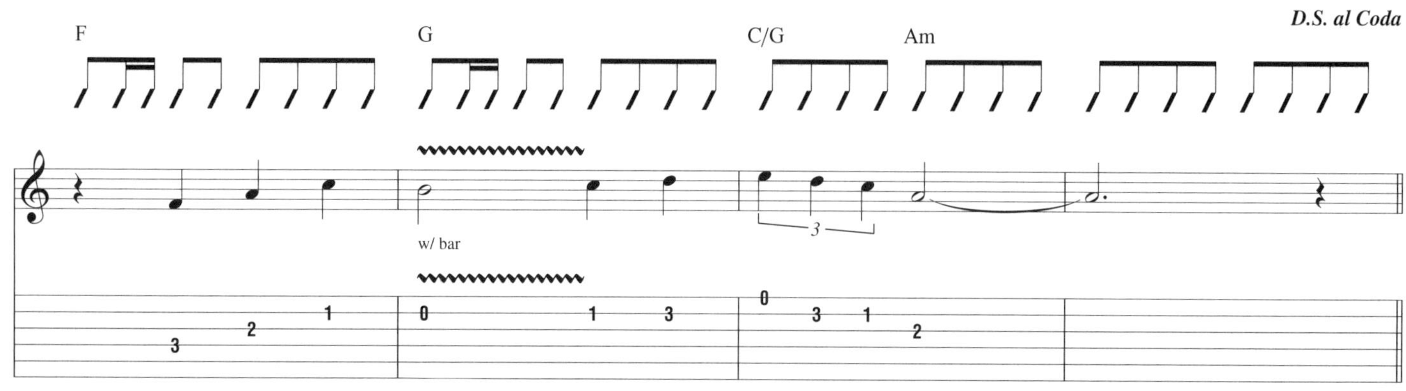
D.S. al Coda
F
G
C/G
Am
w/ bar
3 2 1
0 1 3
0 3 1 2

Coda
F
Am
D
Am
P.M.
D
Am
P.M.
P.M.
G
Dm
G
Dm
Em11
let ring
P.M.
Am
D
Am
P.M.
w/ bar

H

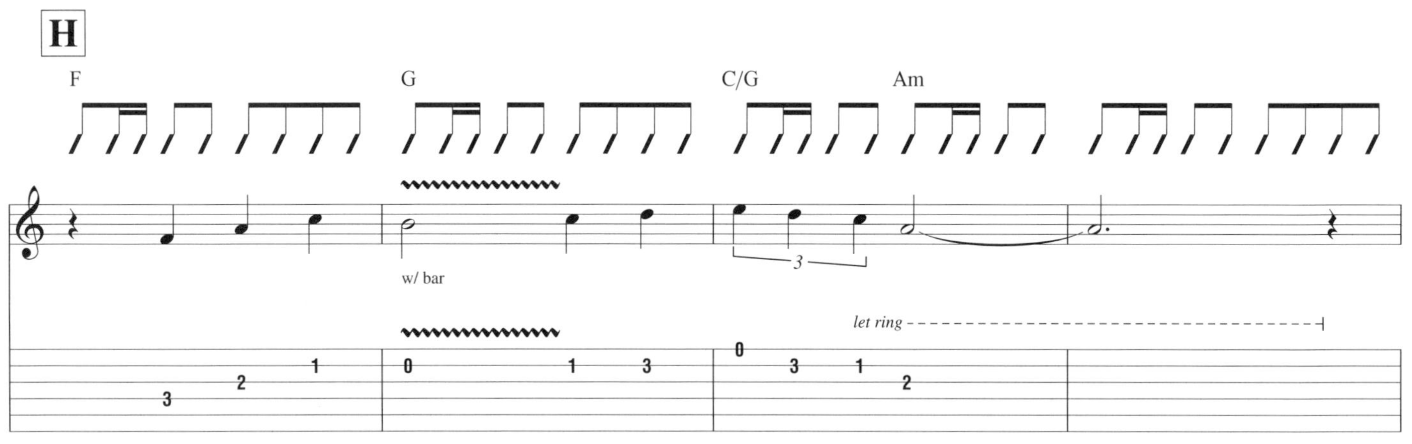

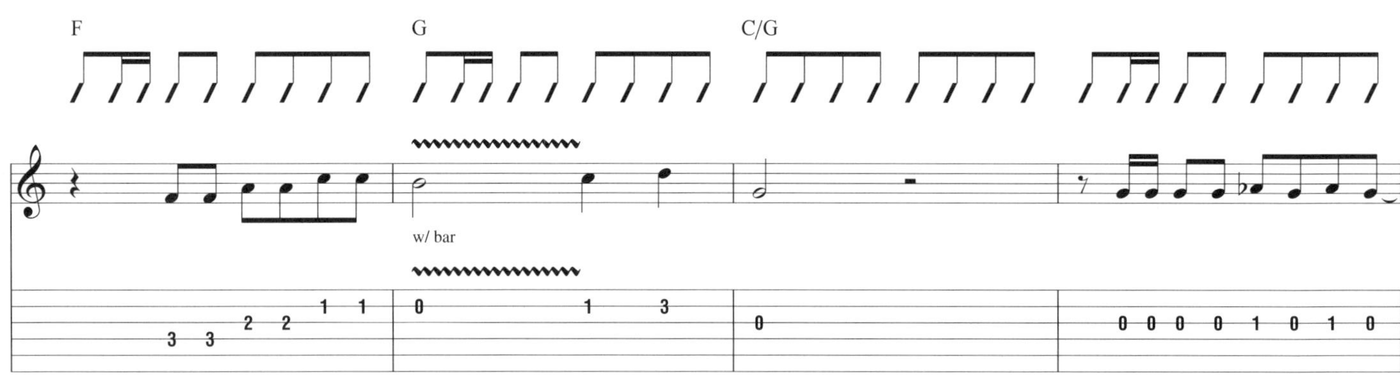

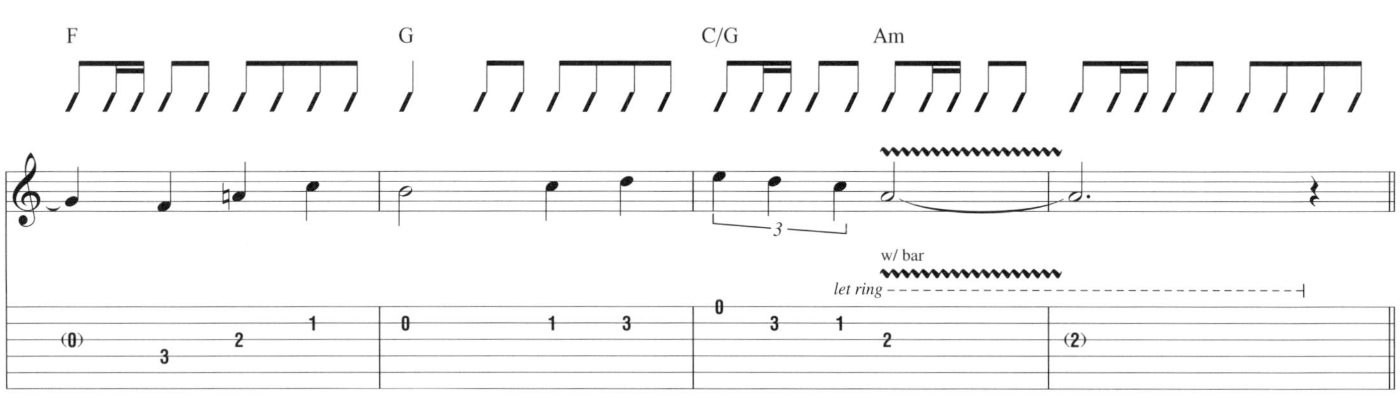

I

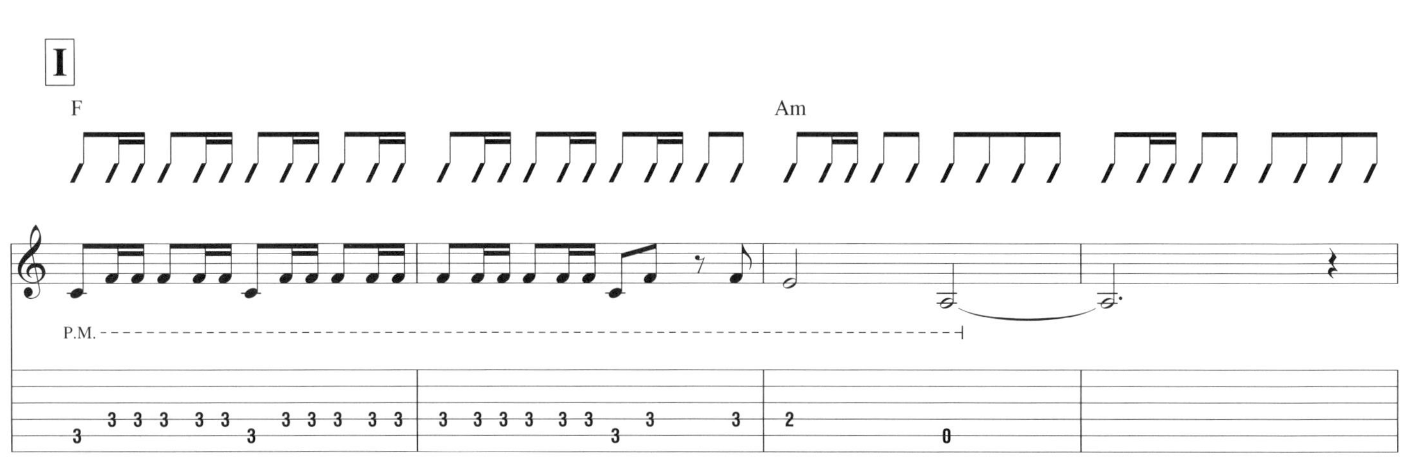

F
Am

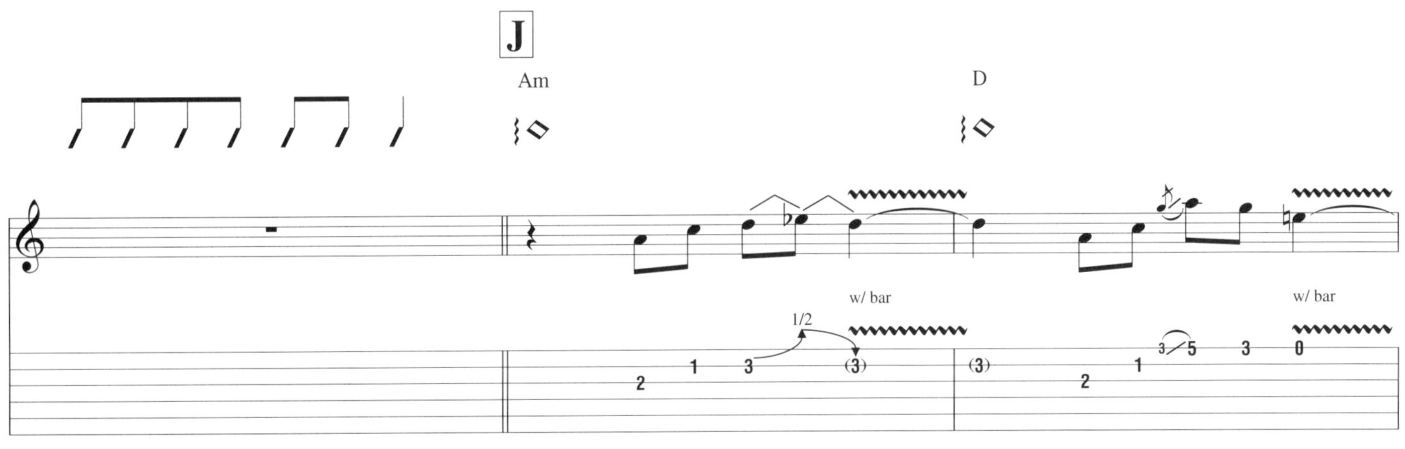
J
Am
D
w/ bar
w/ bar
1/2

Am
D
Am
D
w/ bar
w/ bar
w/ bar
w/ bar
1/2
1/2

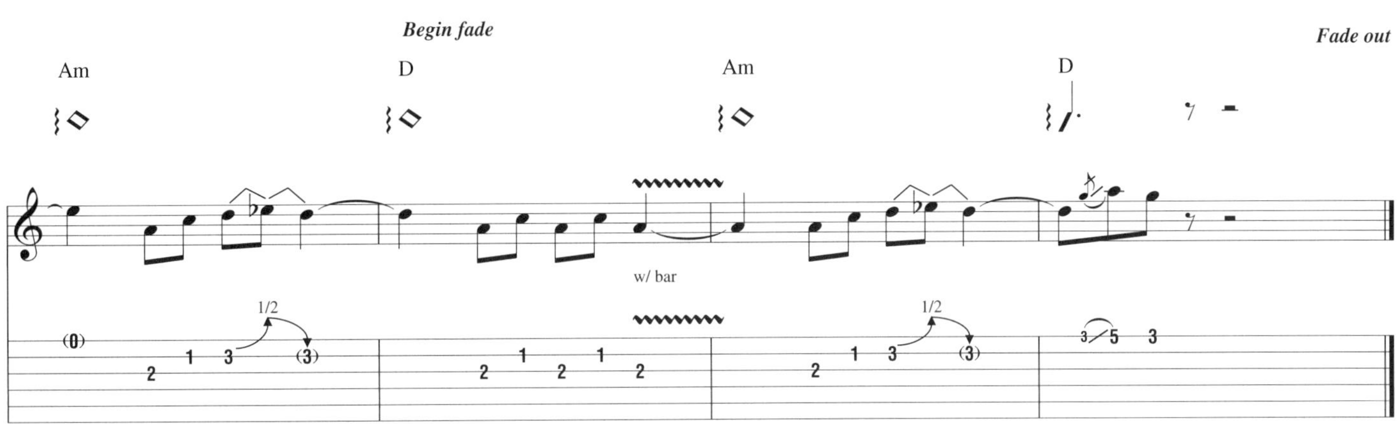
Begin fade
Fade out
Am
D
Am
D
w/ bar
1/2
1/2

Beck's Bolero

By Jimmy Page

*Two gtrs. (elec. w/ clean tone & 12-str. acous.) arr. for one.

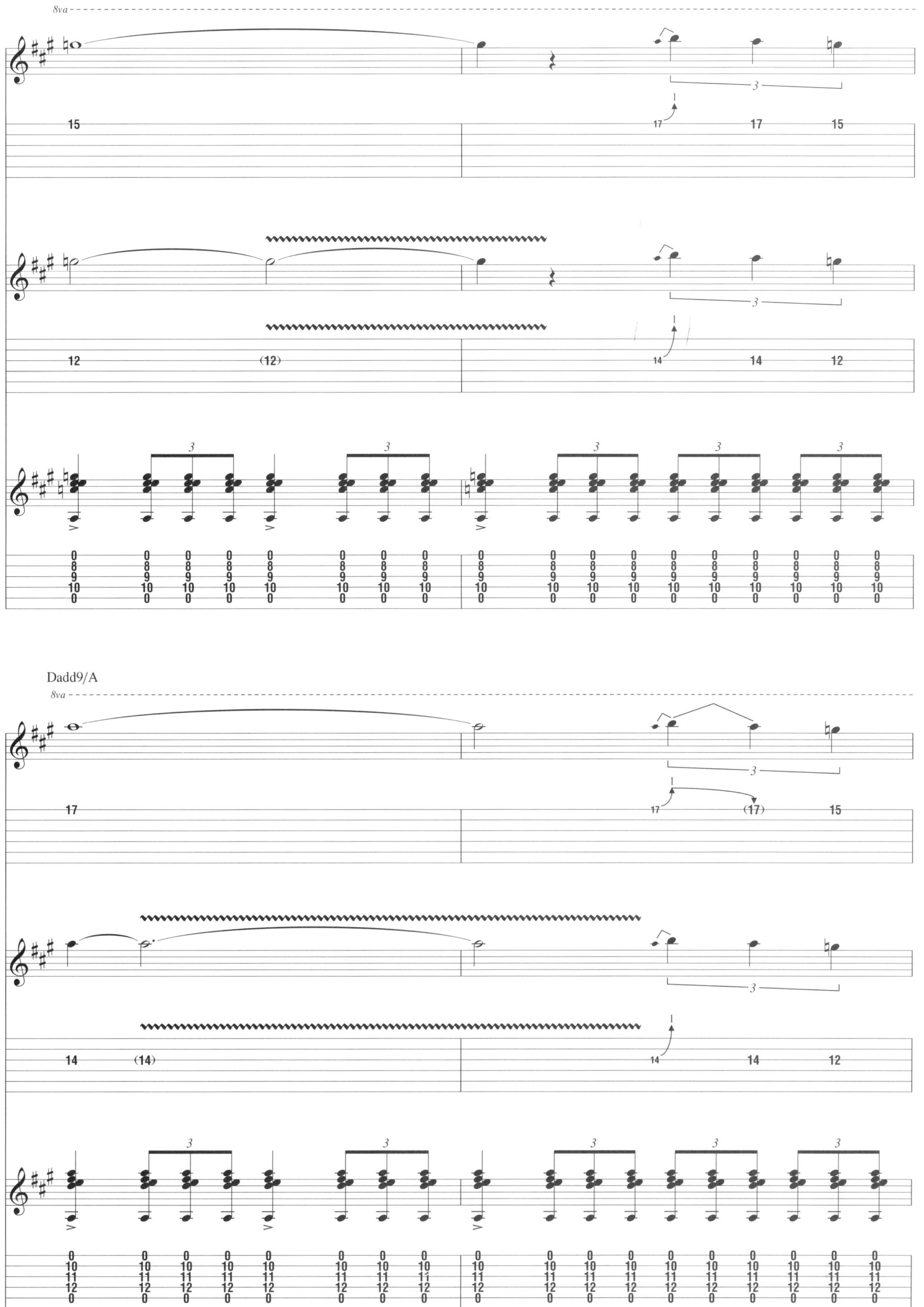

C/A
8va
Dadd9/A
8va

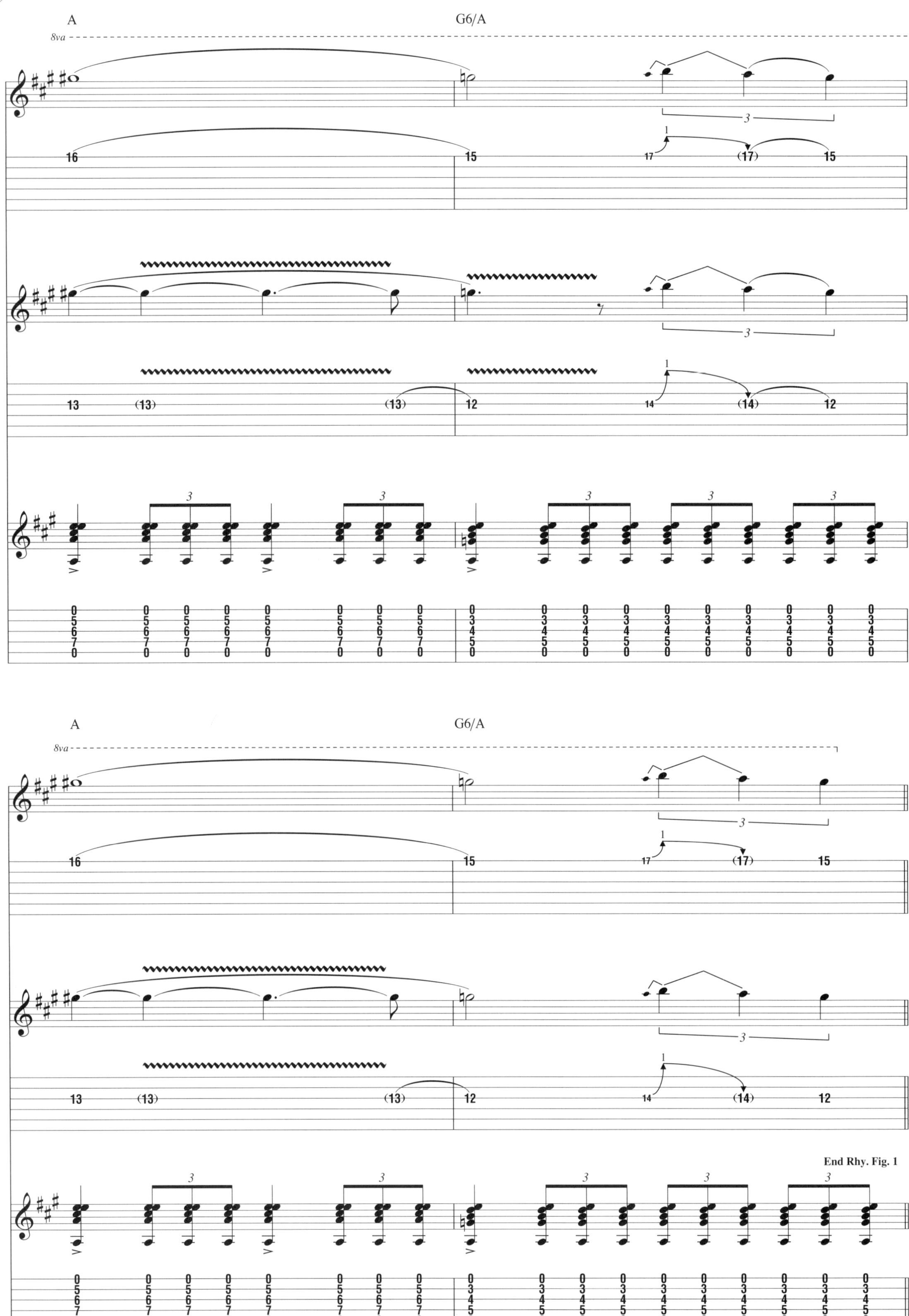

A
G6/A
8va
End Rhy. Fig. 1

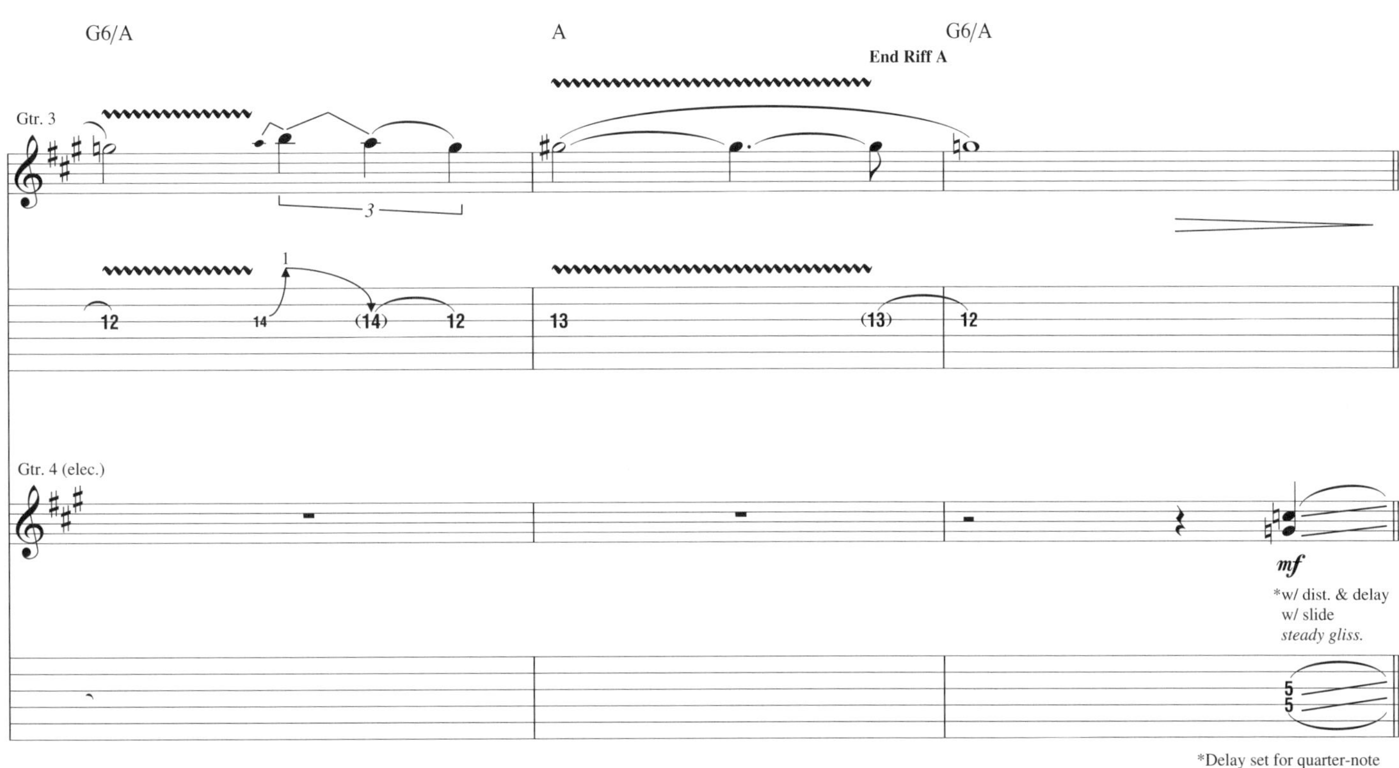

*Delay set for quarter-note regeneration w/ 1 repeat.

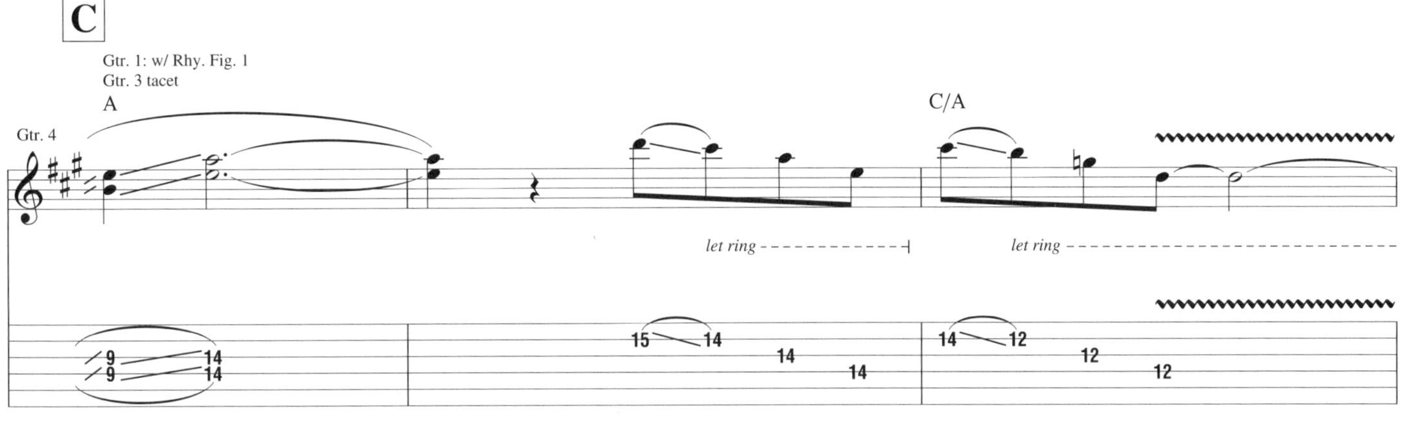

Dadd9/A
let ring
A
G6/A
A
G6/A
D
Gtr. 1: w/ Rhy. Fig. 1
A
C/A
Gtr. 4
steady gliss.
steady gliss.
steady gliss.
steady gliss.
Gtr. 3
f
Dadd9/A
A
steady gliss.

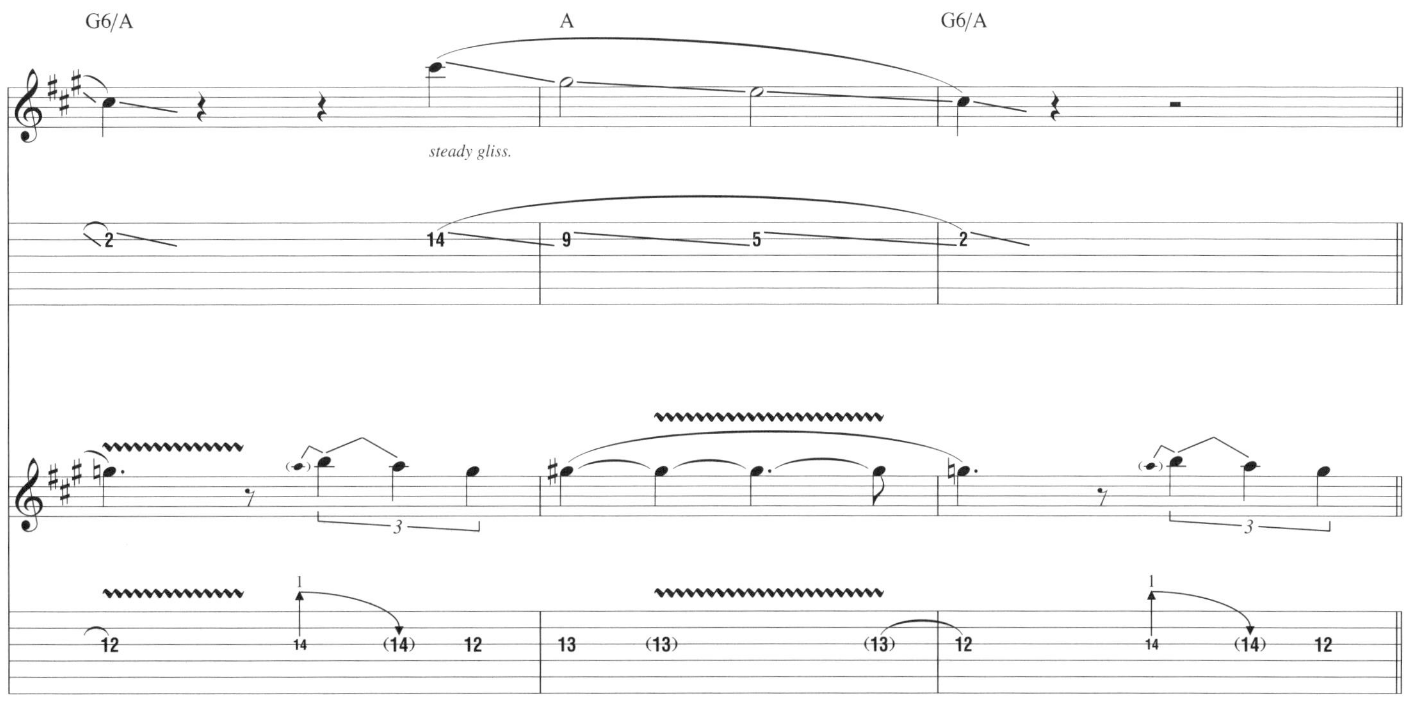
G6/A
A
G6/A
steady gliss.

E

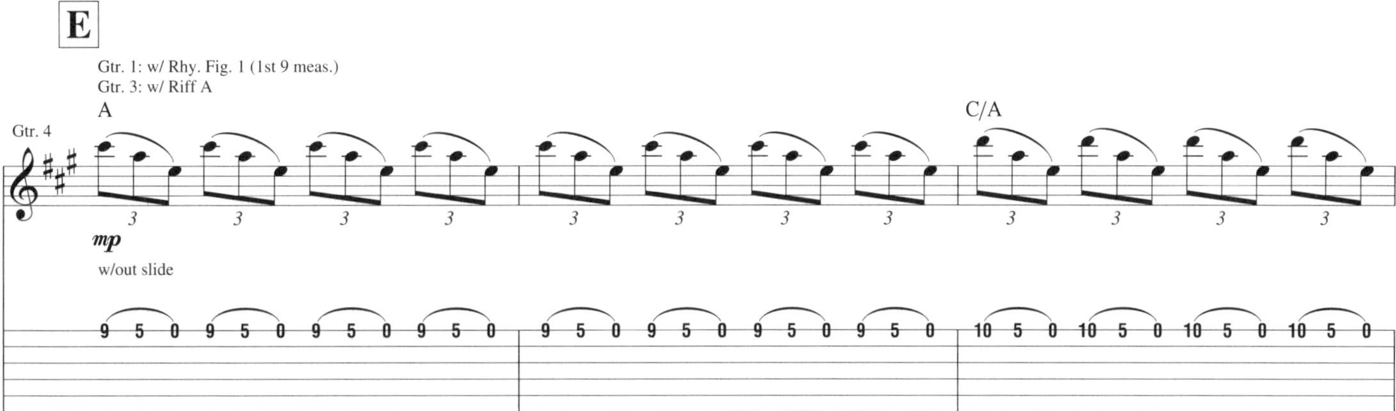
Gtr. 1: w/ Rhy. Fig. 1 (1st 9 meas.)
Gtr. 3: w/ Riff A
A
C/A
Gtr. 4
mp
w/out slide

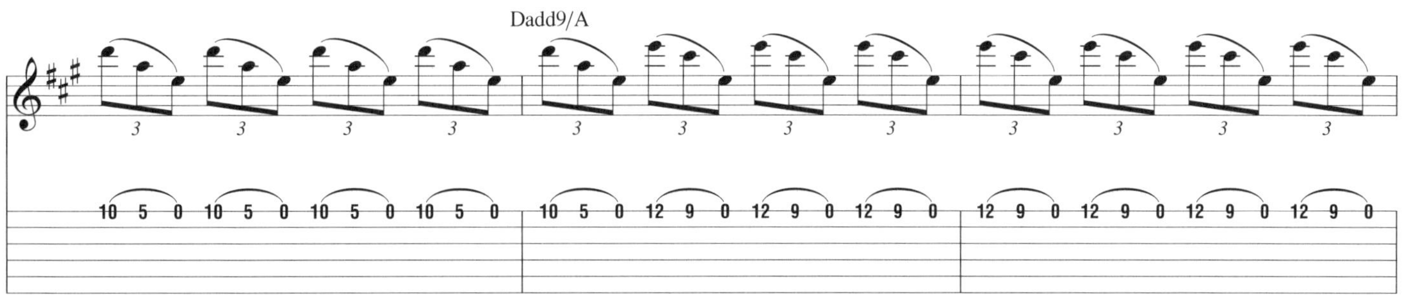
Dadd9/A

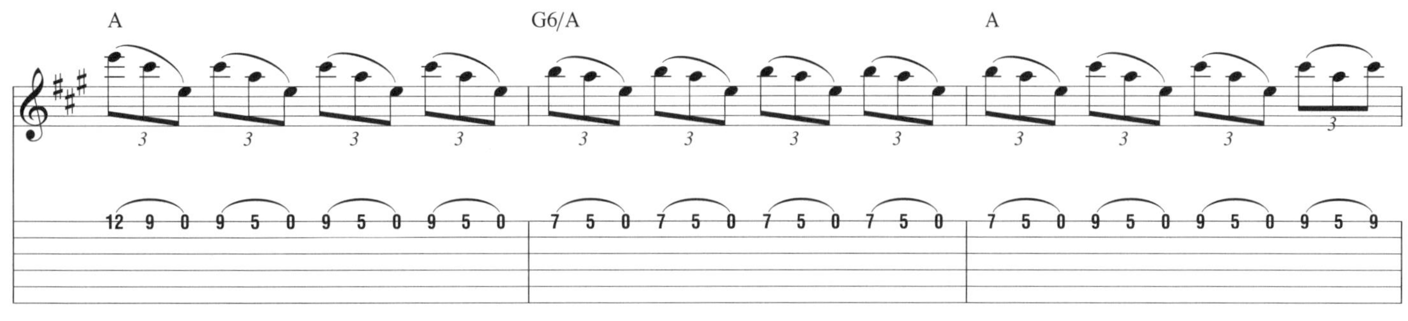
A
G6/A
A

Gtrs. 1 & 4 tacet
G6/A
A
N.C.
Gtr. 4
Gtr. 3
F
*A5 C5 A5 A♭5 G5 E5 D5 C5 G5 A5 C5 A5 A♭5 G5 E5 D5 C5
mf
P.M.
*Chord symbols reflect implied harmony.
C5 E♭5 C5 B5 B♭5 G5 F5 E♭5 C5 E♭5 C5 B5 B♭5
G5 F5 E♭5 D5 F5 D5 D♭5 C5 A5 G5 F5
P.H.
Pitch: F♯

D5
F5
D5
D♭5
C5
A5
G5
F5
D5
E5
P.H.
G
Gtr. 1: w/ Rhy. Fig. 1
A
Gtr. 4
C/A
Gtr. 3
f
Dadd9/A
A

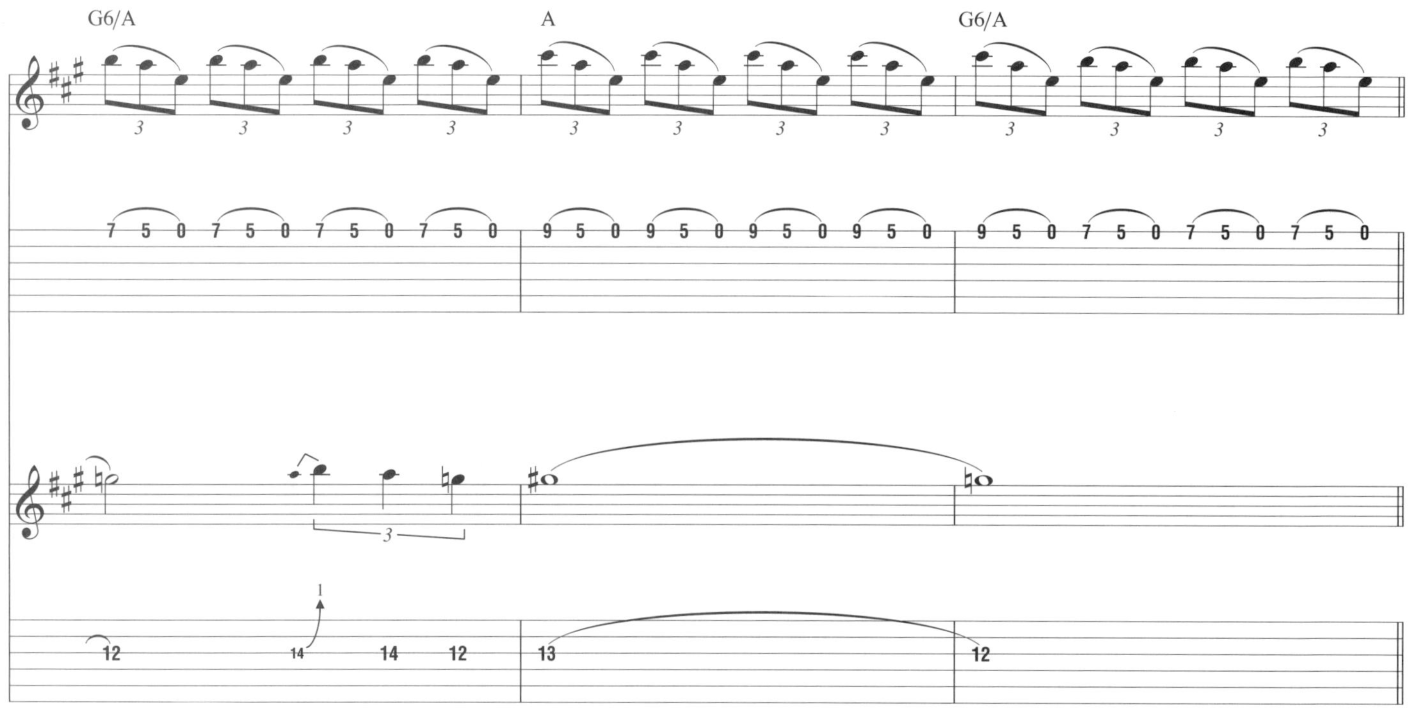

H

Gtr. 4 tacet

A G6/A A G6/A

Gtr. 4

Gtr. 3

8va

*fdbk.

Pitch: G

*Microphonic fdbk., not caused by string vibration (next 9 meas.).

Rhy. Fig. 2

End Rhy. Fig. 2

Gtr. 1

Gtr. 1: w/ Rhy. Fig. 2 (2 1/2 times)
A
G6/A
Gtr. 3
8va
loco
fdbk.
Gtr. 3 tacet
Gtr. 4
w/ heavy reverb
w/ bar
N.C.
*fdbk.
*Microphonic fdbk., not caused by string vibration.
Gtr. 1

Dee

Music by Randy Rhoads

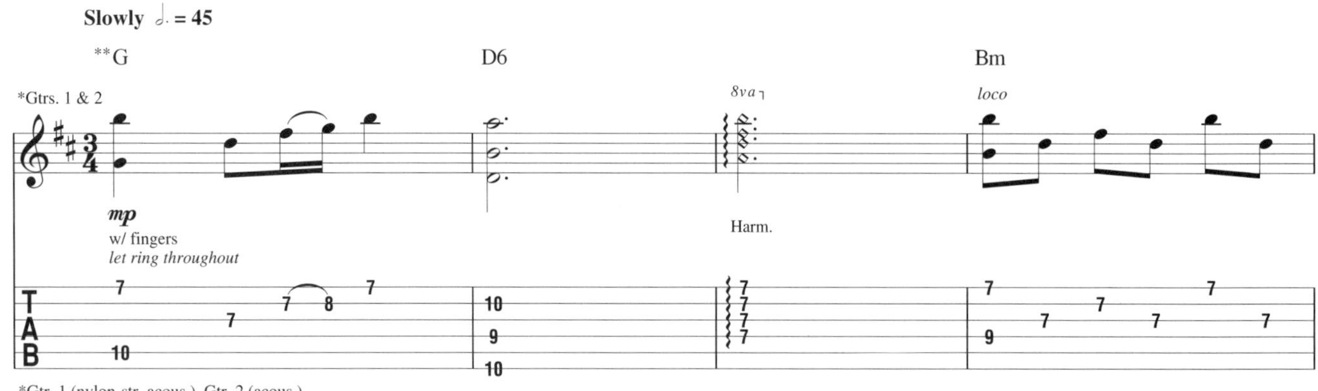

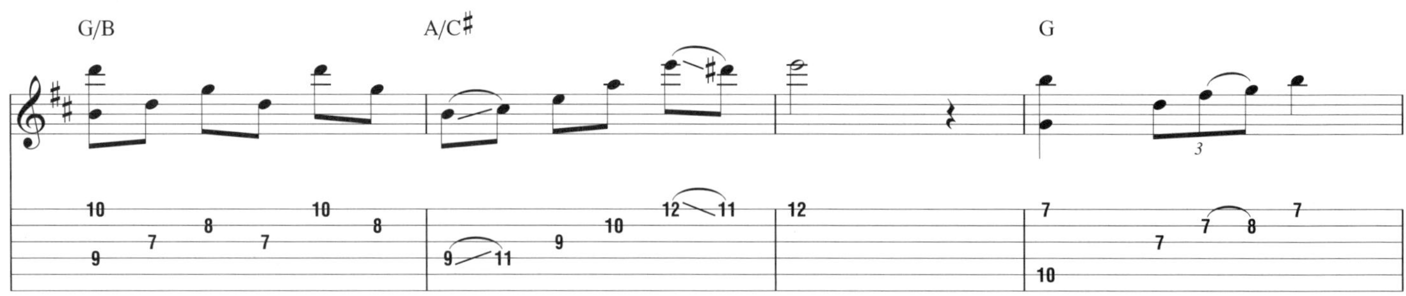

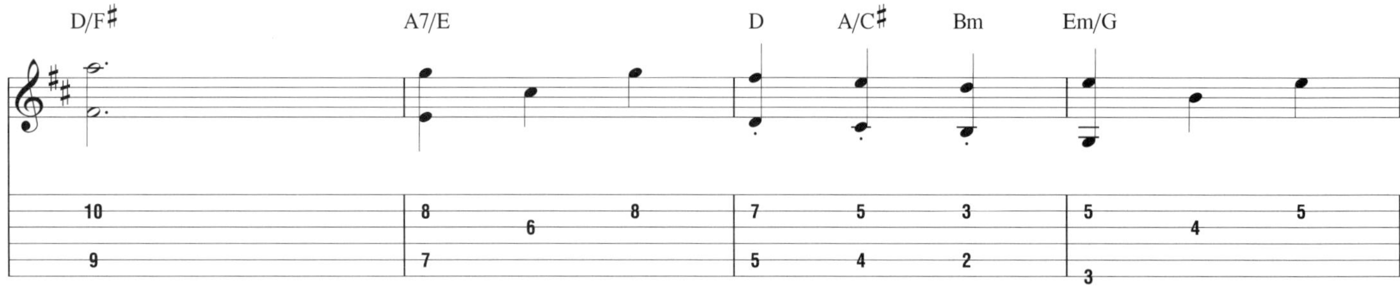

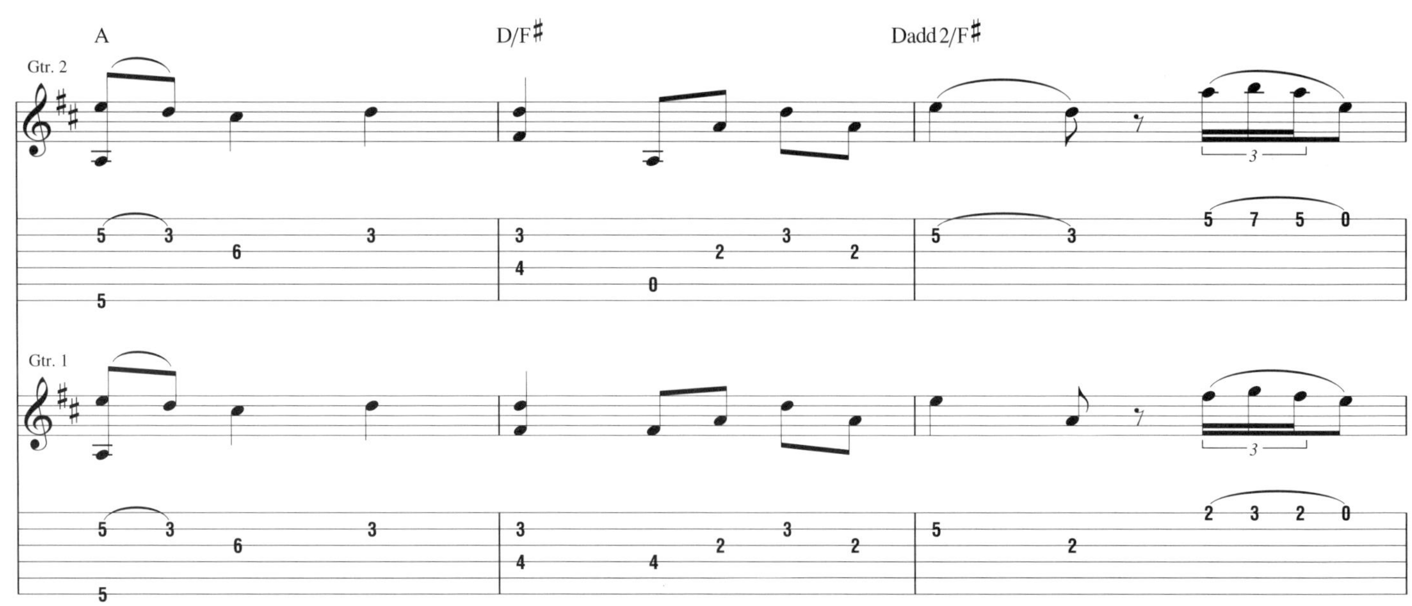

B7/D♯
B7
Em
E7
A7
Gtrs. 1 & 2
Harm.
D
G/B
D
A7
D
Gtr. 2
Gtr. 1
divisi
*Gtr. 2 to left of slashes in tab.
A/C♯
Gtrs. 1 & 2
Bm
Bm/A
Gtr. 2
Gtr. 1
divisi
A7
Gtrs. 1 & 2
D/F♯
Em
A7/C♯
D6
Gtr. 2
8va
rit.
Harm.
Gtr. 1
8va
rit.
Harm.

Eruption

Music by David Lee Roth, Edward Van Halen, Alex Van Halen and Michael Anthony

Gtr. 2 tacet
8va
Gtr. 1
grad. bend
E
loco
w/ bar
1 hold bend
N.C.
w/ bar
grad. dive
B
Am
P.M.
Em
rake

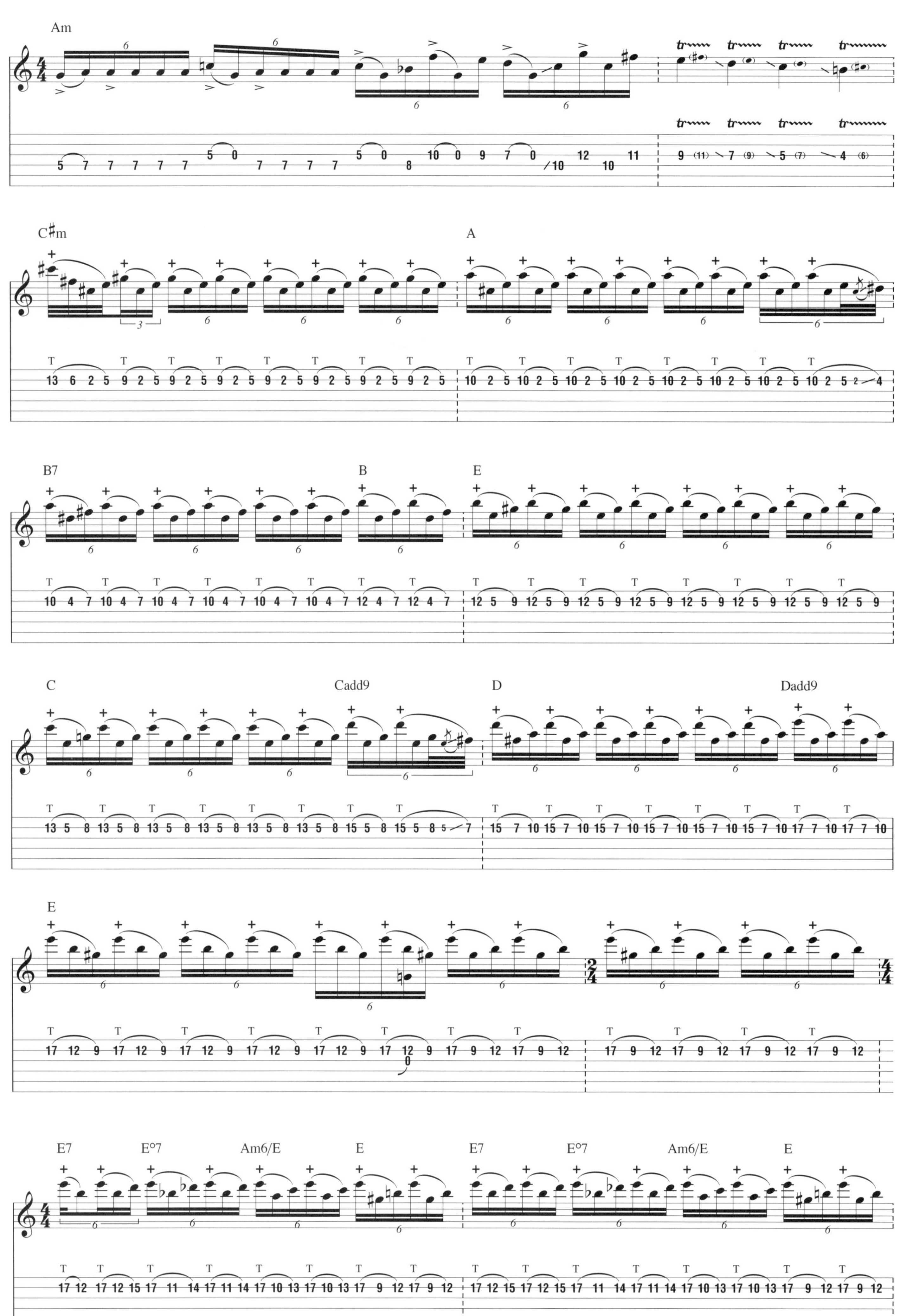
Am
C♯m
A
B7
B
E
C
Cadd9
D
Dadd9
E
E7
E°7
Am6/E
E
E7
E°7
Am6/E
E

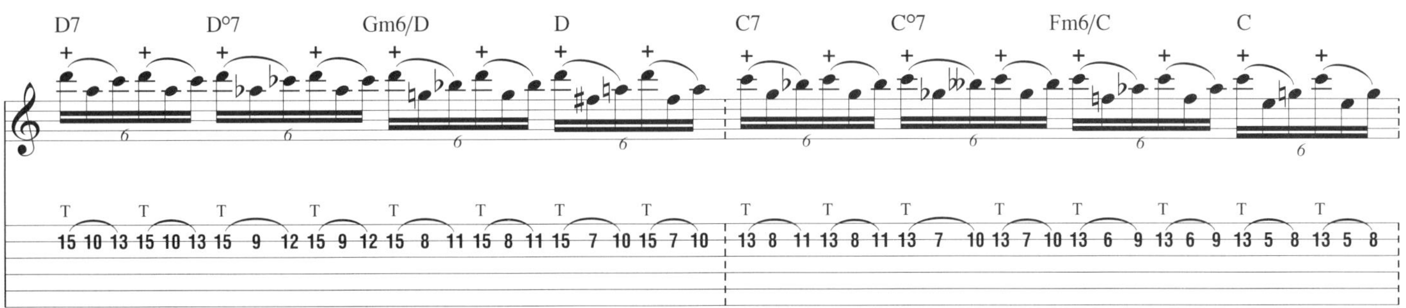
D7
D°7
Gm6/D
D
C7
C°7
Fm6/C
C

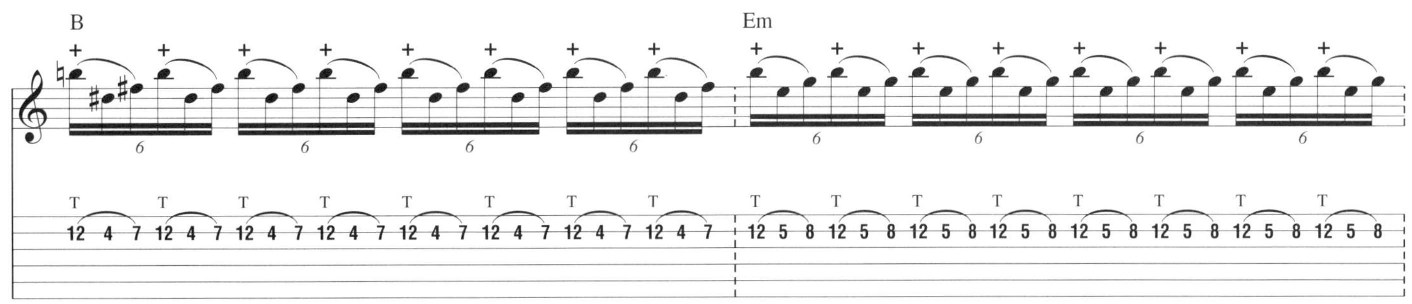
B
Em

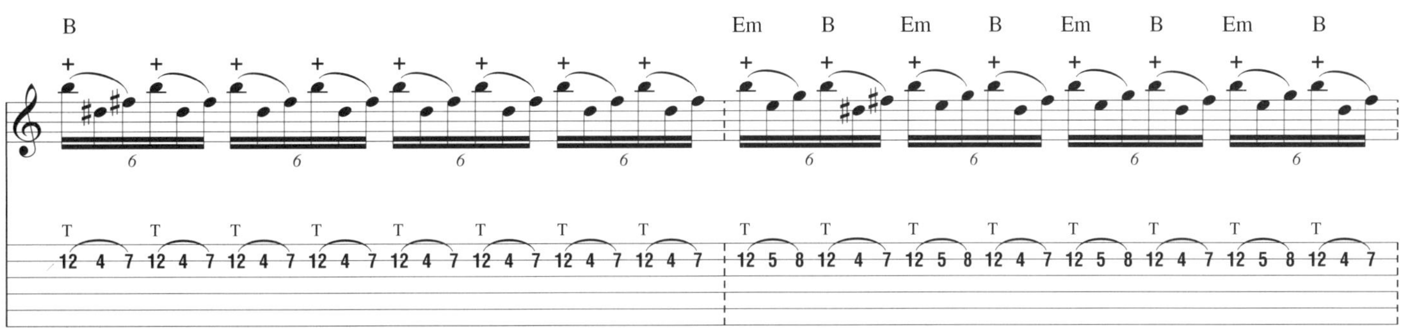
B
Em B Em B Em B Em B

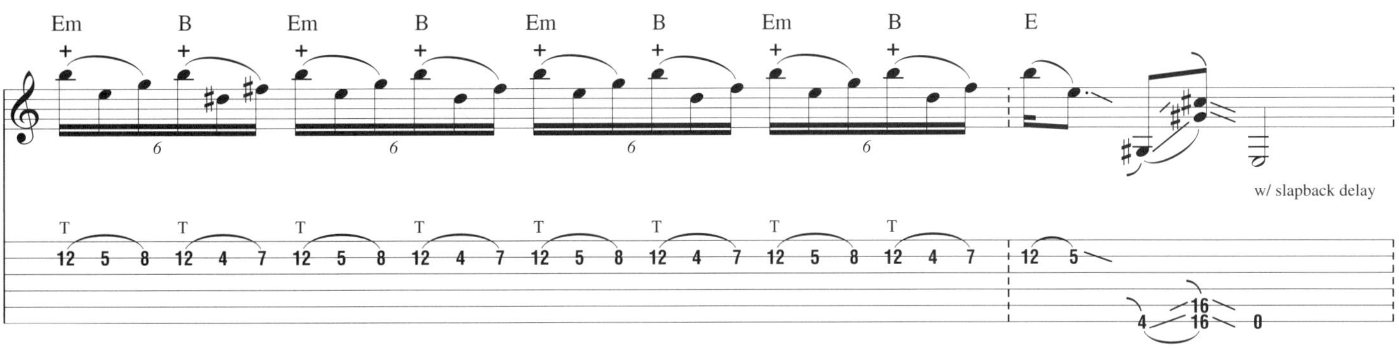
Em B Em B Em B Em B
E
w/ slapback delay

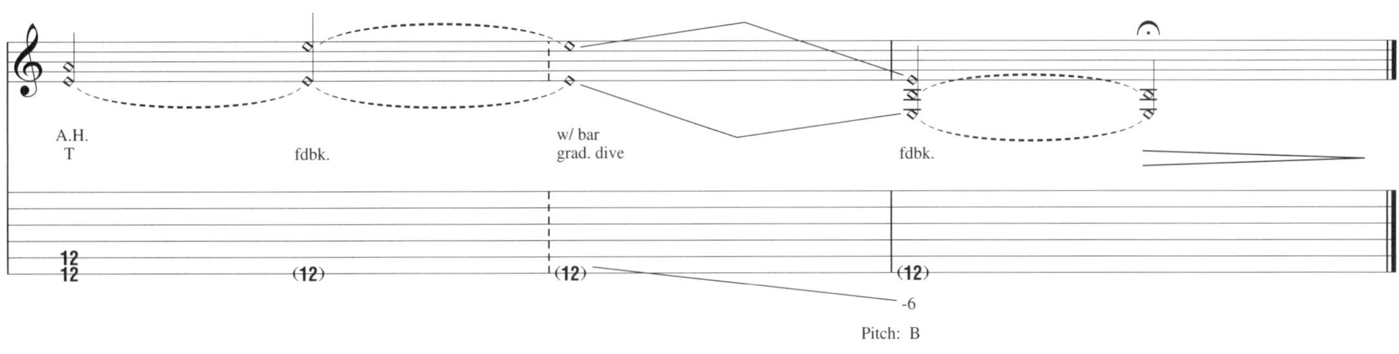
A.H.
fdbk.
w/ bar
grad. dive
fdbk.
Pitch: B

Frankenstein

By Edgar Winter

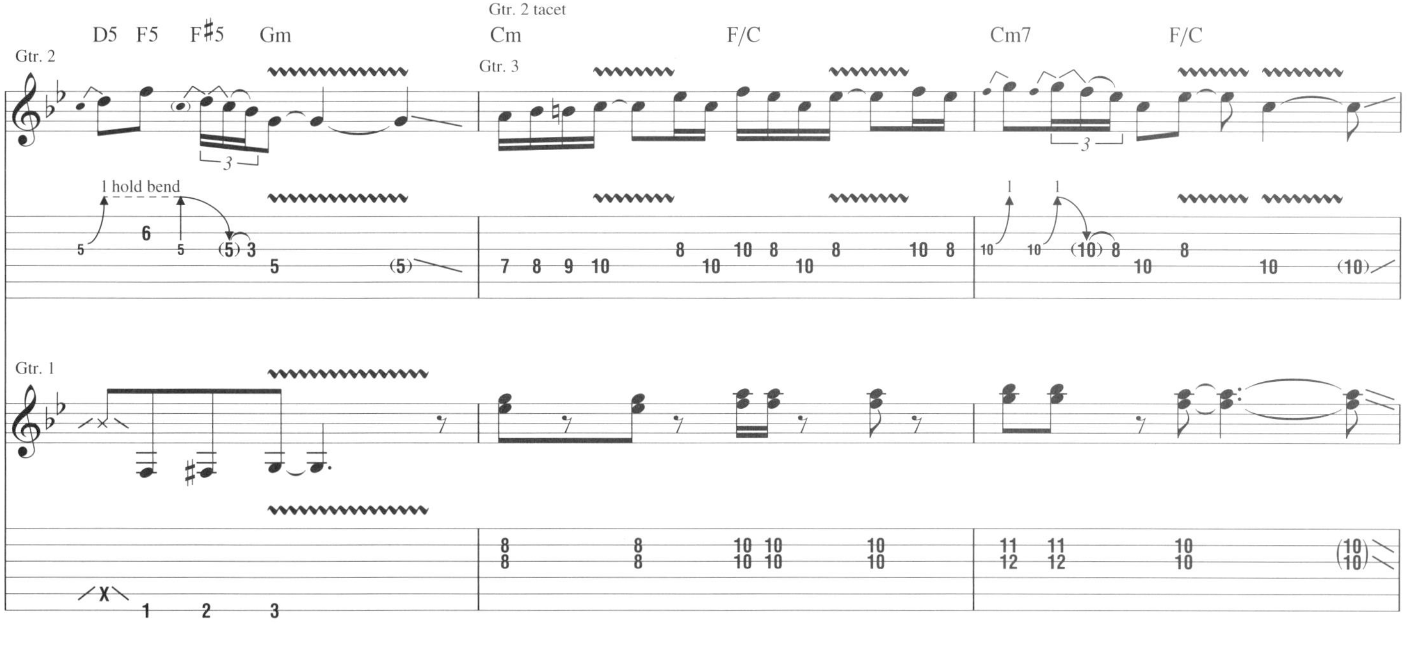
Gtr. 2 tacet
D5 F5 F♯5 Gm
Cm
F/C
Cm7
F/C
Gtr. 2
Gtr. 3
1 hold bend
Gtr. 1

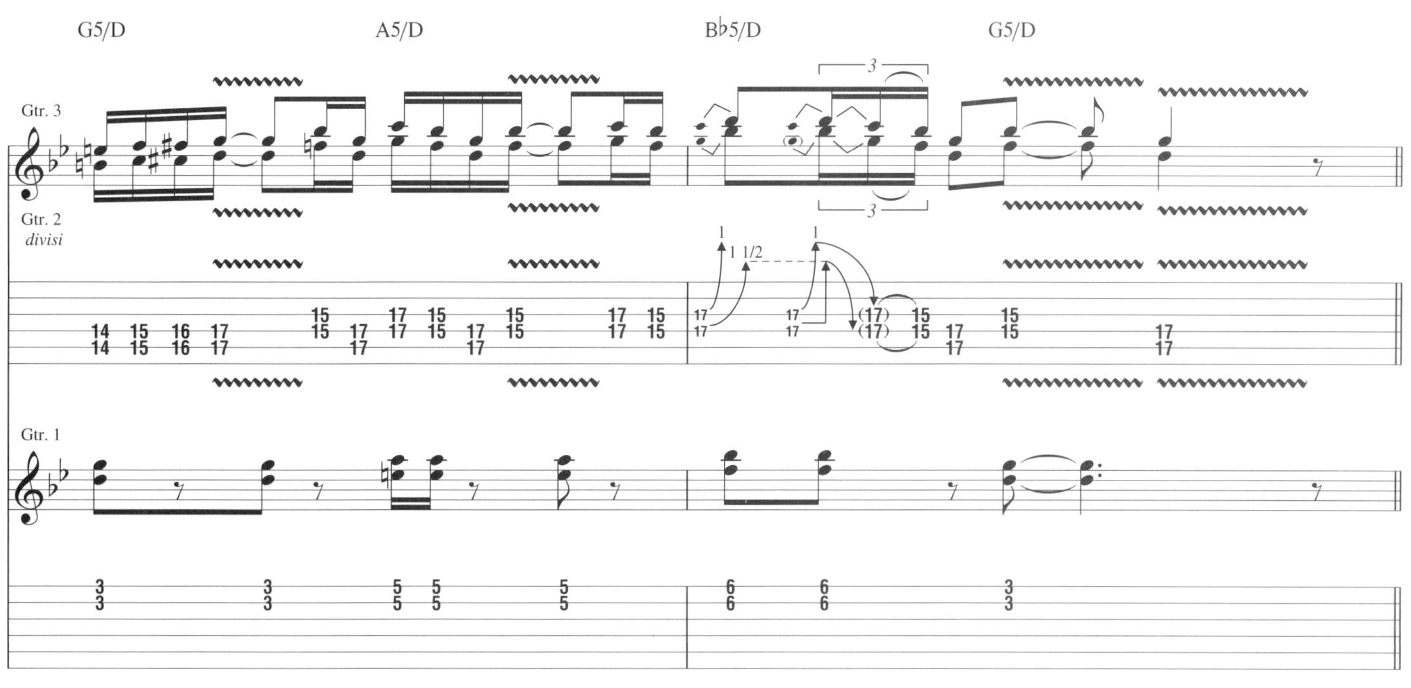
G5/D
A5/D
B♭5/D
G5/D
Gtr. 3
Gtr. 2
divisi
Gtr. 1

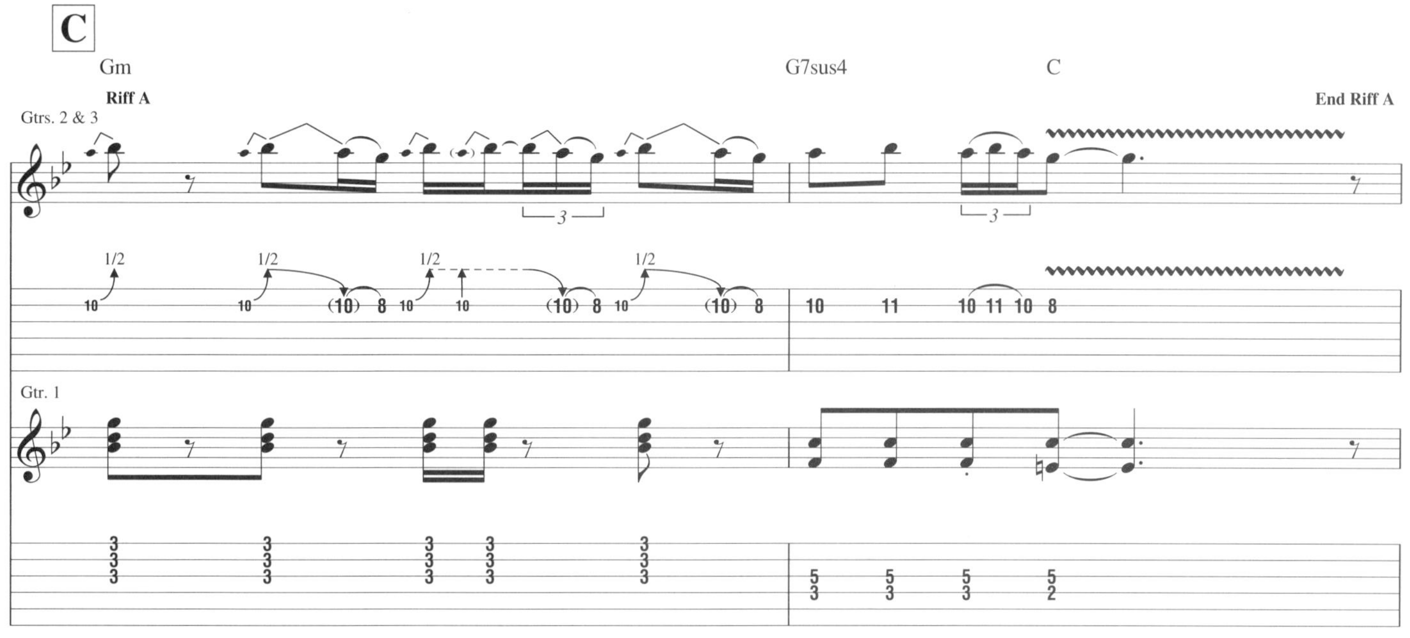
C
Gm
G7sus4
C
Riff A
End Riff A
Gtrs. 2 & 3
Gtr. 1

Gtr. 2: w/ Riff A
*C♯°7
Gm/D
E♭
C/E
Gtr. 3
Gtr. 1
*Chord symbols reflect implied harmony (next 2 meas.)
D
Gtr. 3 tacet
G5
F5 G5
B♭5
G5
F5 G5
N.C.
Gtr. 2 tacet
G5
F5 G5
B♭5
Gtr. 1
Gtr. 2 divisi
1., 2., 3.
E
G5
F5 G5 N.C.
Gm
C9
Gm
C9
mf
w/ clean tone
1/2
4.
Gm
C
Gm9
C9
Gm9
C9
1/2
F
Gtr. 1
Gm
C
Gm7
C9
Gtr. 2

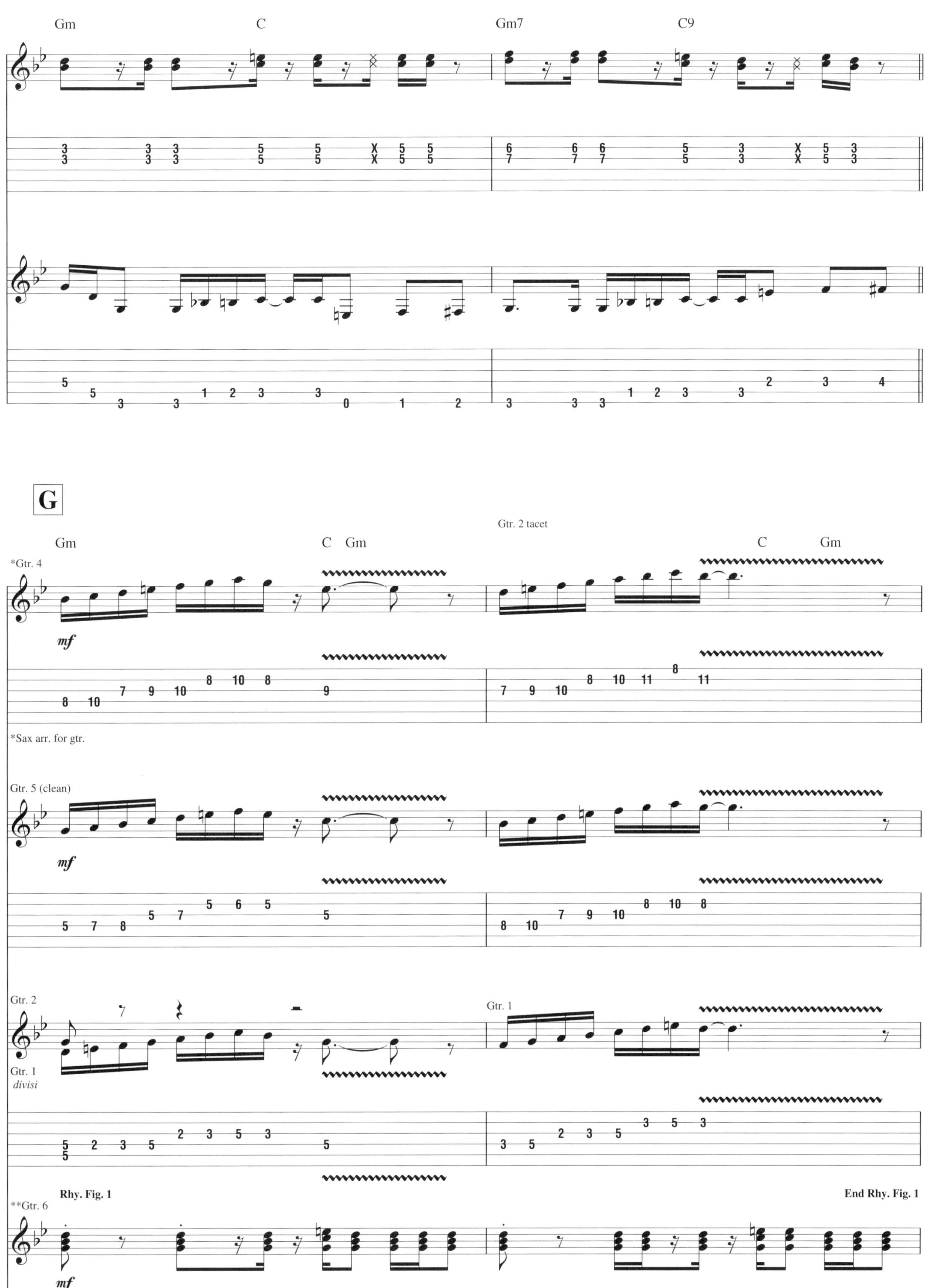

Gm
C
Gm7
C9
G
Gtr. 2 tacet
Gm
C Gm
C
Gm
*Gtr. 4
mf
*Sax arr. for gtr.
Gtr. 5 (clean)
mf
Gtr. 2
Gtr. 1
divisi
Gtr. 1
Rhy. Fig. 1
End Rhy. Fig. 1
**Gtr. 6
mf
**Organ arr. for gtr.

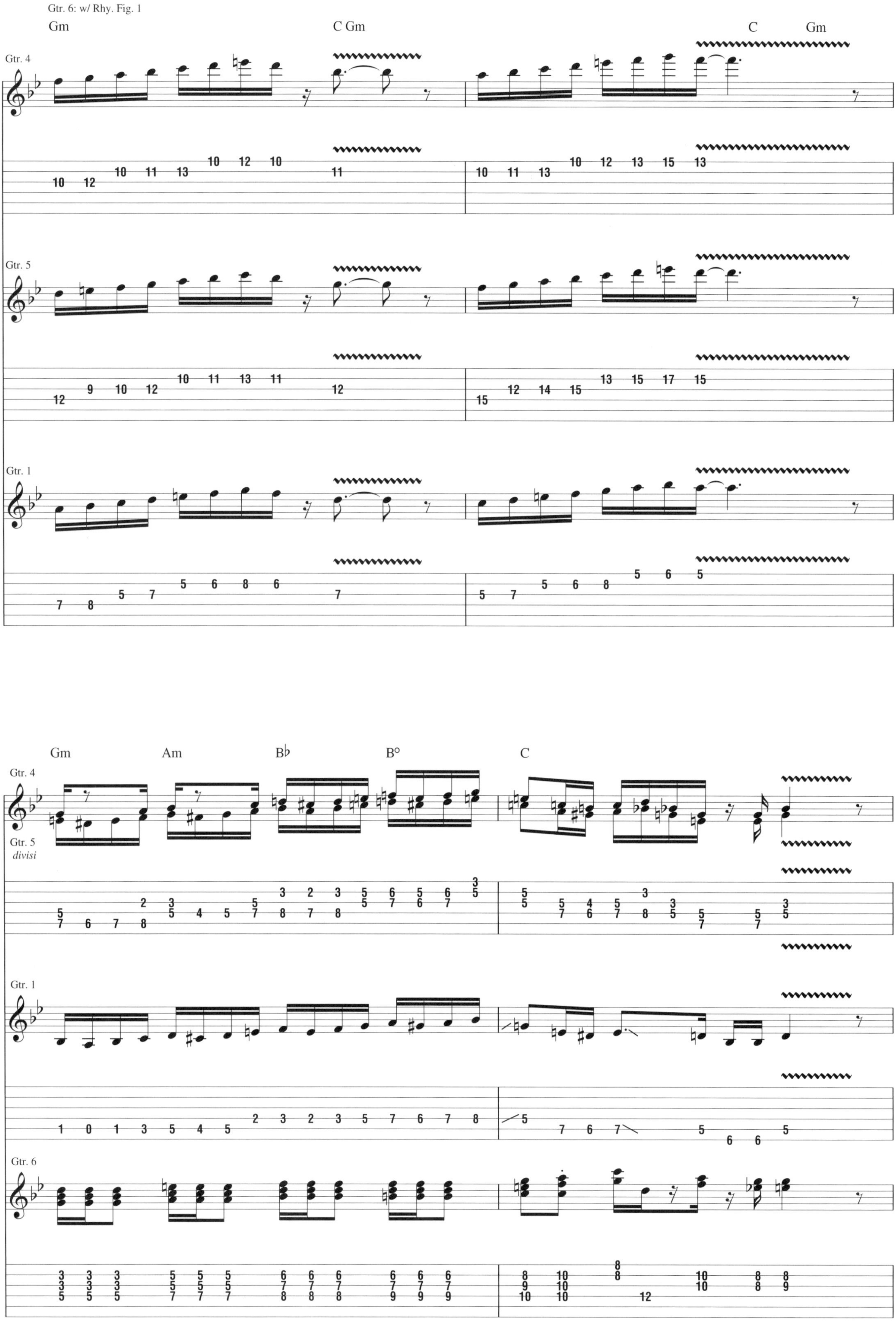

Gtr. 6: w/ Rhy. Fig. 1

Gm C Gm C Gm

Gtr. 4

Gtr. 5

Gtr. 1

Gm Am B♭ B° C

Gtr. 4

Gtr. 5
divisi

Gtr. 1

Gtr. 6

Gm Am B♭ C Dm Em9 F Gm C6
*Gtr. 4 to left of slashes in tab.
w/ dist.
(cont. on lower staff)
(cont. on upper staff)
H
Gtrs. 4 & 5 tacet
G7(no3rd)
Gtr. 6
Gtr. 1
I
G5 F5 G5 F5 N.C. G5 F5 G5 B♭5 N.C.

J
Gm
Am/G
B♭/G
C/G
Gtrs. 1 & 5 (dist.)
*w/ wah-wah
*Gtr. 1 only
** ○ = open (toe up): + = closed (toe down)
Gtr. 6
K
Double-time 𝅗𝅥 = 162
Gtrs. 1, 5 & 6 tacet
N.C.
8va
(Drums)
wah-wah off
L
A tempo
G5
B♭5
F5
Gtr. 1
Play 3 times
M

N.C.
(Drums enter)
Synth.
Hi-hat
N
G5
F5 G5
B♭5
Gtr. 1
Gtr. 2
divisi
N.C.
Gtr. 2 tacet
P.S.
Gm
C
Free time
C5
fdbk.
*fdbk.
Pitch: F
*Using a guitar with Les Paul style electronics, set lead volume to 0 and rhythm volume to 10. Strike the strings while the pickup selector switch is in the lead position, then flip the switch in the rhythm indicated to simulate the re-attack.

Green Onions

Written by Al Jackson, Jr., Lewis Steinberg, Booker T. Jones and Steve Cropper

C
Organ Solo
Riff A
P.M.
End Rhy. Fig. 2
let ring

Bb5 Db5 Eb5 F5 Ab5 Bb5 F5 Ab5 Bb5
End Riff A
P.M.

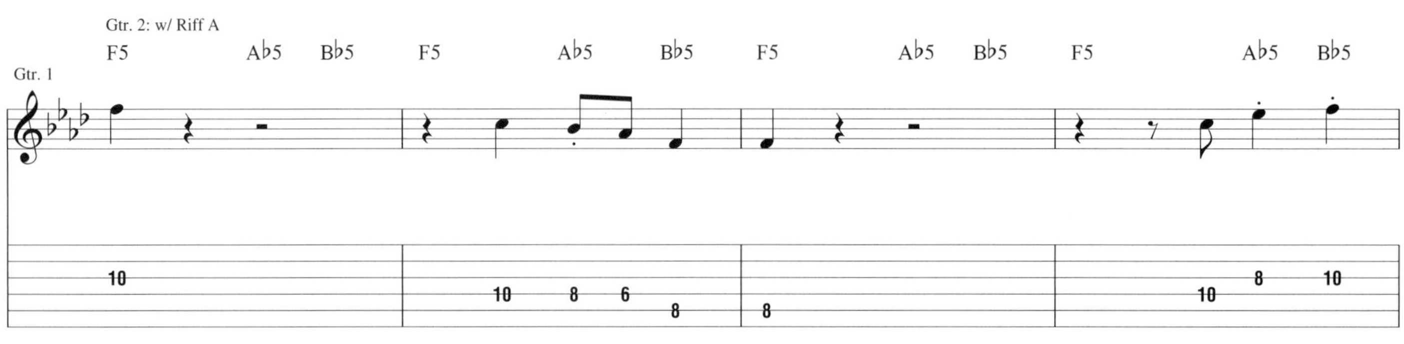
Gtr. 2: w/ Riff A
Gtr. 1
F5 Ab5 Bb5 F5 Ab5 Bb5 F5 Ab5 Bb5 F5 Ab5 Bb5

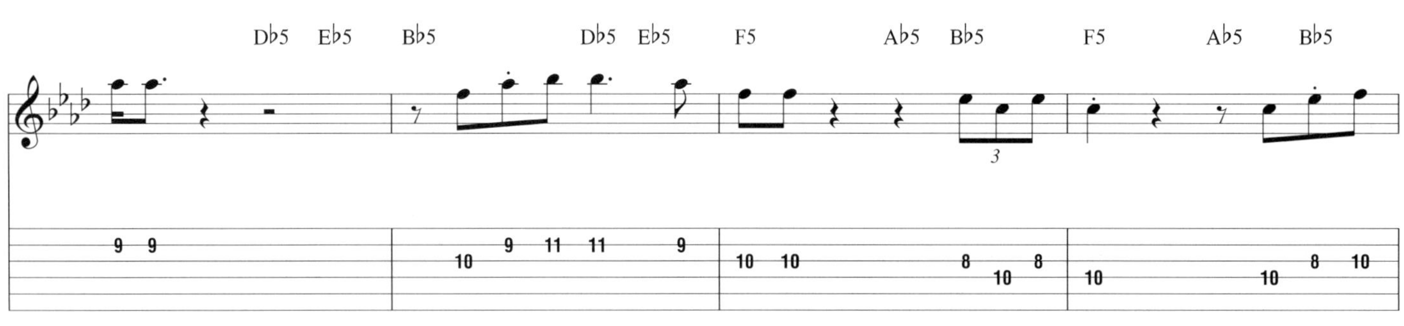
Db5 Eb5 Bb5 Db5 Eb5 F5 Ab5 Bb5 F5 Ab5 Bb5

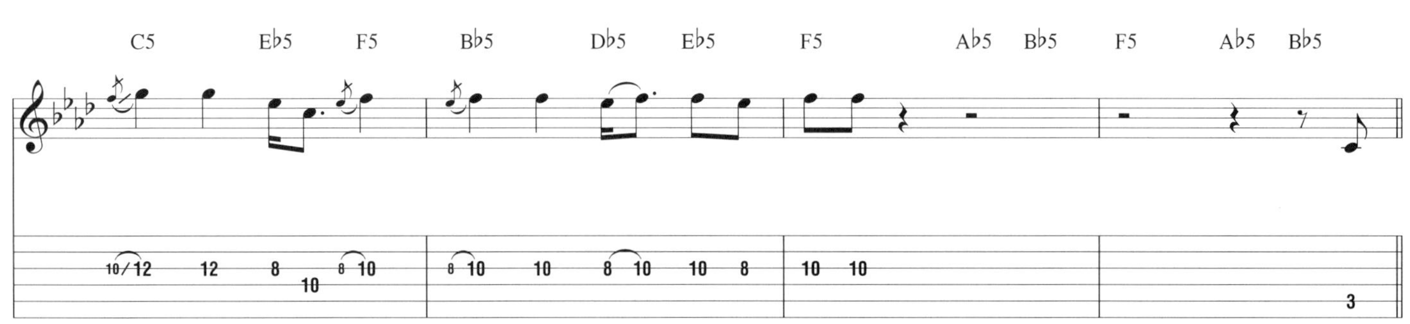
C5 Eb5 F5 Bb5 Db5 Eb5 F5 Ab5 Bb5 F5 Ab5 Bb5

D
Guitar Solo
Gtr. 1: w/ Rhy. Fig. 2 (2 times)
Gtr. 2
w/ reverb

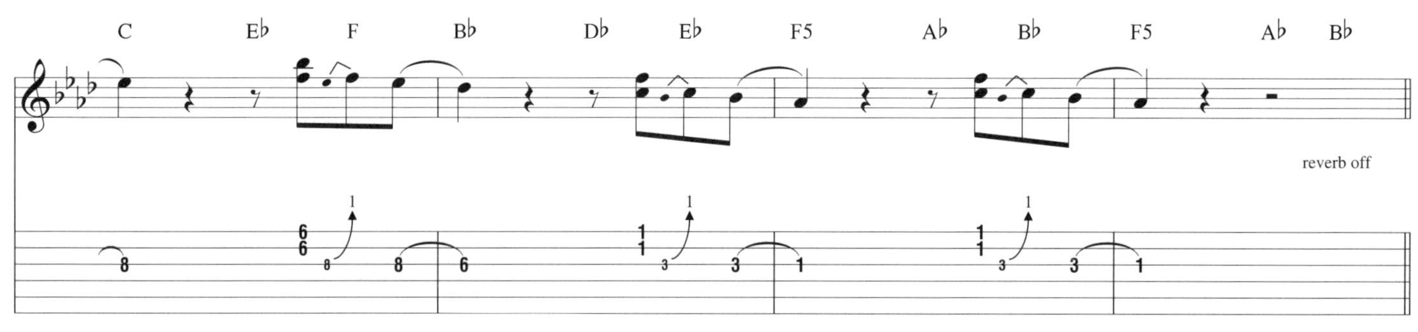
C Eb F Bb Db Eb F5 Ab Bb F5 Ab Bb
reverb off

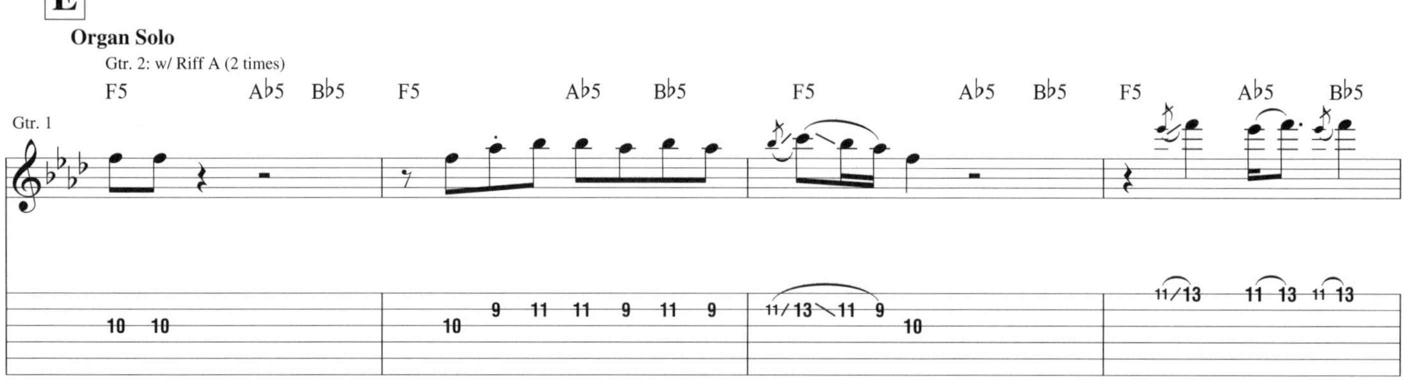
E
Organ Solo
Gtr. 2: w/ Riff A (2 times)
F5 Ab5 Bb5 F5 Ab5 Bb5 F5 Ab5 Bb5 F5 Ab5 Bb5
Gtr. 1

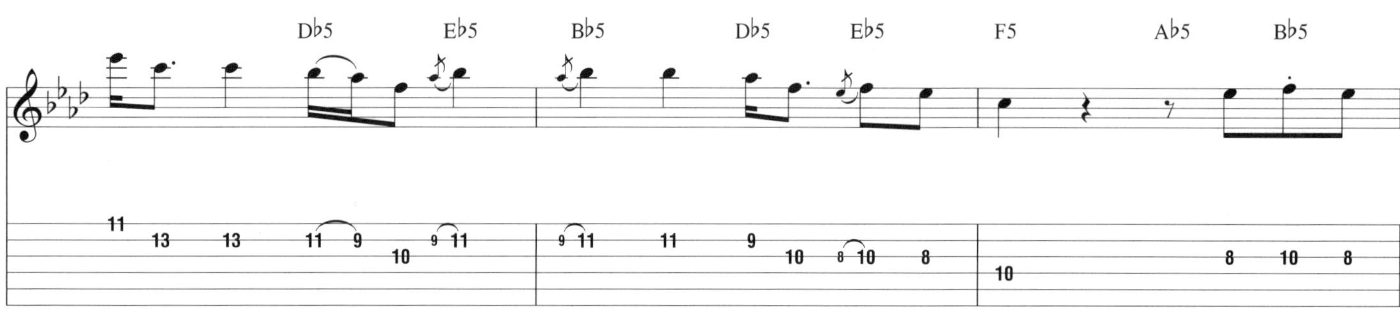
Db5 Eb5 Bb5 Db5 Eb5 F5 Ab5 Bb5

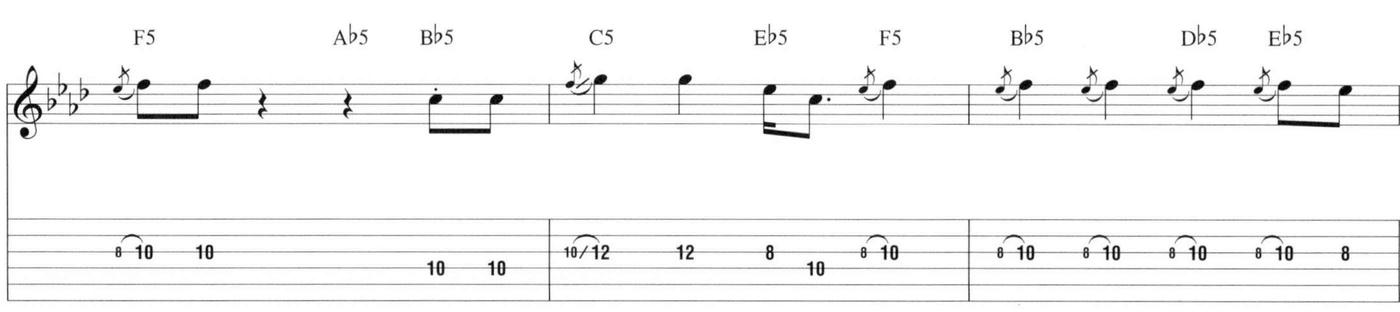
F5 Ab5 Bb5 C5 Eb5 F5 Bb5 Db5 Eb5

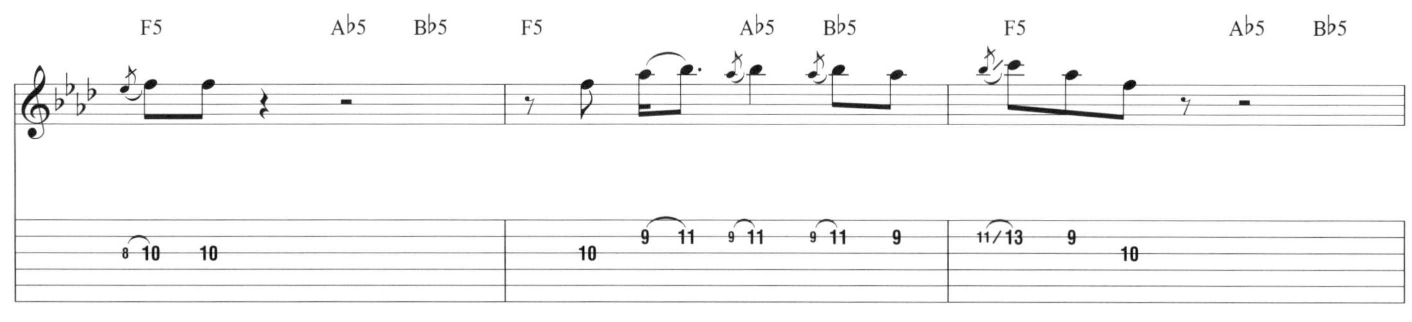
F5 Ab5 Bb5 F5 Ab5 Bb5 F5 Ab5 Bb5

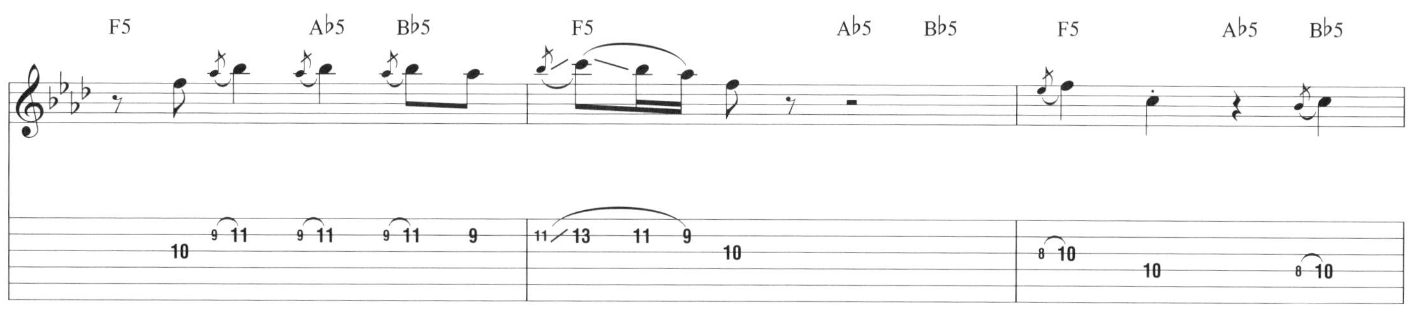
F5
A♭5
B♭5
F5
A♭5
B♭5
F5
A♭5
B♭5

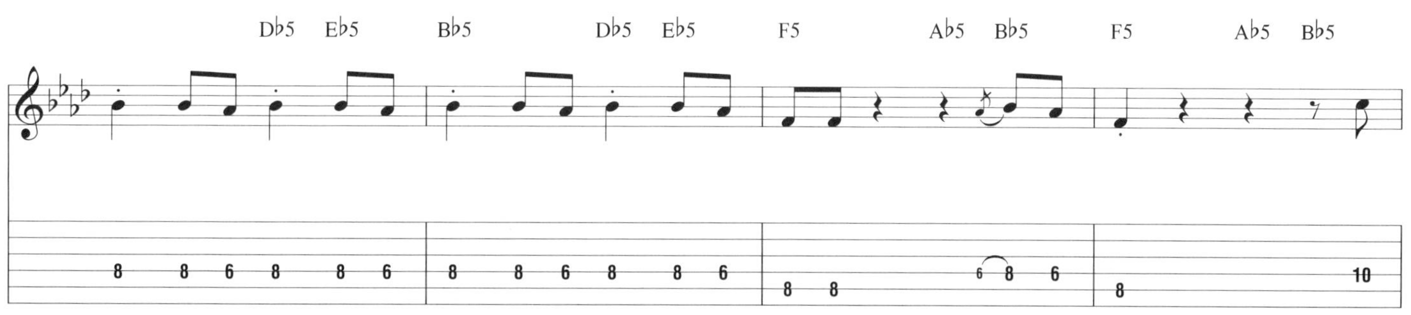
D♭5
E♭5
B♭5
D♭5
E♭5
F5
A♭5
B♭5
F5
A♭5
B♭5

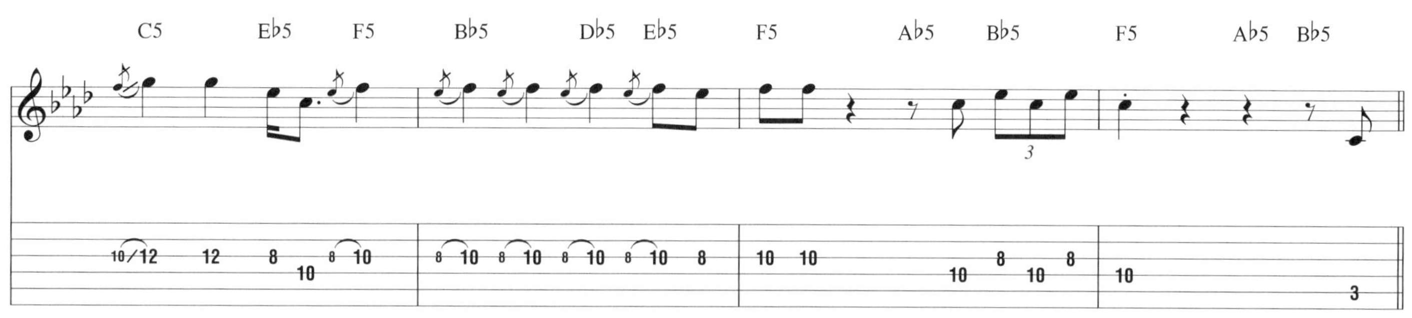
C5
E♭5
F5
B♭5
D♭5
E♭5
F5
A♭5
B♭5
F5
A♭5
B♭5

F

Outro

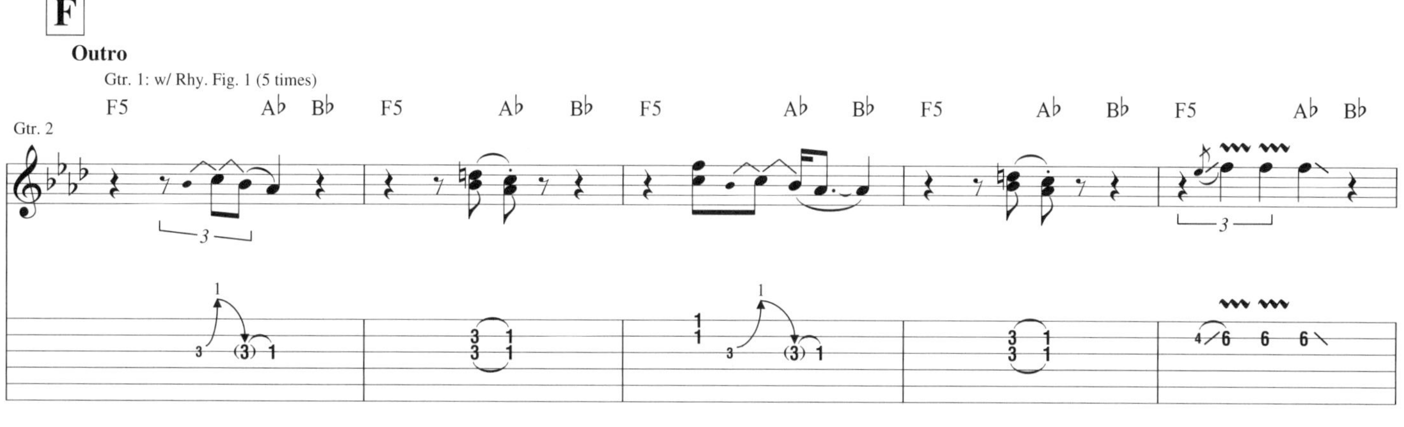
Gtr. 1: w/ Rhy. Fig. 1 (5 times)
Gtr. 2
F5
A♭
B♭
F5
A♭
B♭
F5
A♭
B♭
F5
A♭
B♭
F5
A♭
B♭

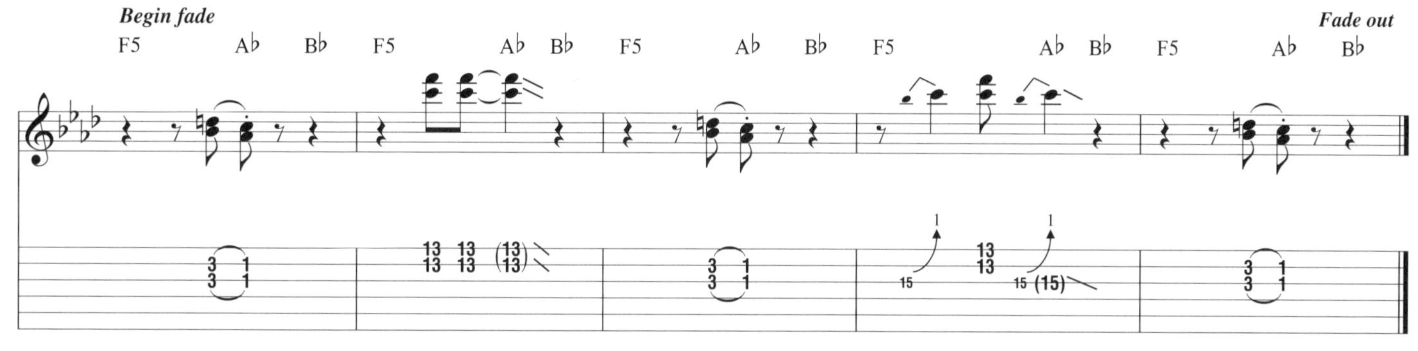
Begin fade
Fade out
F5
A♭
B♭
F5
A♭
B♭
F5
A♭
B♭
F5
A♭
B♭
F5
A♭
B♭

Guitar Boogie Shuffle

By Arthur Smith

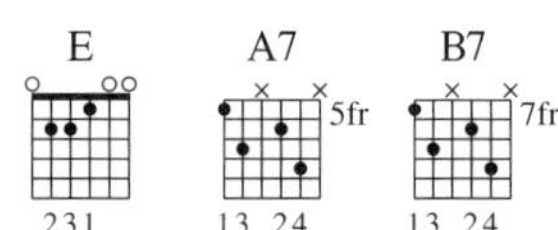

Tune down 1/2 step:
(low to high) E♭-A♭-D♭-G♭-B♭-E♭

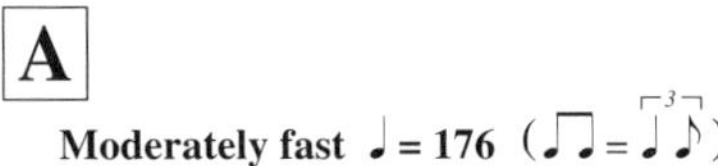

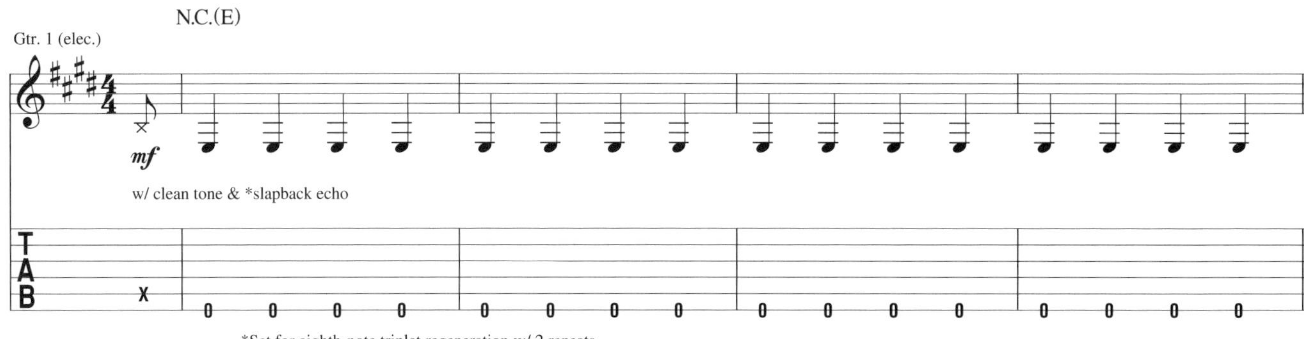

*Set for eighth-note triplet regeneration w/ 2 repeats.

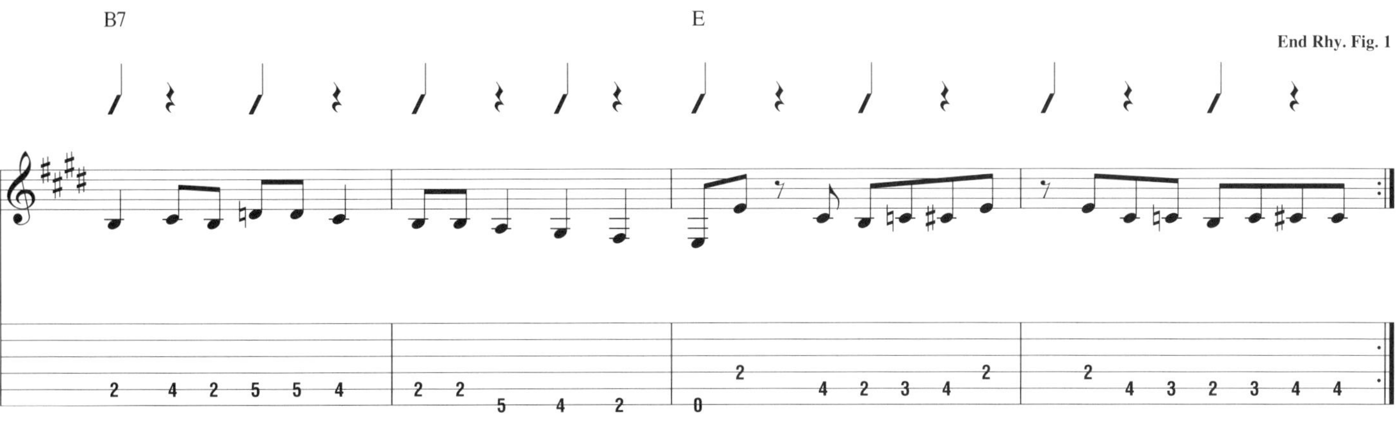
3rd time, Begin fade
B7
E
End Rhy. Fig. 1
2 4 2 5 5 4
2 2 5 4 2
0 2 4 2 3 4 2
2 4 3 2 3 4 4

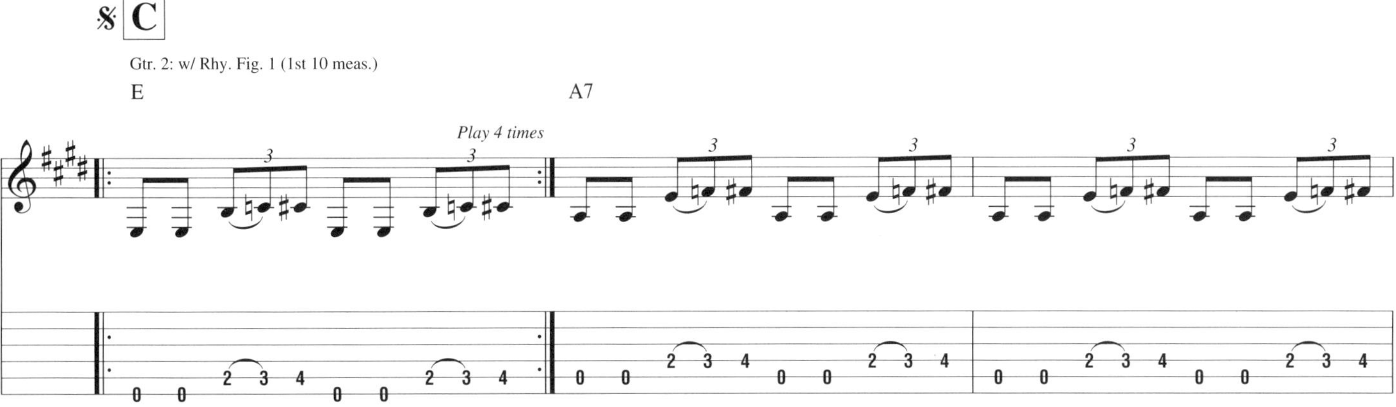
C
Gtr. 2: w/ Rhy. Fig. 1 (1st 10 meas.)
E
A7
Play 4 times

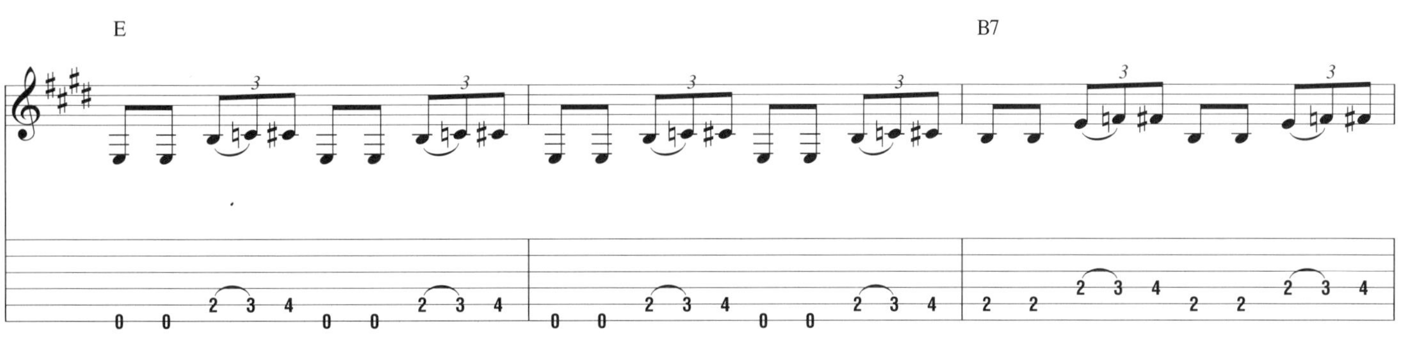
E
B7

To Coda
E
Rhy. Fill 1
End Rhy. Fill 1
Gtr. 2

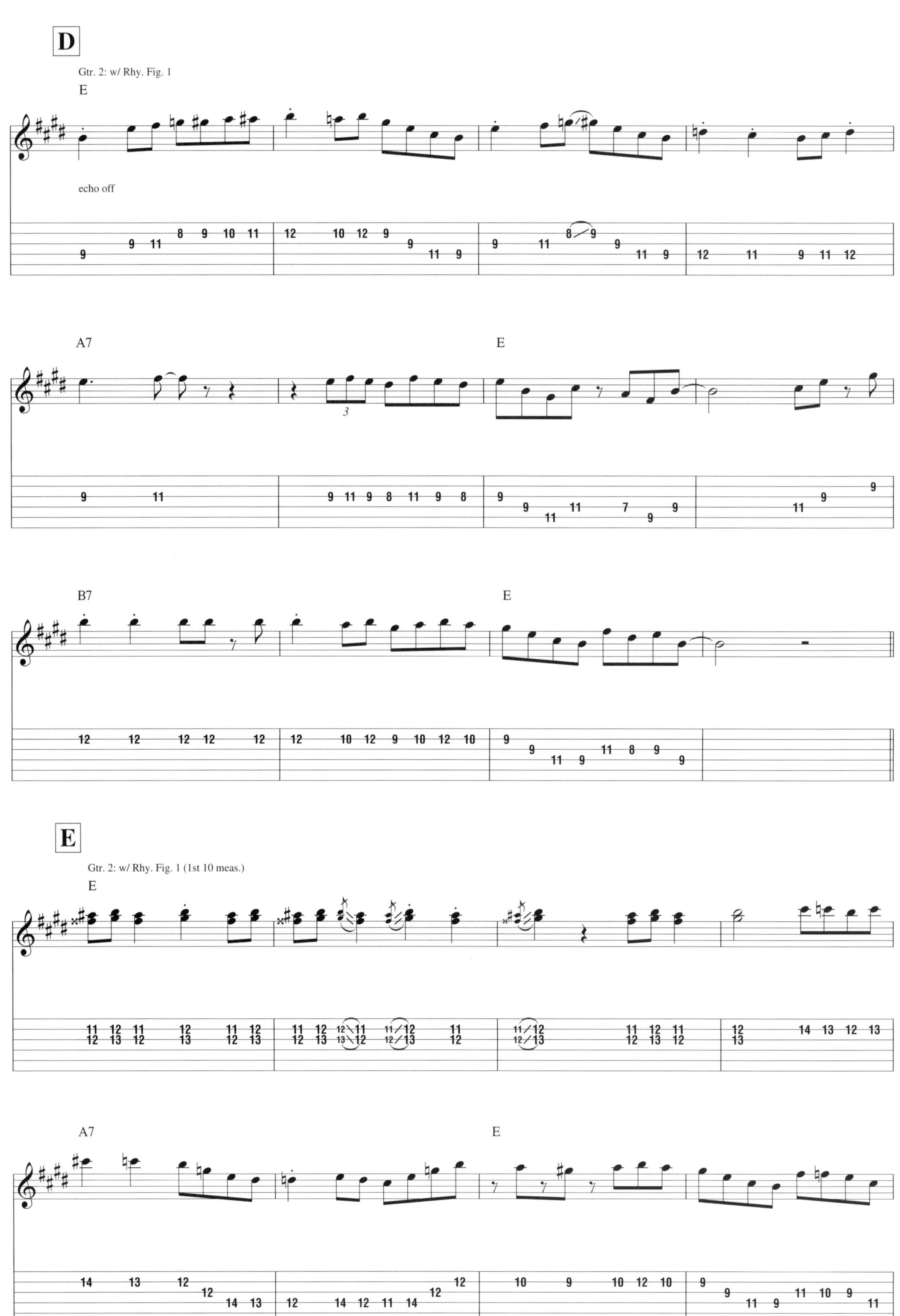
D
Gtr. 2: w/ Rhy. Fig. 1
E
echo off
A7
E
3
B7
E
E
Gtr. 2: w/ Rhy. Fig. 1 (1st 10 meas.)
E
A7
E

D.S. al Coda
(take repeats)

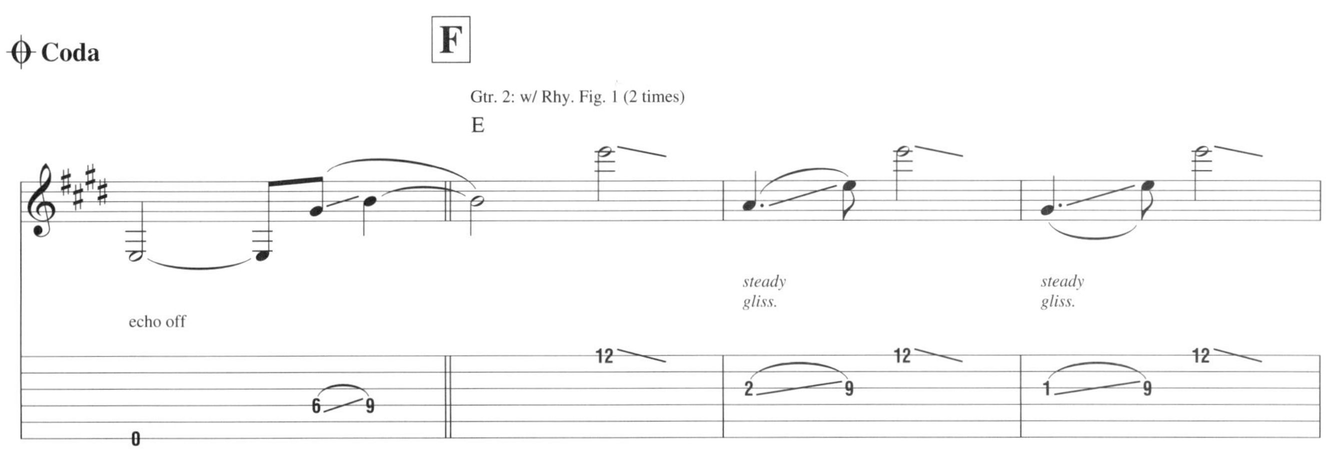

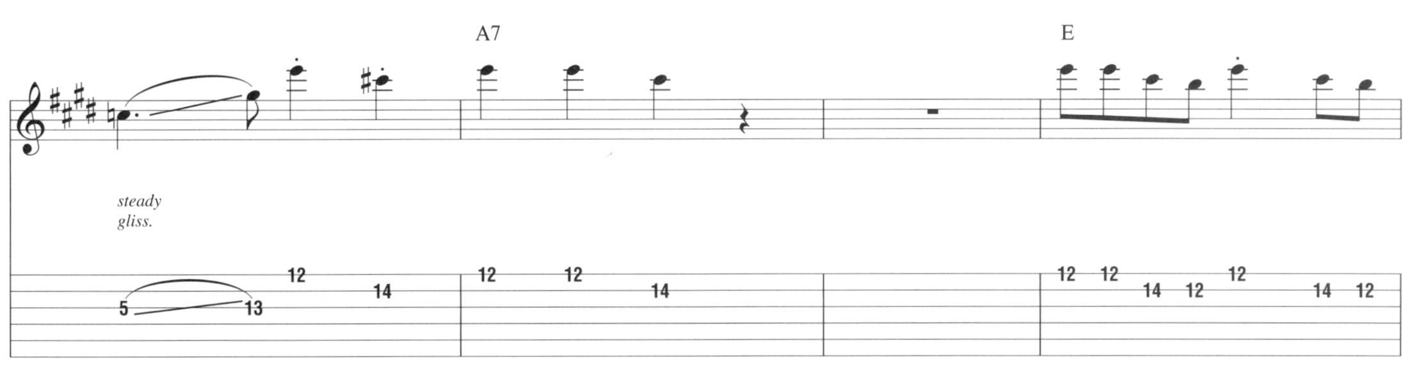

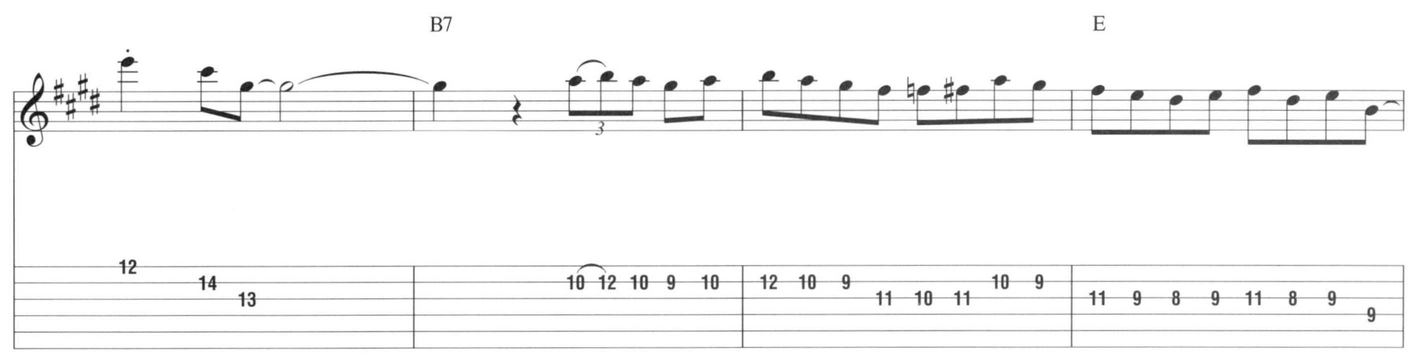

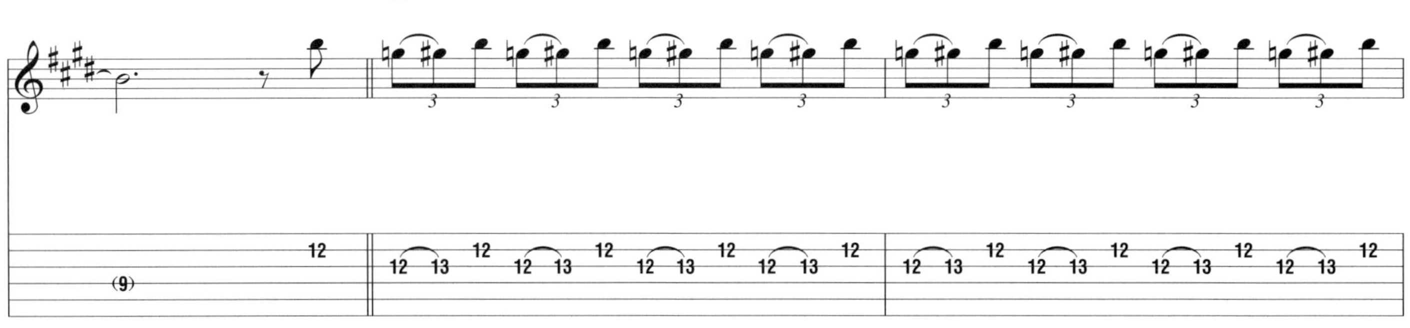

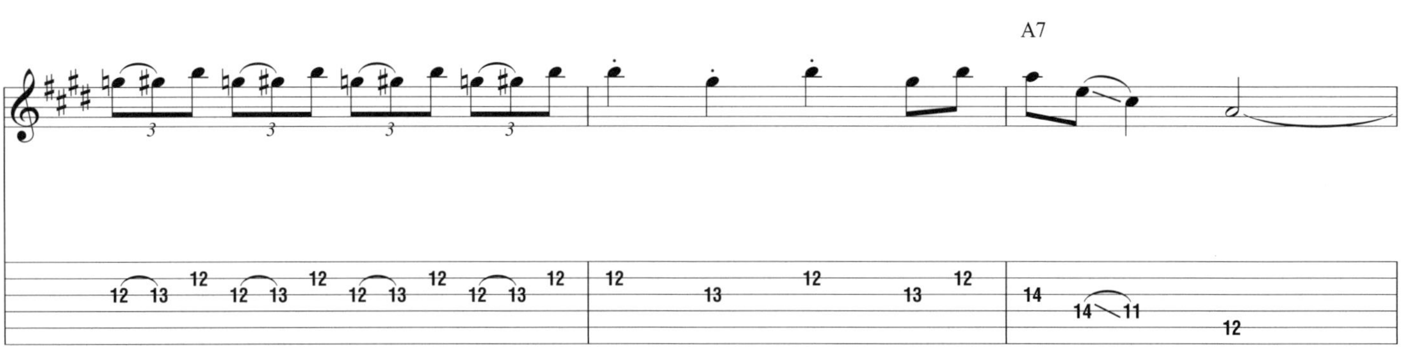

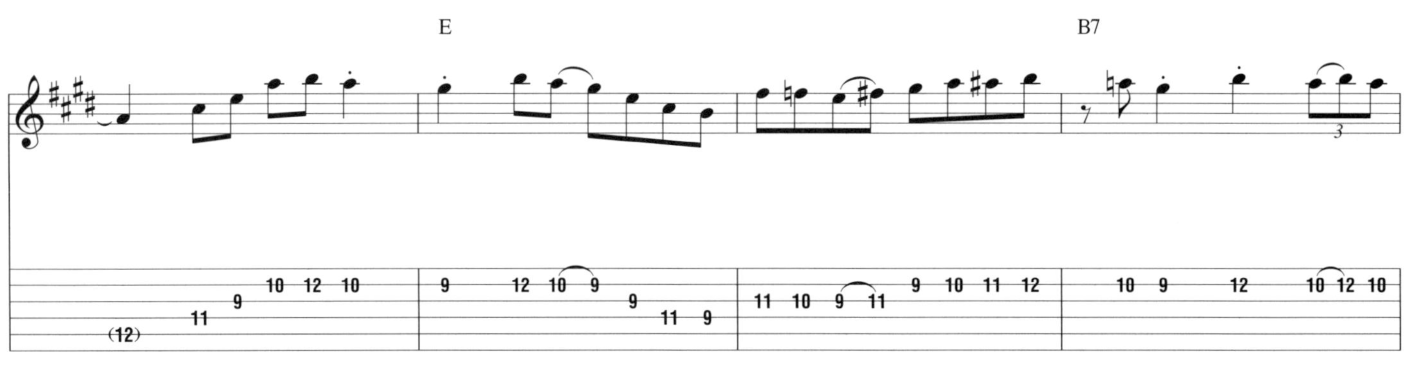

D.S.S. & fade

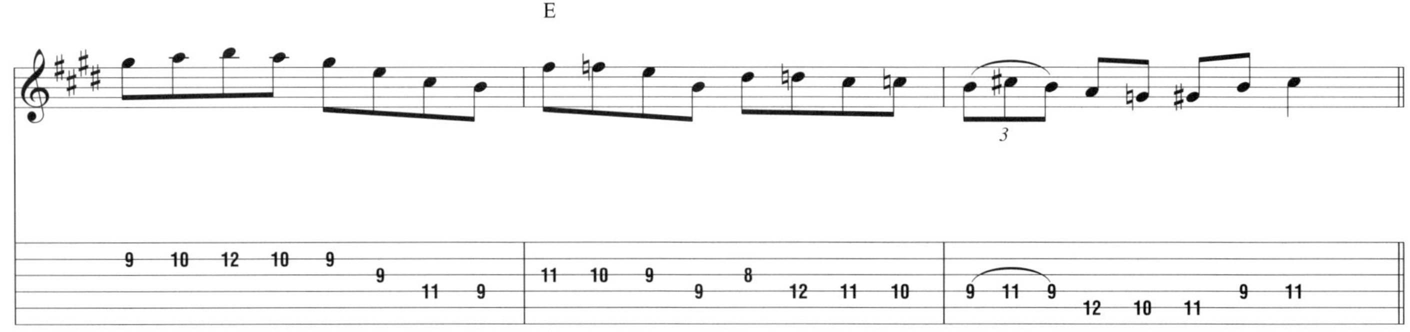

Hawaii Five-O Theme

from the Television Series

By Mort Stevens

C
Cm
F5
F
A♭5
B♭5
C5/G
A♭5
B♭5
C5/G
A♭5
N.C.
D
C♯5/G♯
B5/F♯
C♯5/G♯

E5/B
C♯5/G♯
B5/F♯
E5/B
E
G♯5/D♯
C♯5/G♯
A5
B5
C♯5/G♯
B5/F♯
C♯5/G♯
A5

F
N.C.
D5/A
C5/G
D5/A
F5/C
D5/A
C5/G
F5/C
A5
D5/A

B♭5
C5
D5/A
C5/G
N.C.
G
D5/A
C5/G
D5/A
B♭6
C
Dm

D5/A

A5

N.C.
B♭5
N.C.
C5
N.C.
D5

Hide Away

By Freddie King and Sonny Thompson

A7
E7
P.M.
B7
A7
E7
let ring
C
E7
B7
A7
E7
B7
E7
tr

D
E7
P.M.
A7
E7
P.M.
B7
A7
B7
E
E7
w/ pick & middle finger

A7

w/ pick & middle finger P.M.

B7

w/ pick & middle finger P.M.

A7 E7 B7

let ring

P.M.

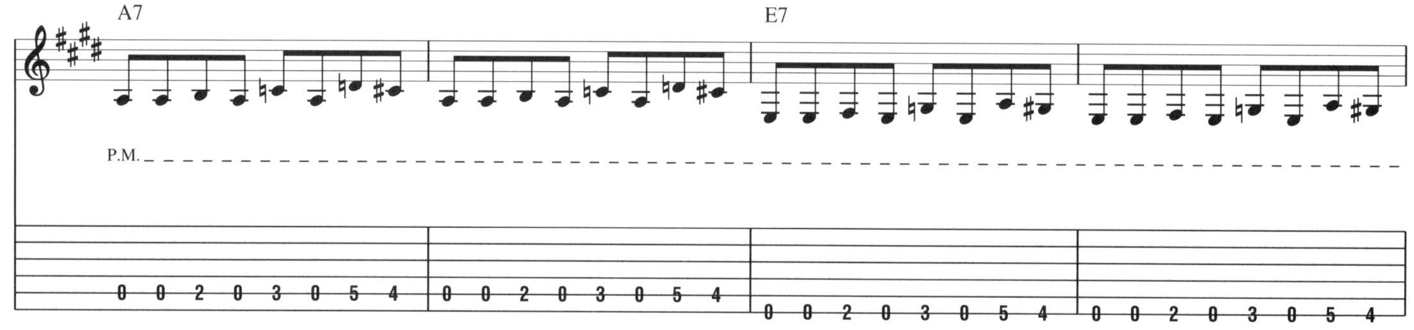

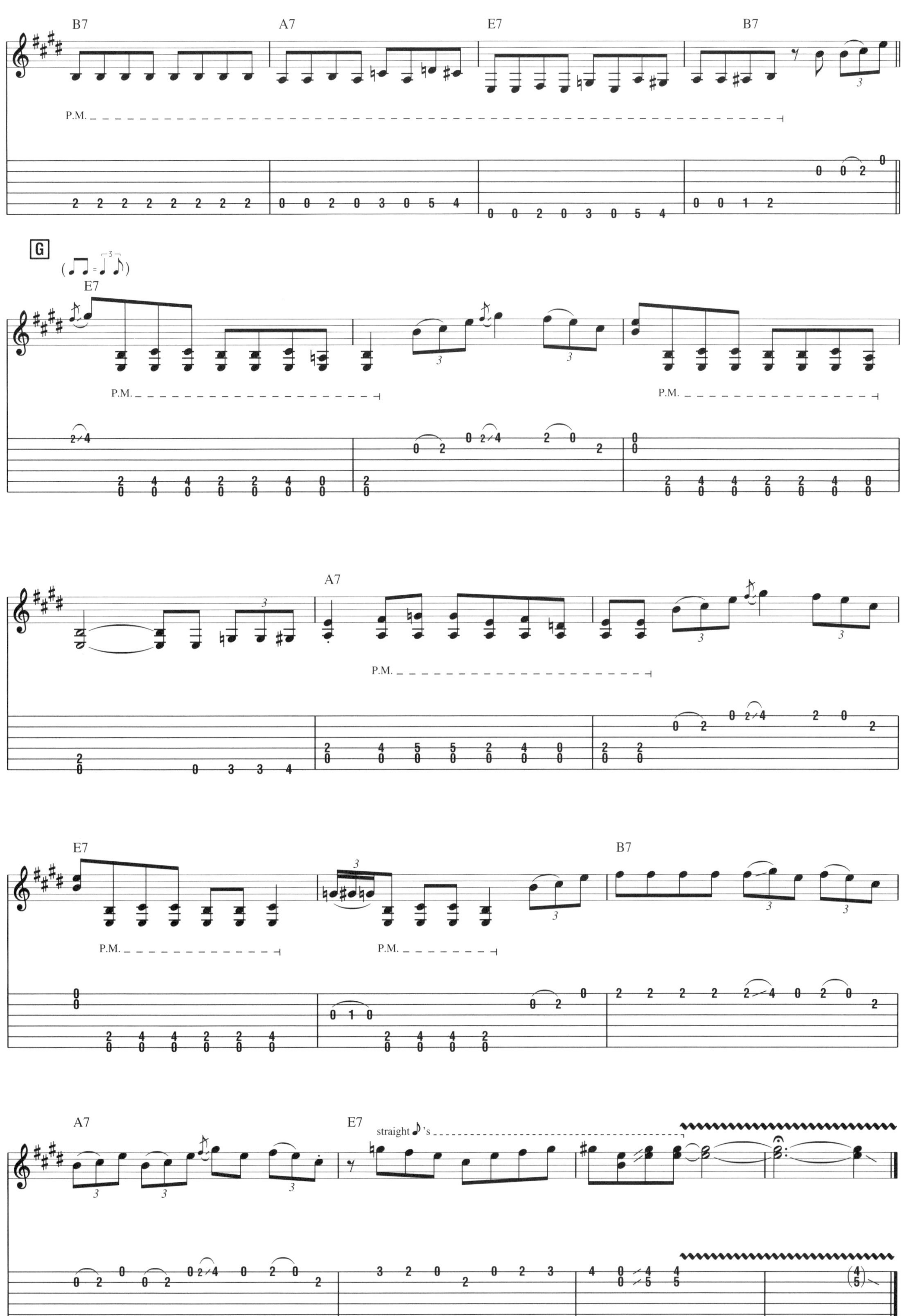

B7
A7
E7
B7
P.M.
G
E7
P.M.
P.M.
A7
P.M.
E7
P.M.
P.M.
B7
A7
E7
straight ♪'s

Jessica

Written by Dickey Betts

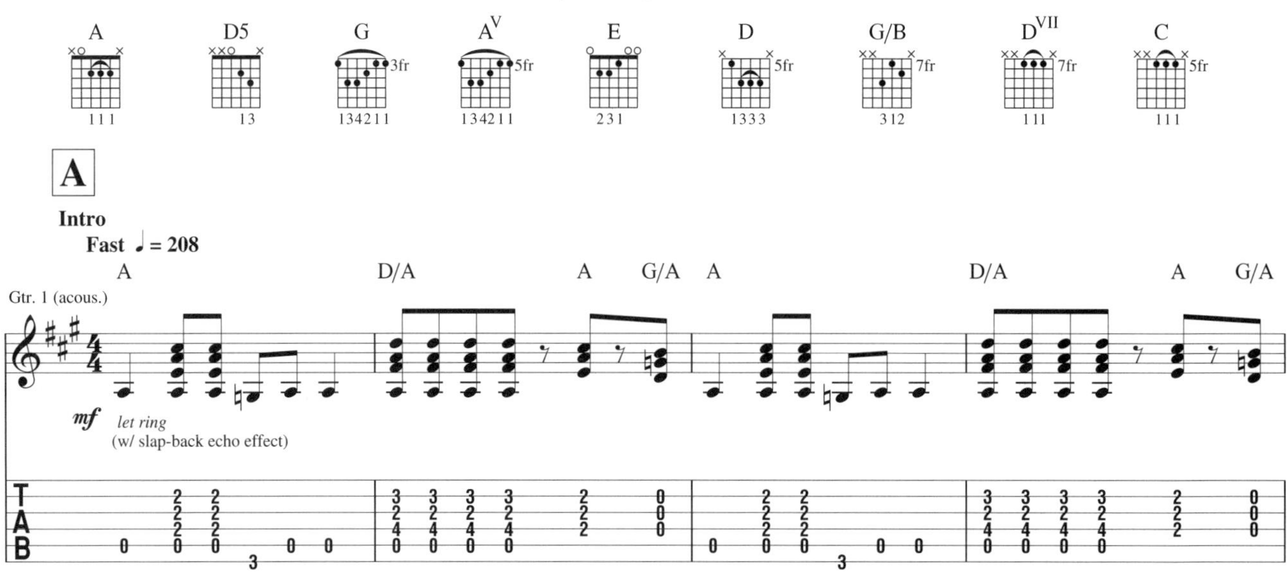

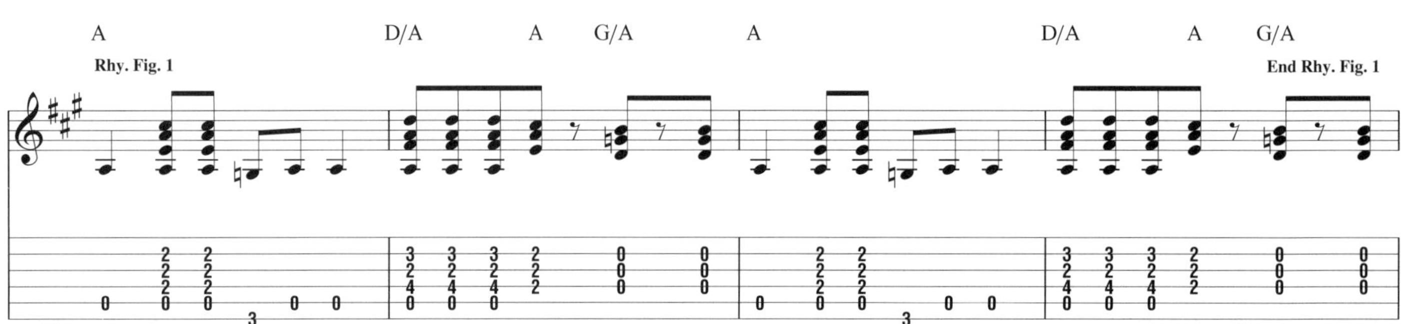

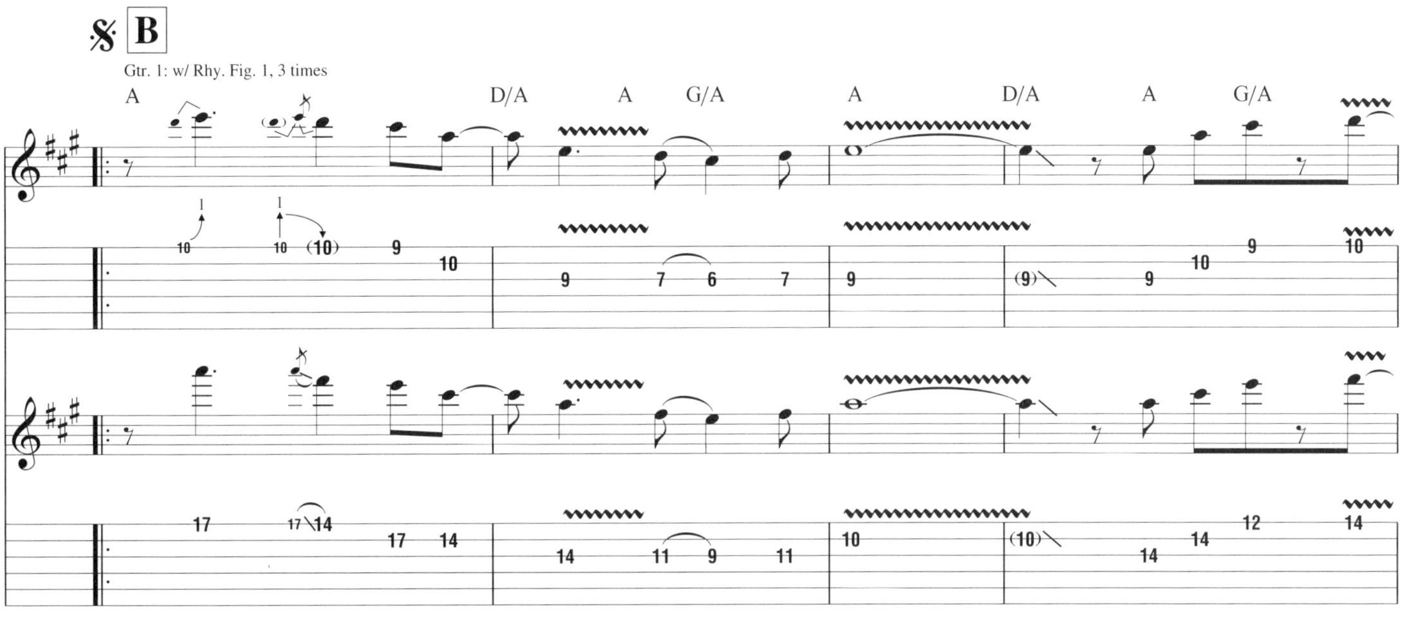
B
Gtr. 1: w/ Rhy. Fig. 1, 3 times
A
D/A
A
G/A
A
D/A
A
G/A

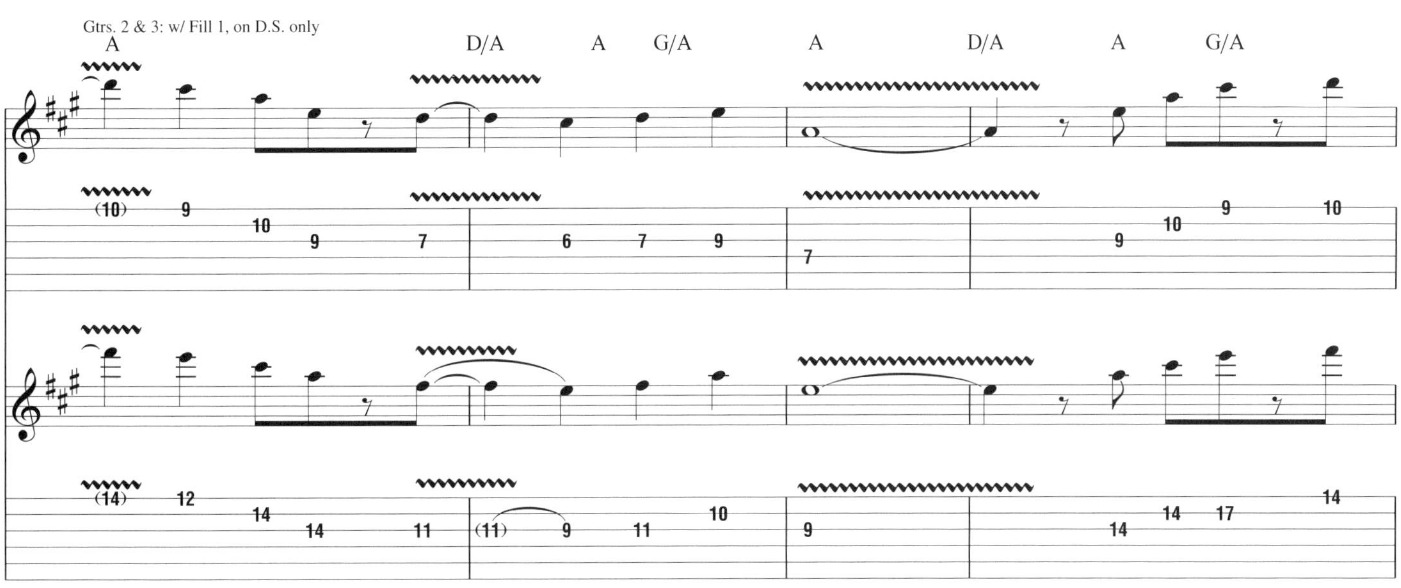
Gtrs. 2 & 3: w/ Fill 1, on D.S. only
A
D/A
A
G/A
A
D/A
A
G/A

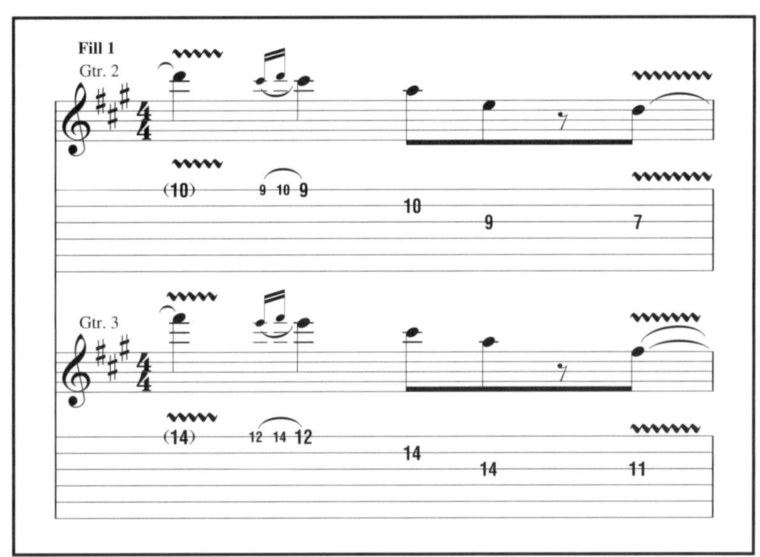
Fill 1
Gtr. 2
Gtr. 3

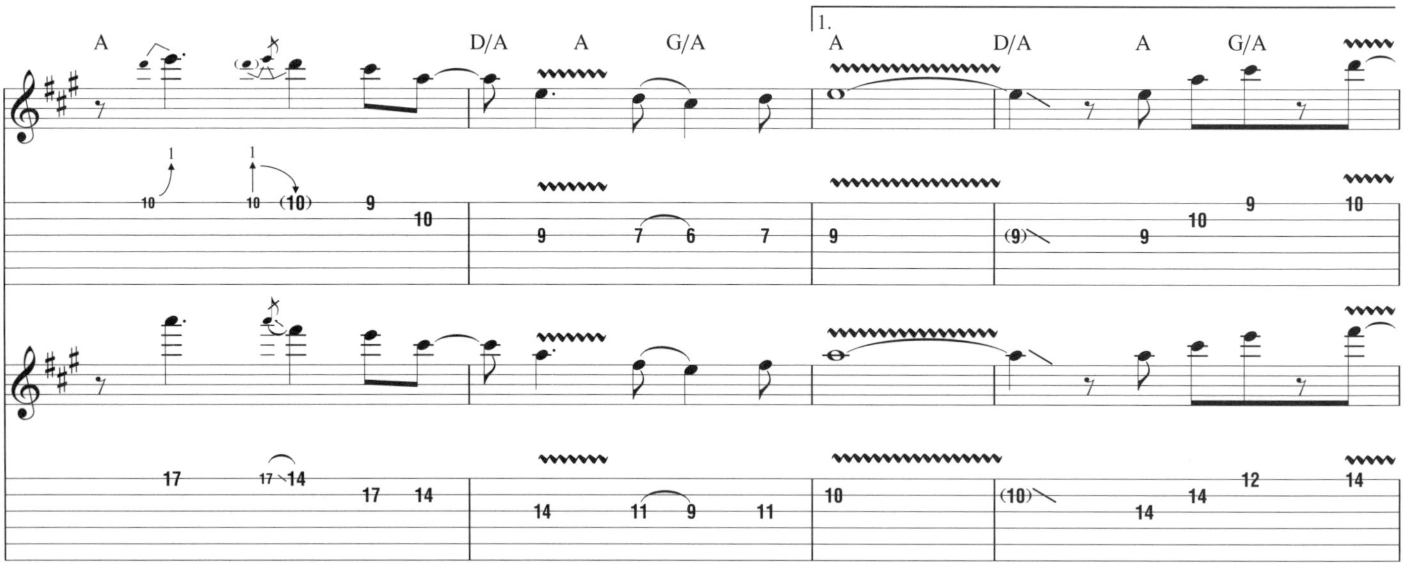
1.
A
D/A
A
G/A
A
D/A
A
G/A

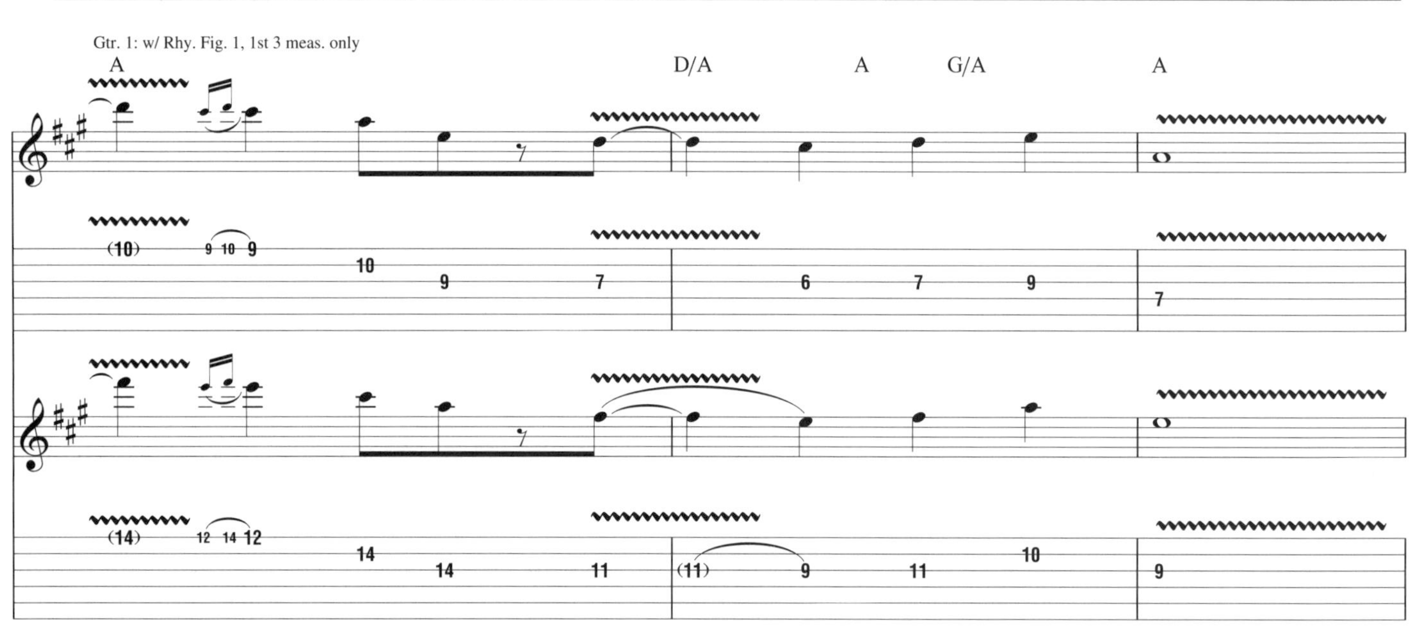
Gtr. 1: w/ Rhy. Fig. 1, 1st 3 meas. only
A
D/A
A
G/A
A

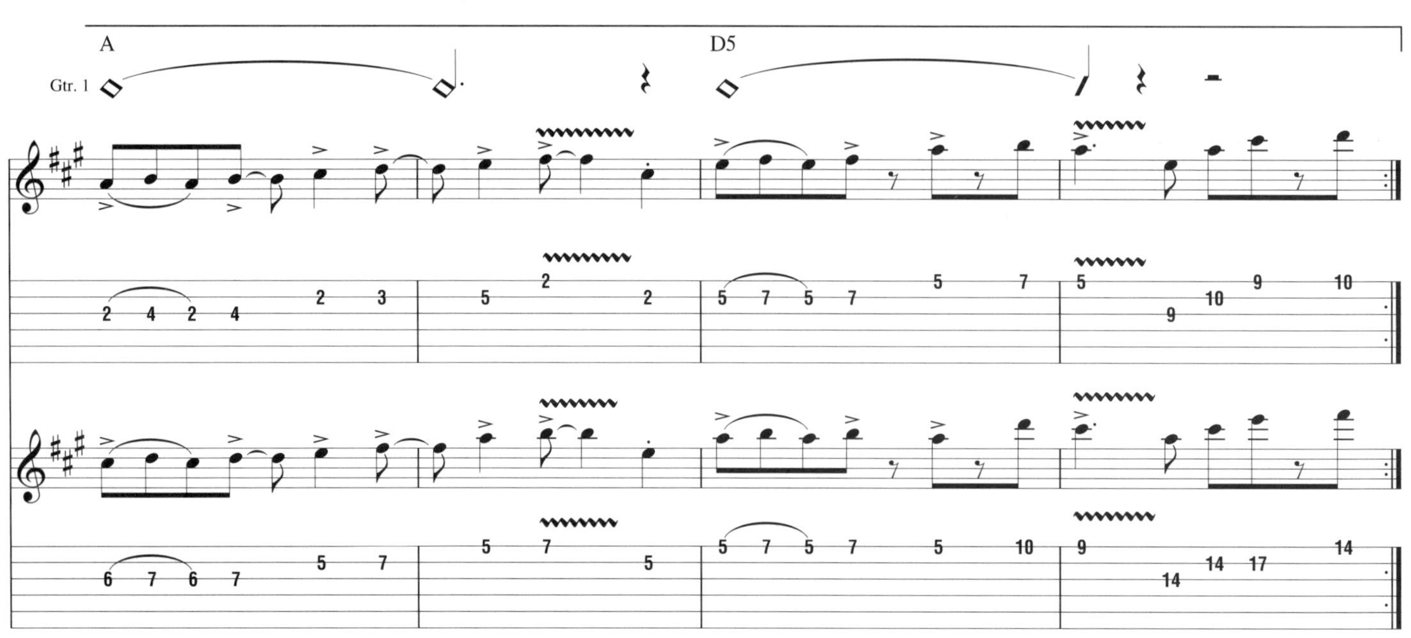
A
D5
Gtr. 1

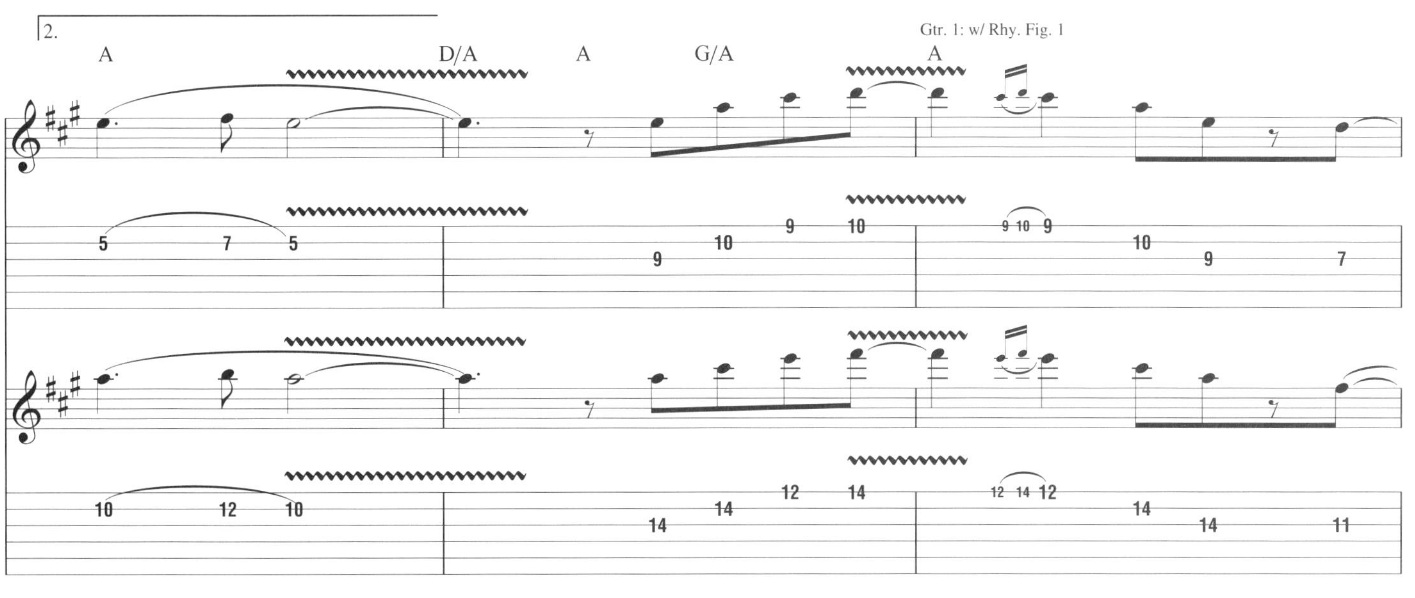
2.
Gtr. 1: w/ Rhy. Fig. 1
A
D/A
A
G/A
A

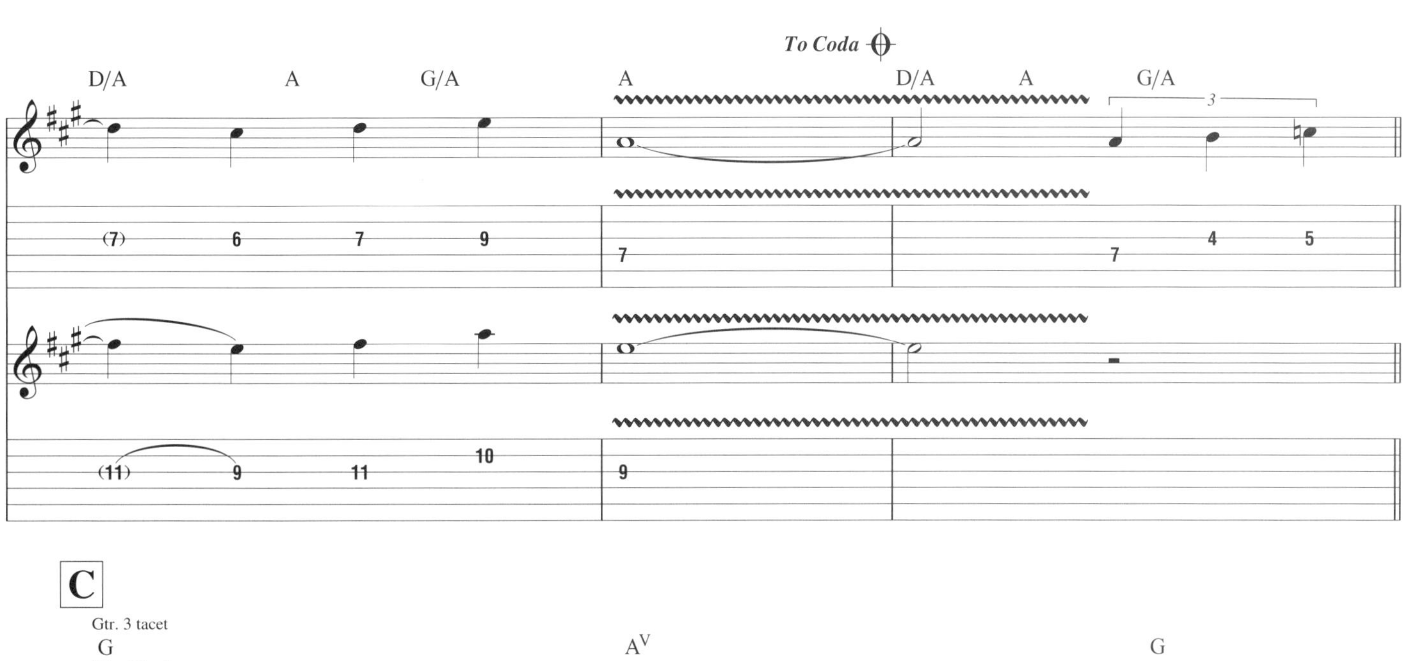
To Coda
D/A
A
G/A
A
D/A
A
G/A

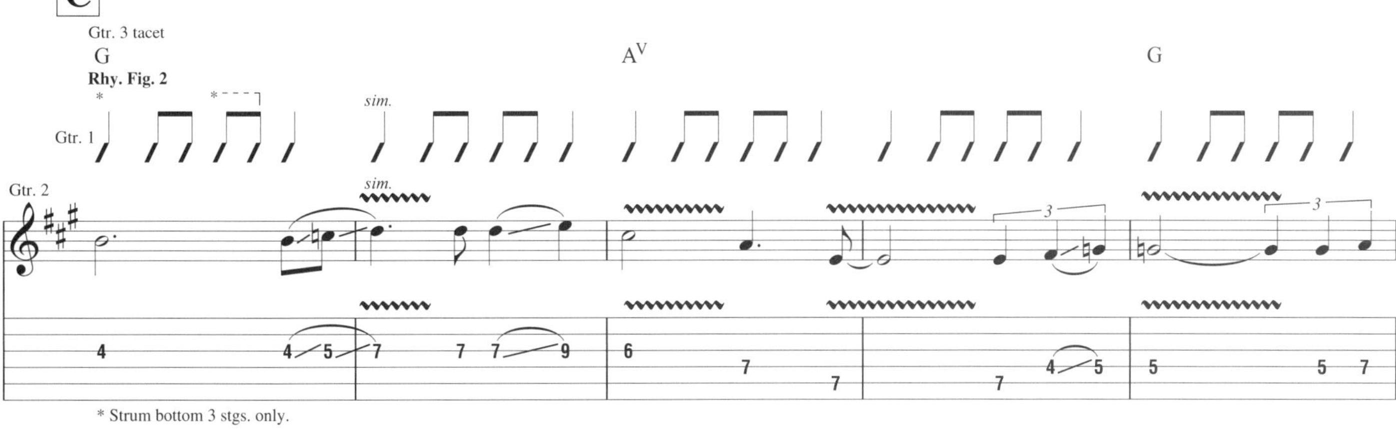
C
Gtr. 3 tacet
G
Rhy. Fig. 2
Gtr. 1
sim.
Gtr. 2
sim.
A^V
G
* Strum bottom 3 stgs. only.

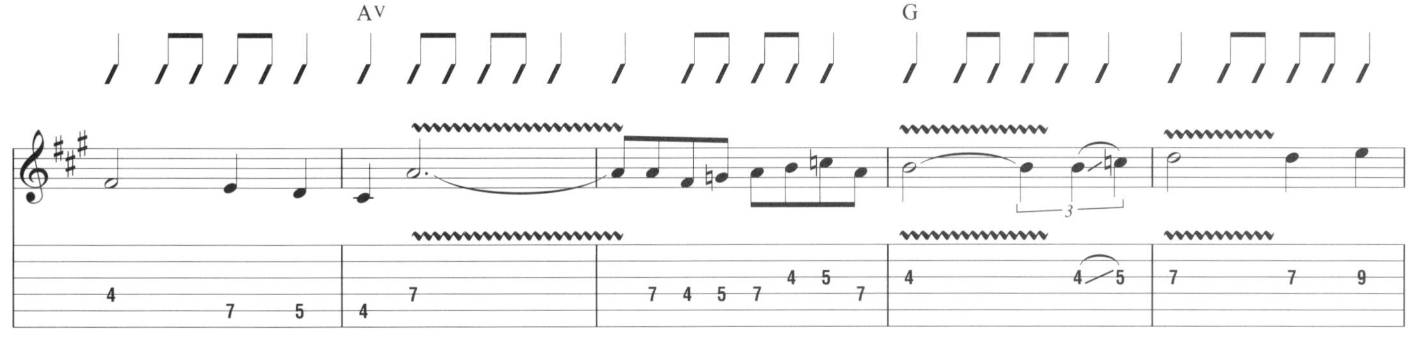
A^V
G

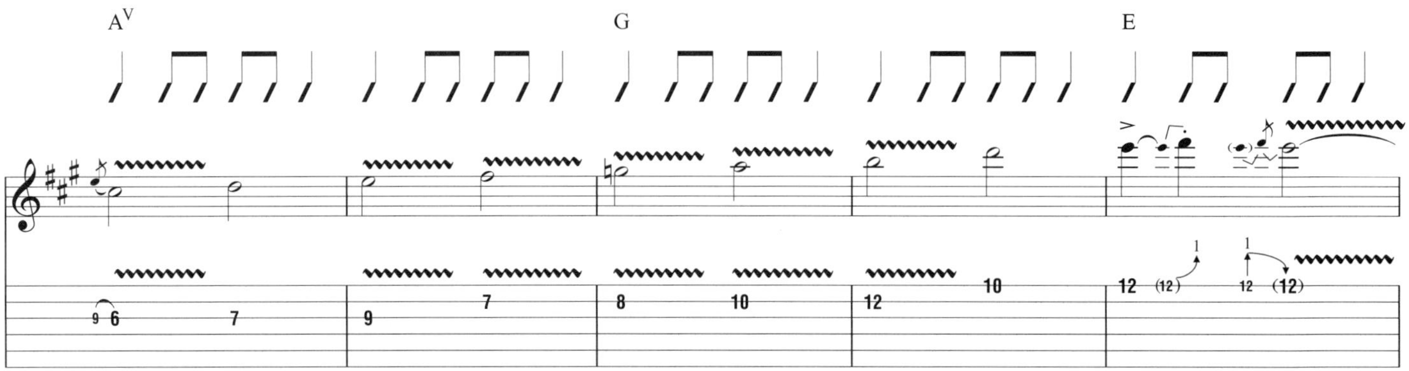
A
G
E

D
Gtr. 1: w/ Rhy. Fig. 1, 3 times
End Rhy. Fig. 2
A
D/A
A
G/A
A
Gtr. 2
Gtr. 3

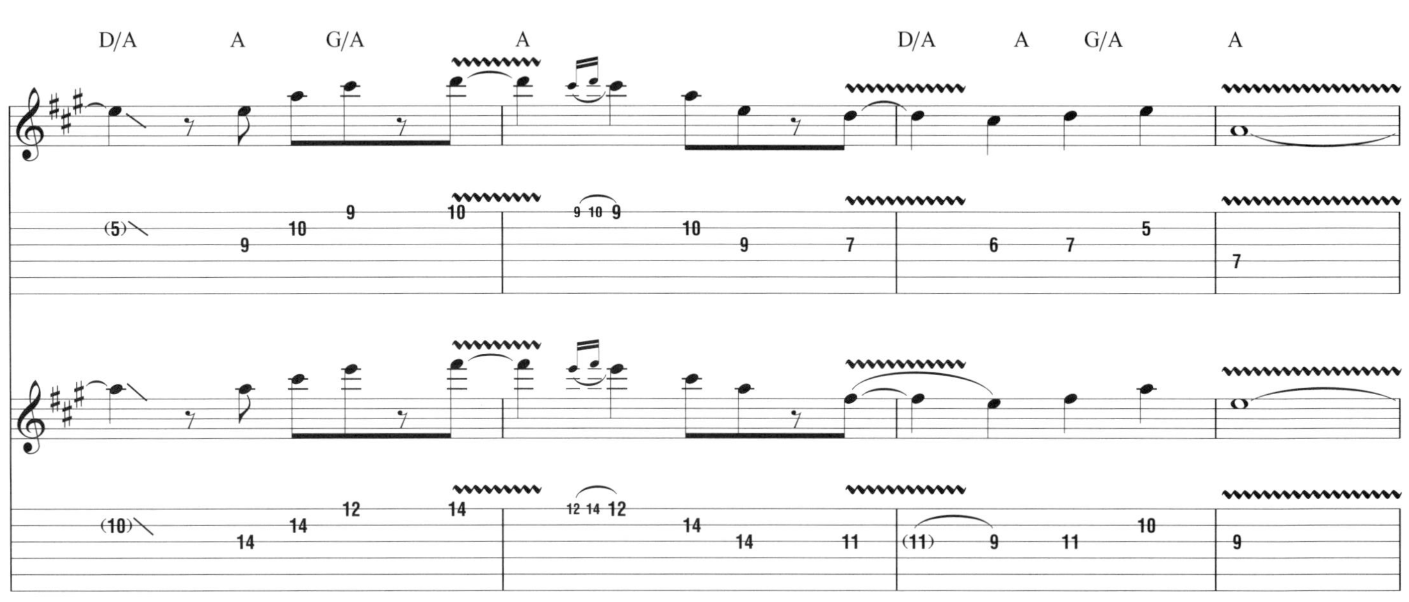
D/A
A
G/A
A
D/A
A
G/A
A

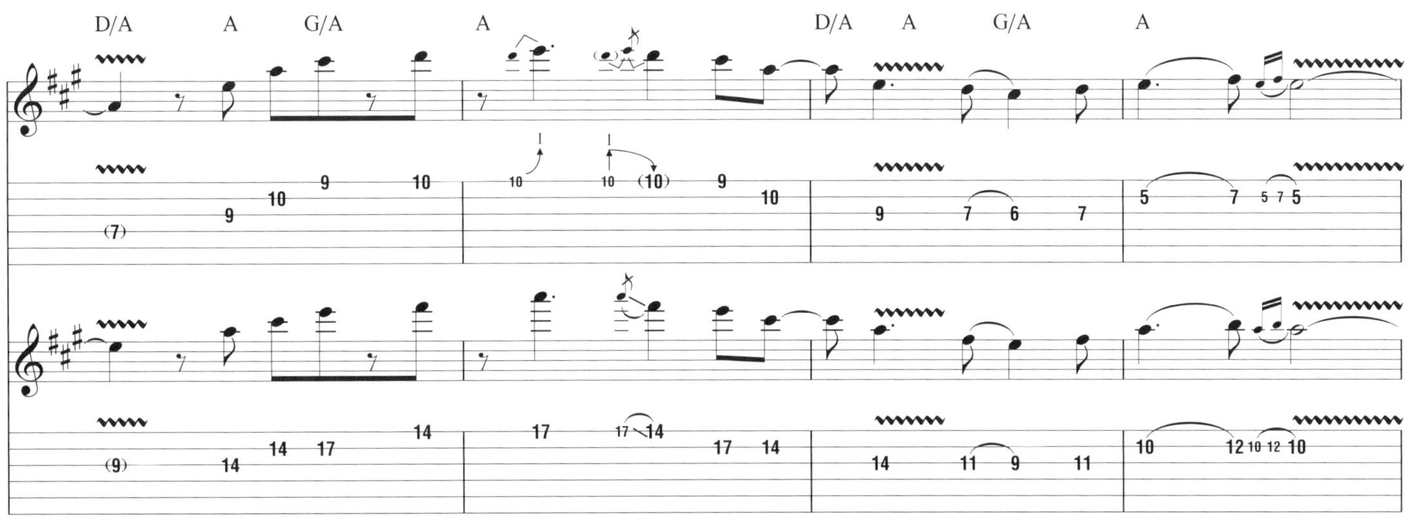
D/A
A
G/A
A
D/A
A
G/A
A

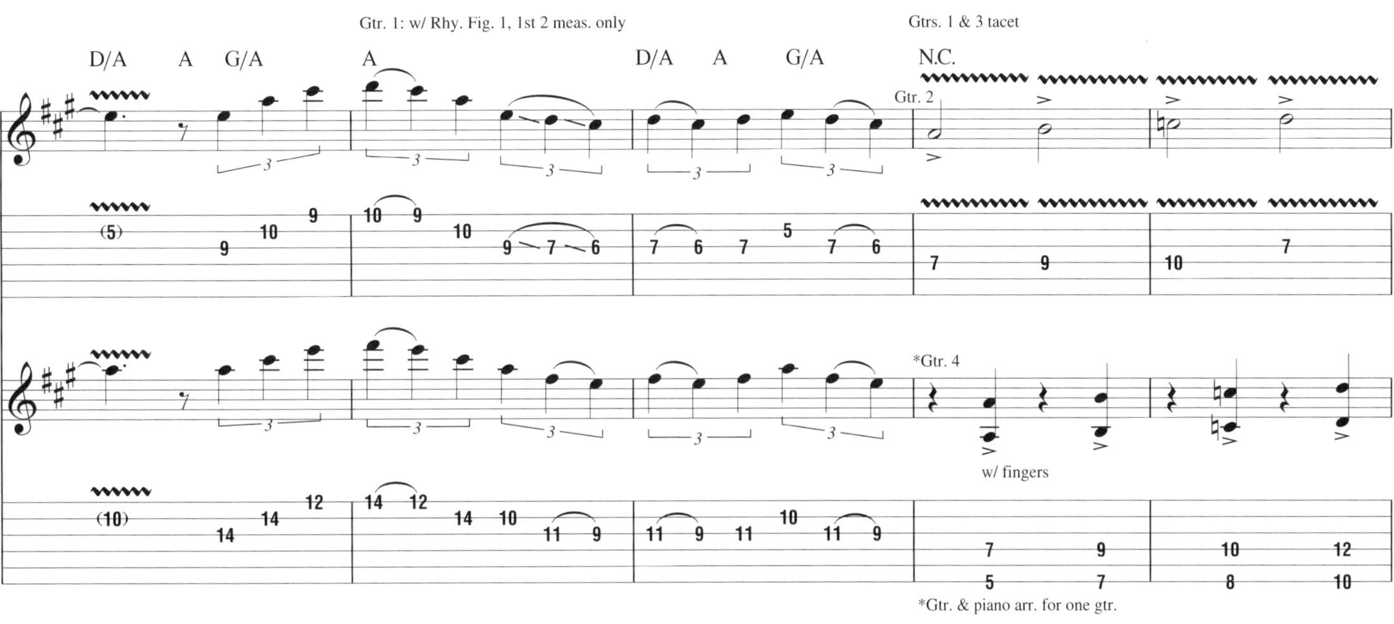
Gtr. 1: w/ Rhy. Fig. 1, 1st 2 meas. only
Gtrs. 1 & 3 tacet
D/A
A
G/A
A
D/A
A
G/A
N.C.
Gtr. 2
*Gtr. 4
w/ fingers
*Gtr. & piano arr. for one gtr.

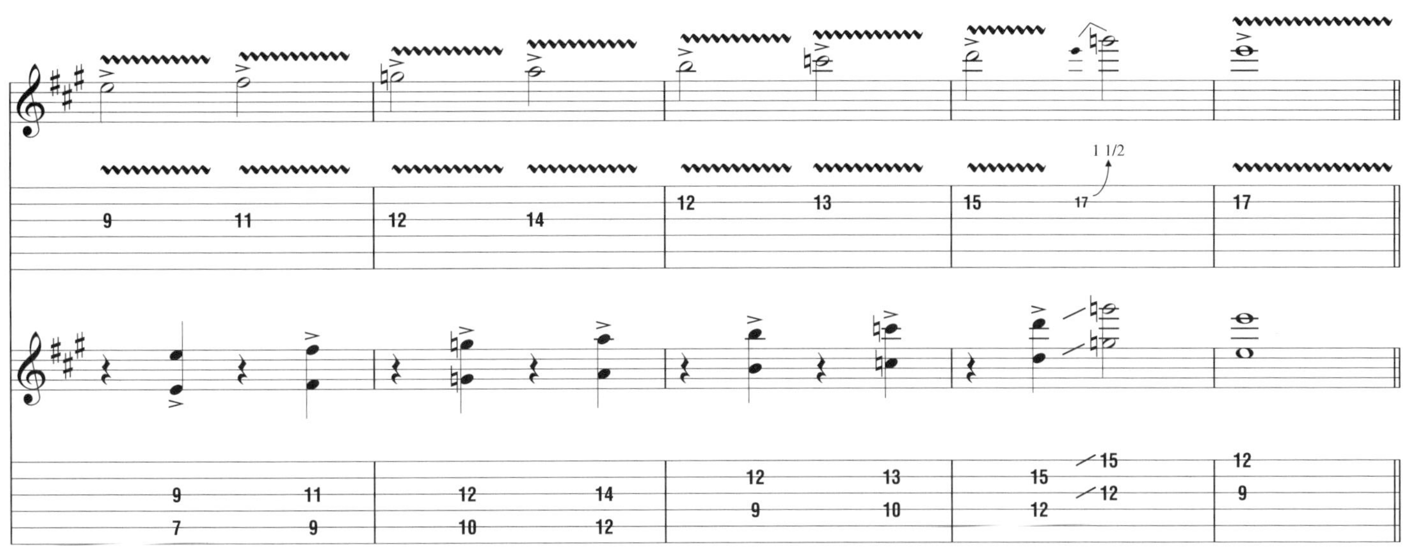
1 1/2

E

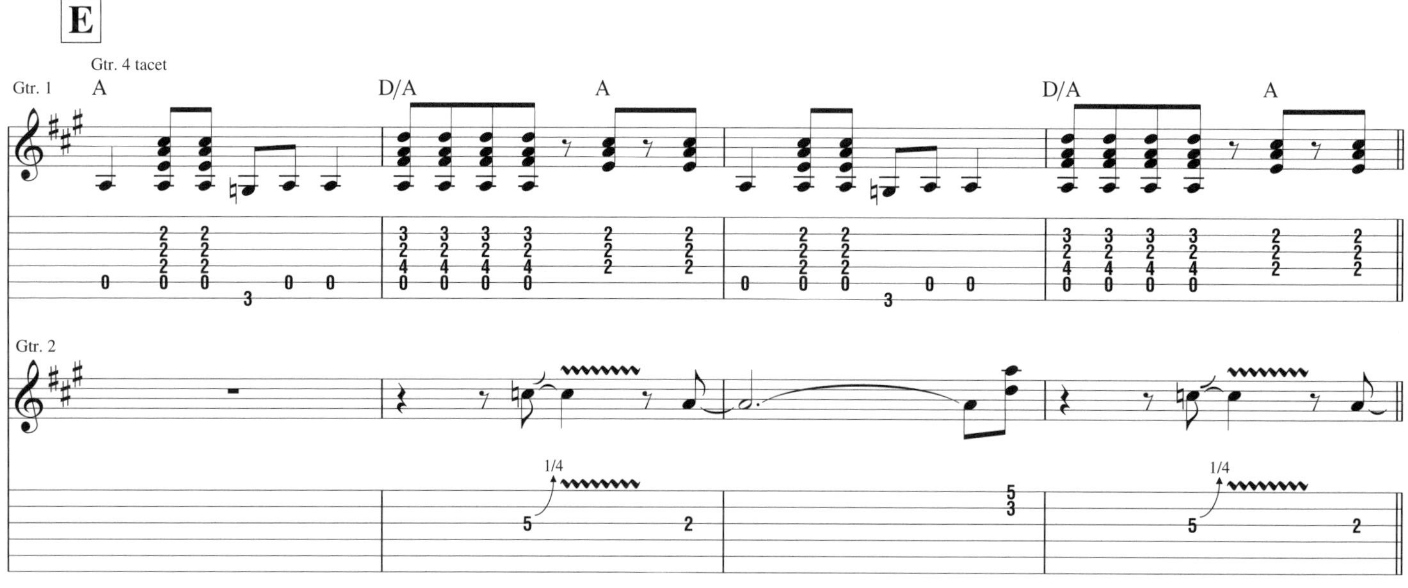

Gtr. 4 tacet
Gtr. 1
A
D/A
A
D/A
A
Gtr. 2
1/4
1/4

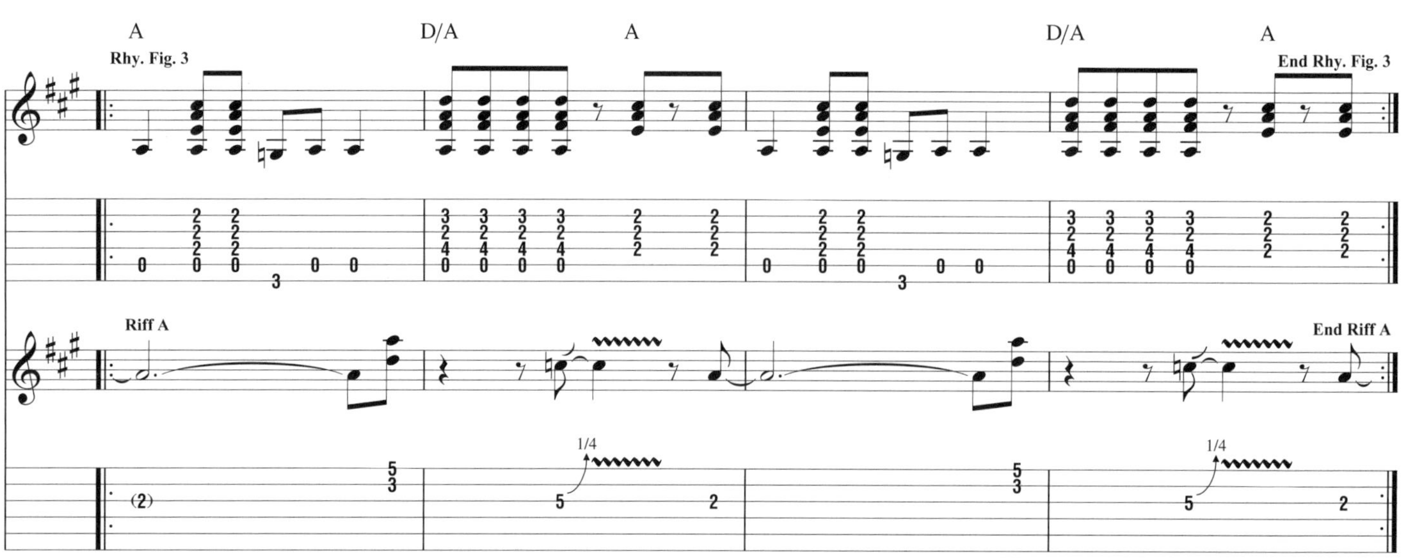

A
D/A
A
D/A
A
Rhy. Fig. 3
End Rhy. Fig. 3
Riff A
End Riff A
1/4
1/4

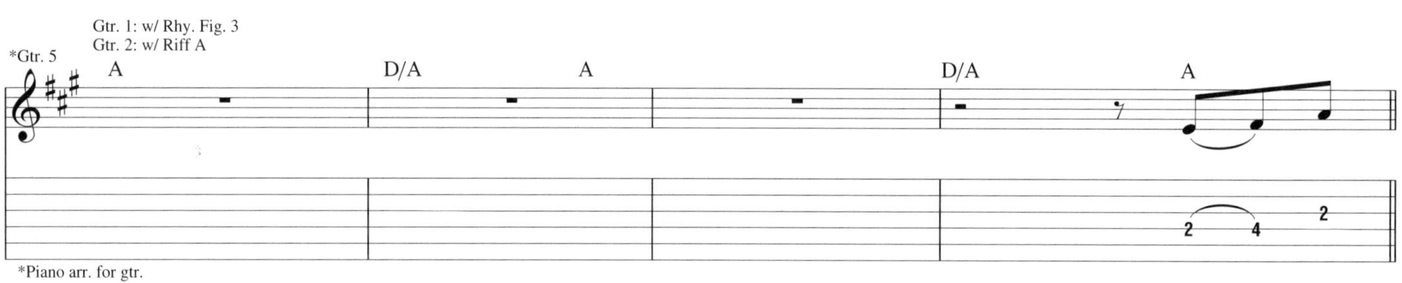

Gtr. 1: w/ Rhy. Fig. 3
Gtr. 2: w/ Riff A
*Gtr. 5
A
D/A
A
D/A
A
*Piano arr. for gtr.

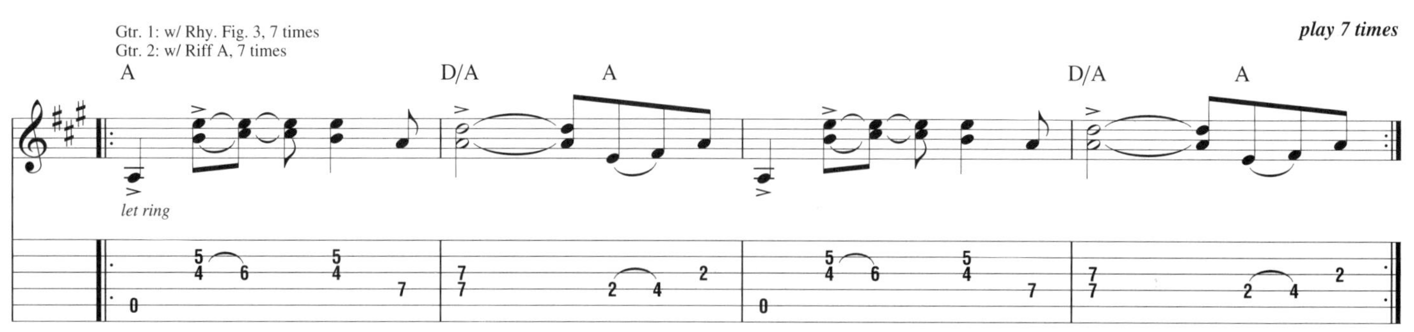

Gtr. 1: w/ Rhy. Fig. 3, 7 times
Gtr. 2: w/ Riff A, 7 times
play 7 times
A
D/A
A
D/A
A
let ring

F
Gtr. 1
A
D/A
A
D/A
play 16 times
N.C.
Gtrs. 1 & 2
G
D
D
5fr
Rhy. Fig. 4
Gtr. 1
Gtr. 2
f
(Gtr. 1 cont. in slashes)
Gtr. 1: w/ Rhy. Fig. 4, 49 times
G/B
DVII
C
D
End Rhy. Fig. 4

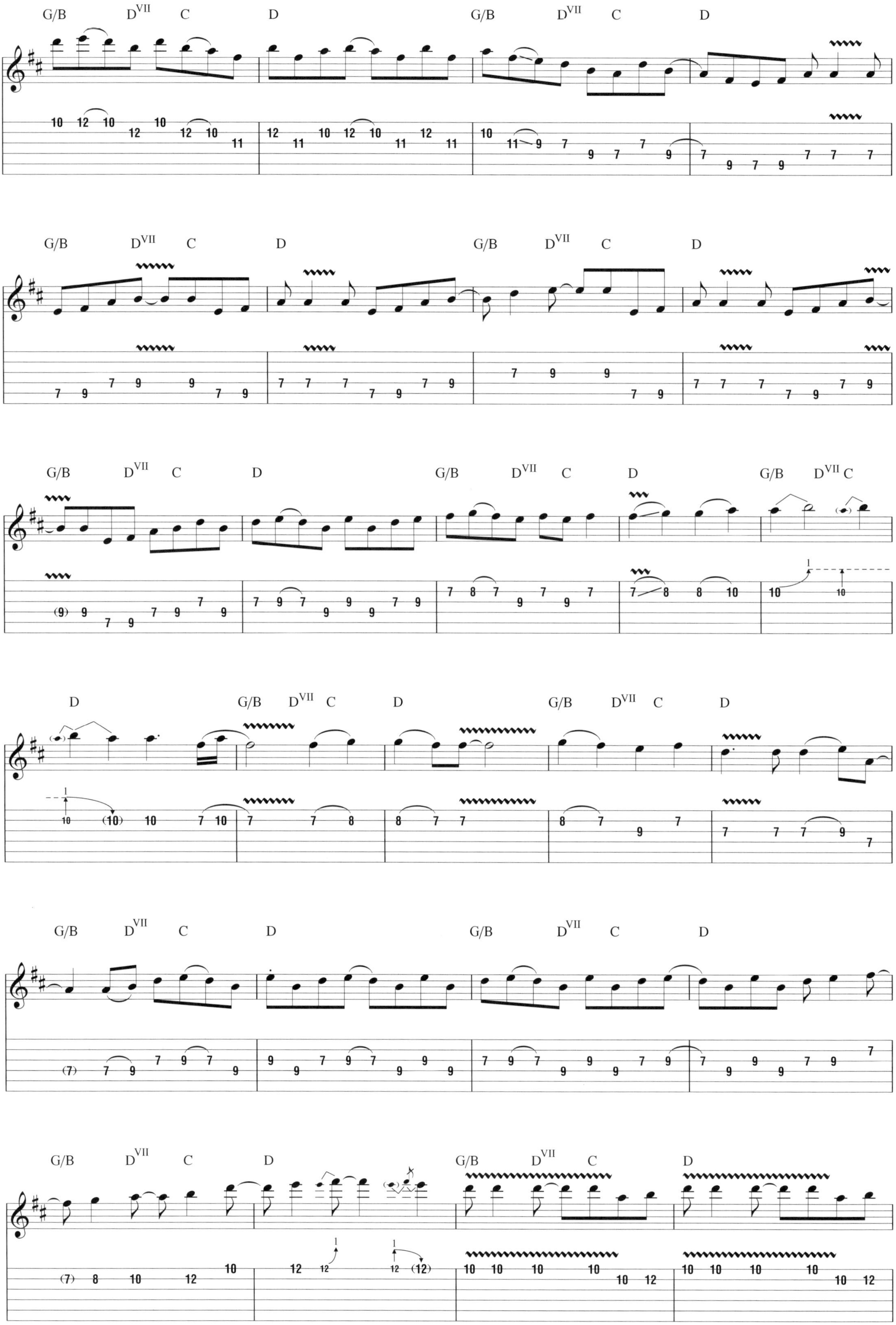

G/B D^VII C D G/B D^VII C D
G/B D^VII C D G/B D^VII C D
G/B D^VII C D G/B D^VII C D G/B D^VII C
D G/B D^VII C D G/B D^VII C D
G/B D^VII C D G/B D^VII C D
G/B D^VII C D G/B D^VII C D

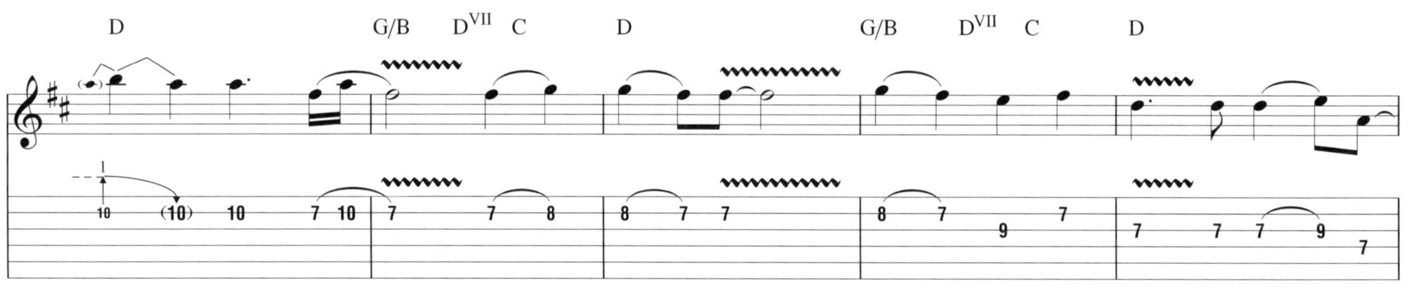

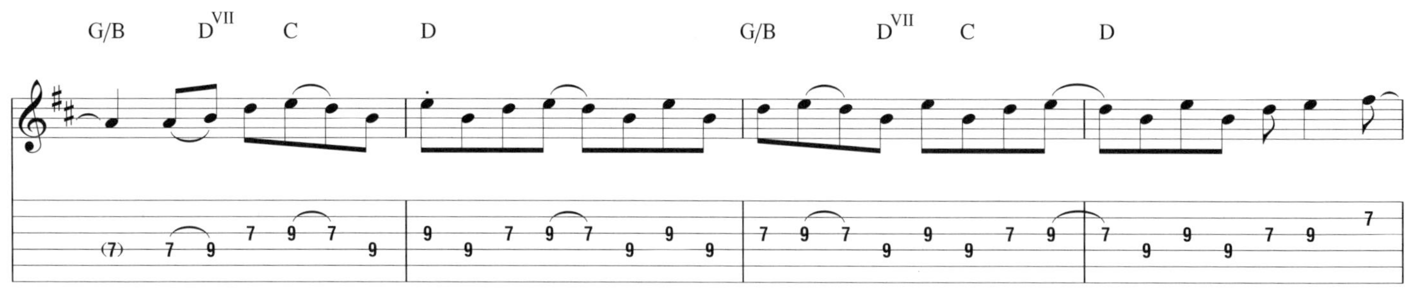

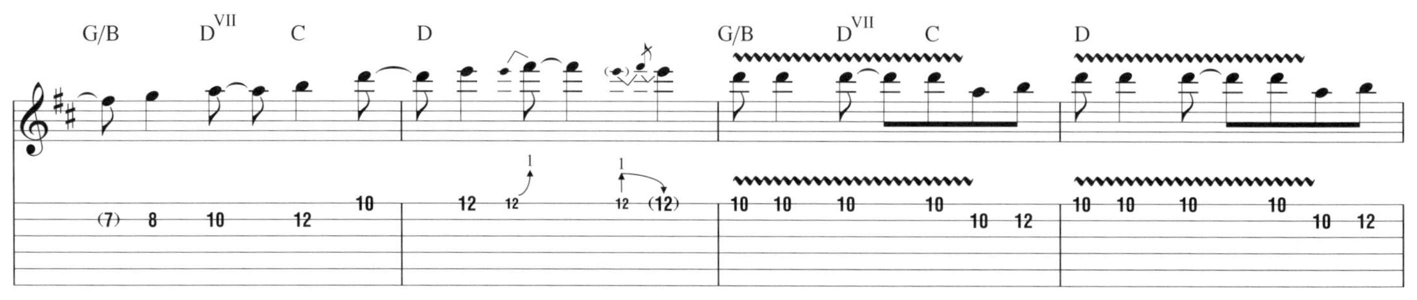

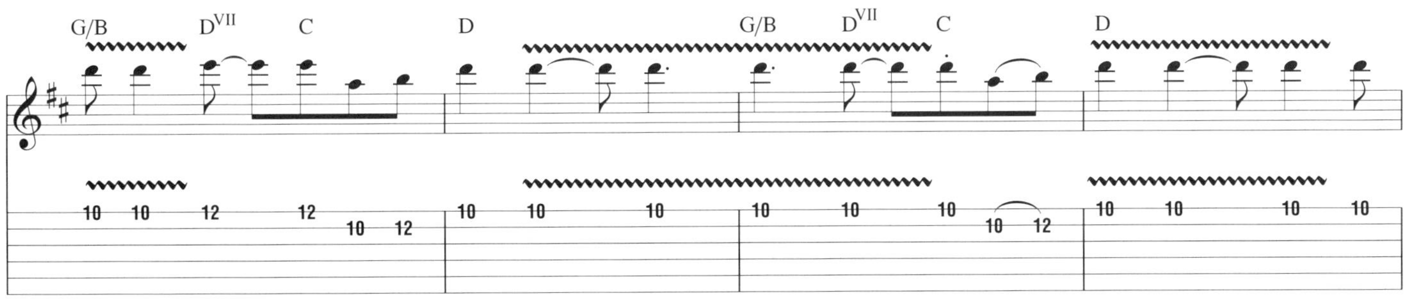
G/B DVII C D G/B DVII C D

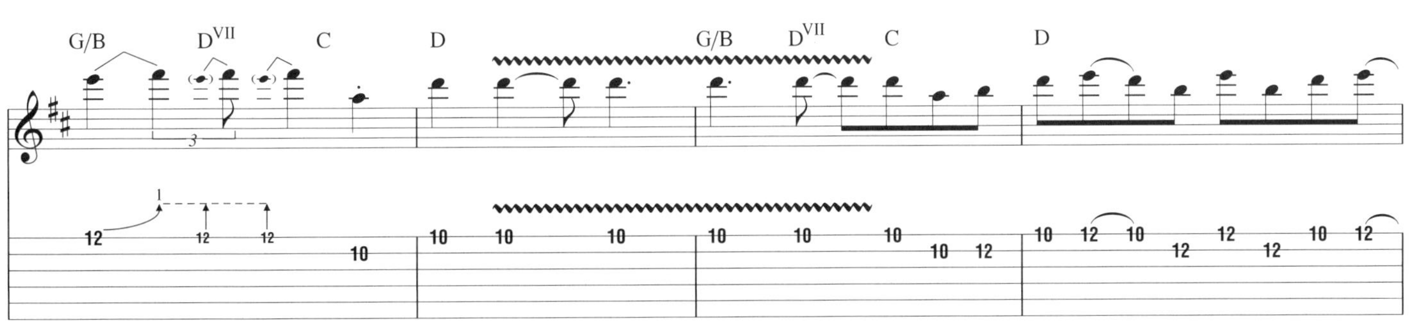
G/B DVII C D G/B DVII C D

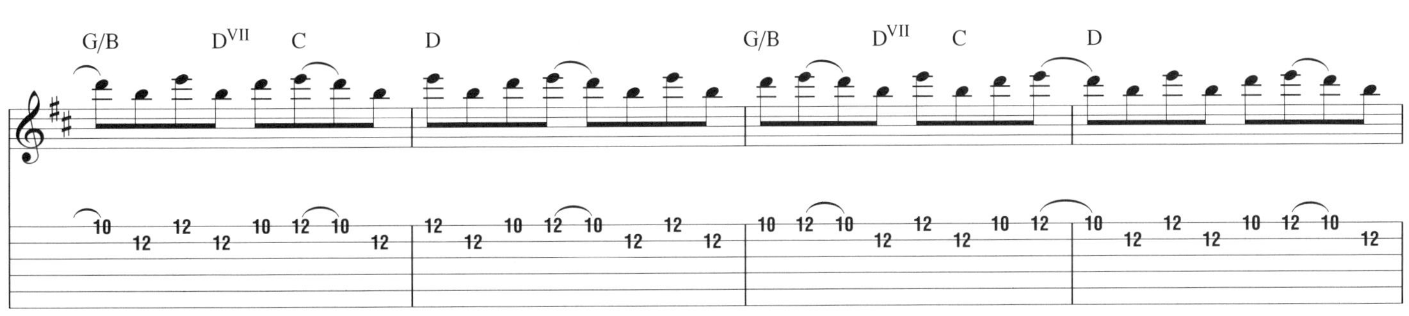
G/B DVII C D G/B DVII C D

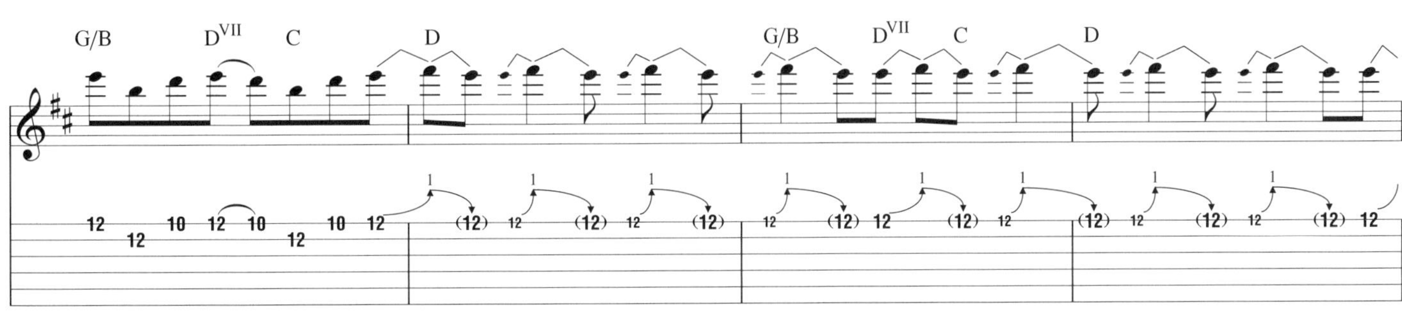
G/B DVII C D G/B DVII C D

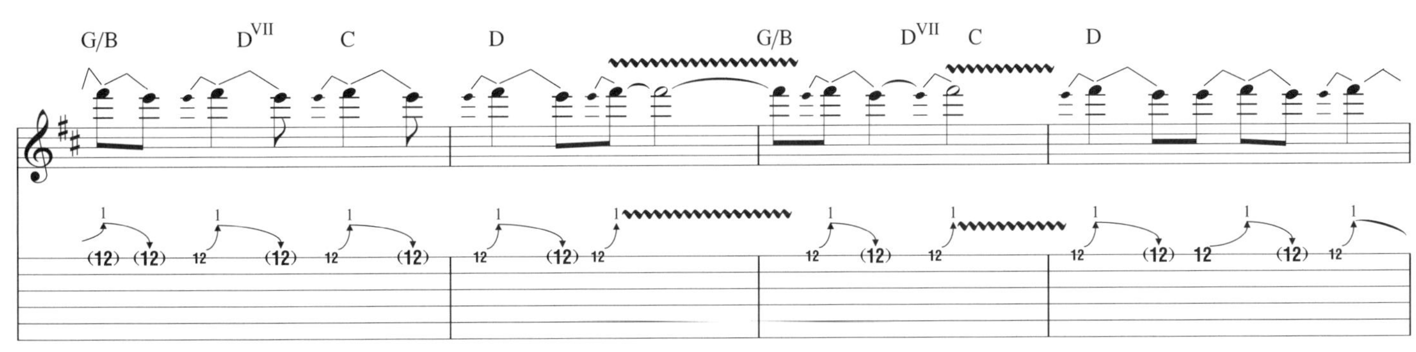
G/B DVII C D G/B DVII C D

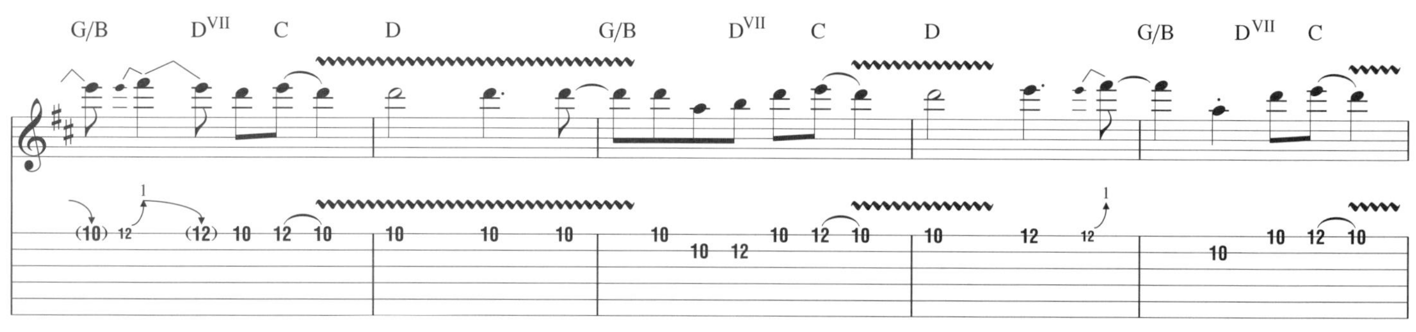
G/B D^{VII} C D G/B D^{VII} C D G/B D^{VII} C

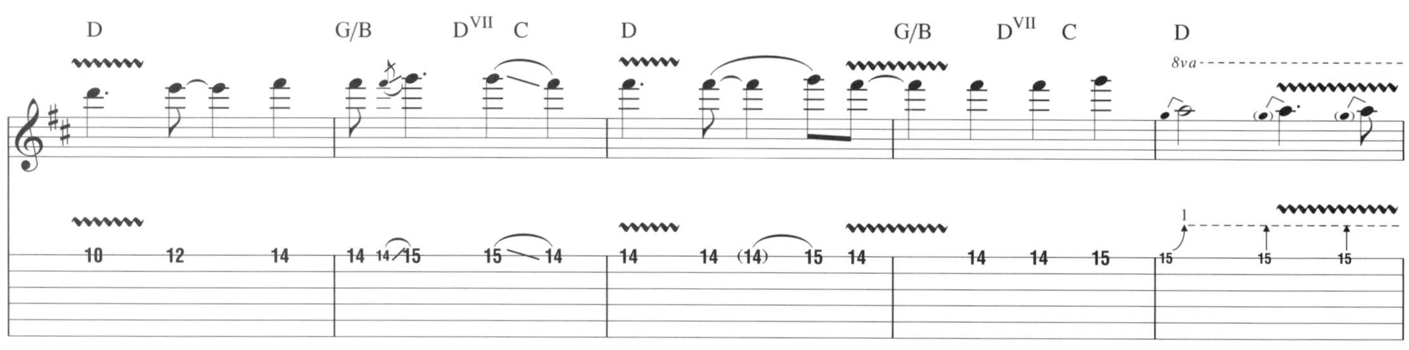
D G/B D^{VII} C D G/B D^{VII} C D
8va

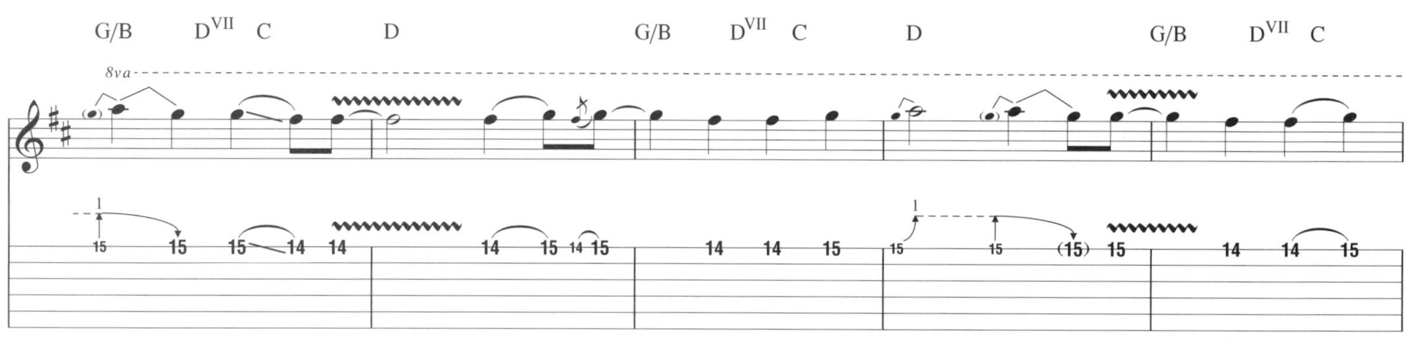
G/B D^{VII} C D G/B D^{VII} C D G/B D^{VII} C
8va

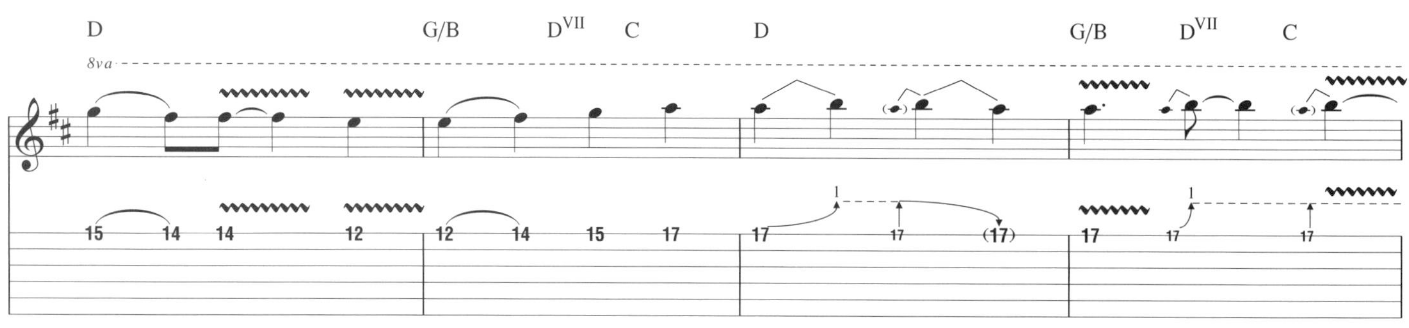
D G/B D^{VII} C D G/B D^{VII} C
8va

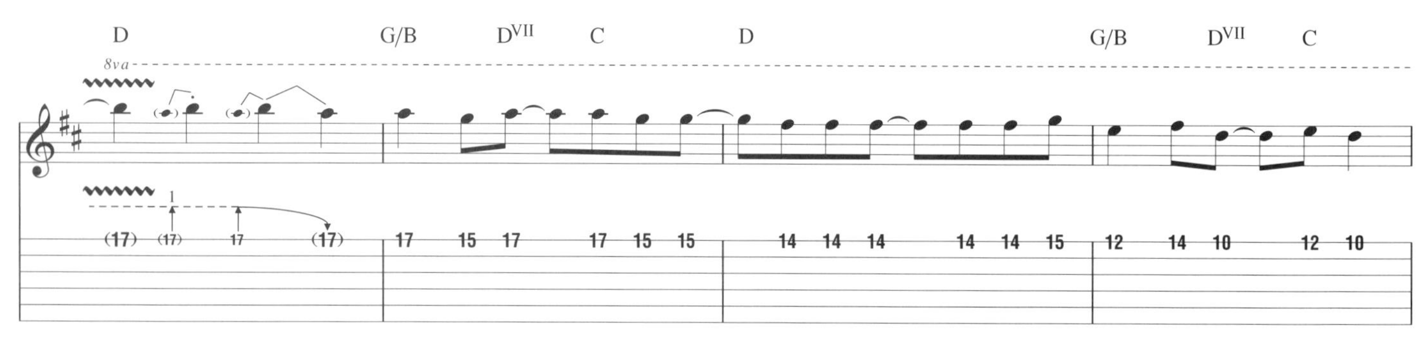
D G/B D^{VII} C D G/B D^{VII} C
8va

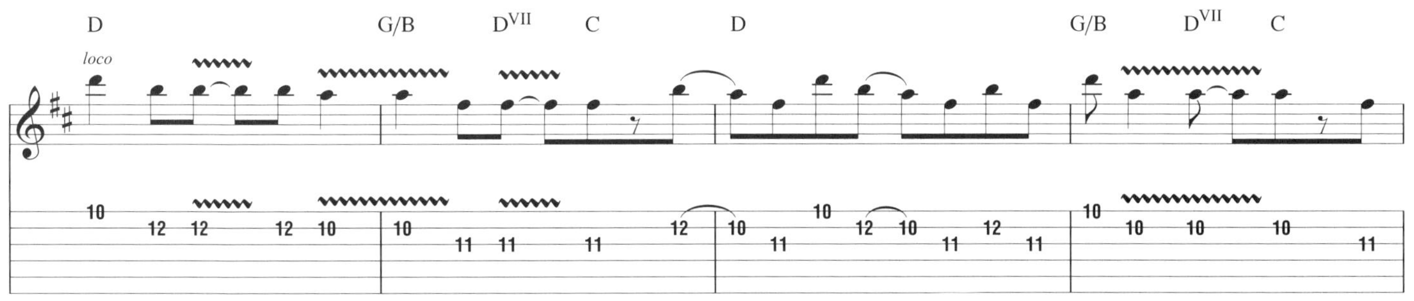
D G/B D^VII C D G/B D^VII C
loco

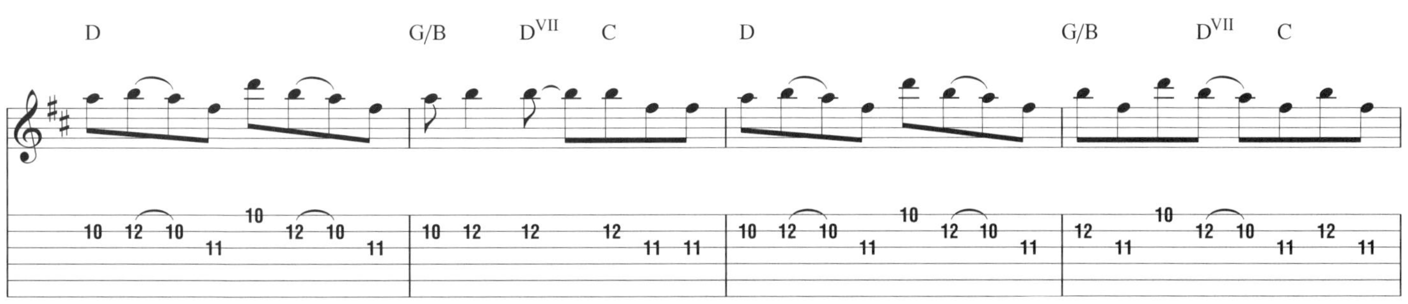
D G/B D^VII C D G/B D^VII C

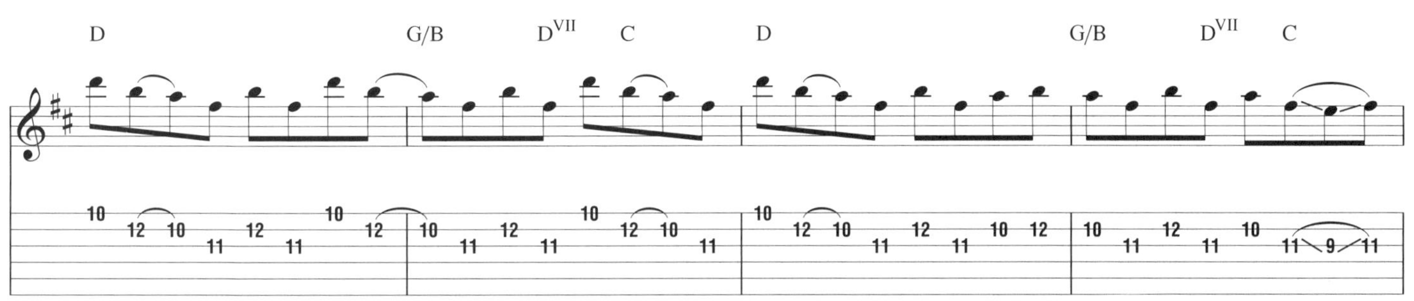
D G/B D^VII C D G/B D^VII C

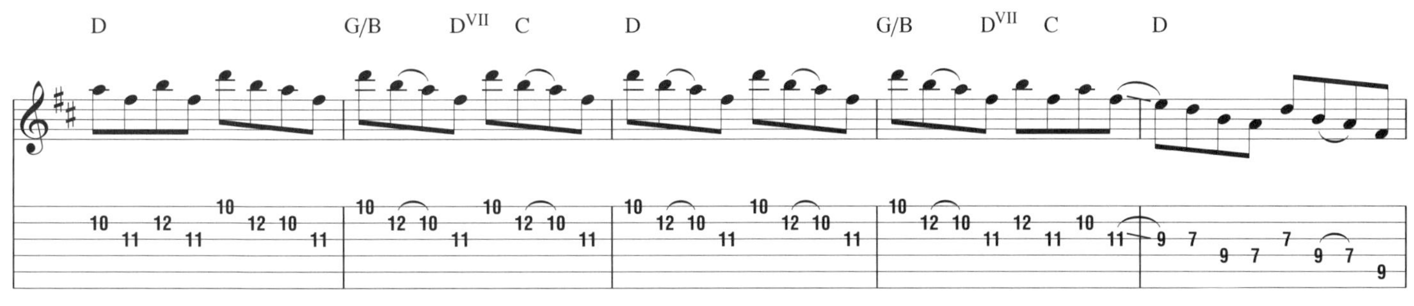
D G/B D^VII C D G/B D^VII C D

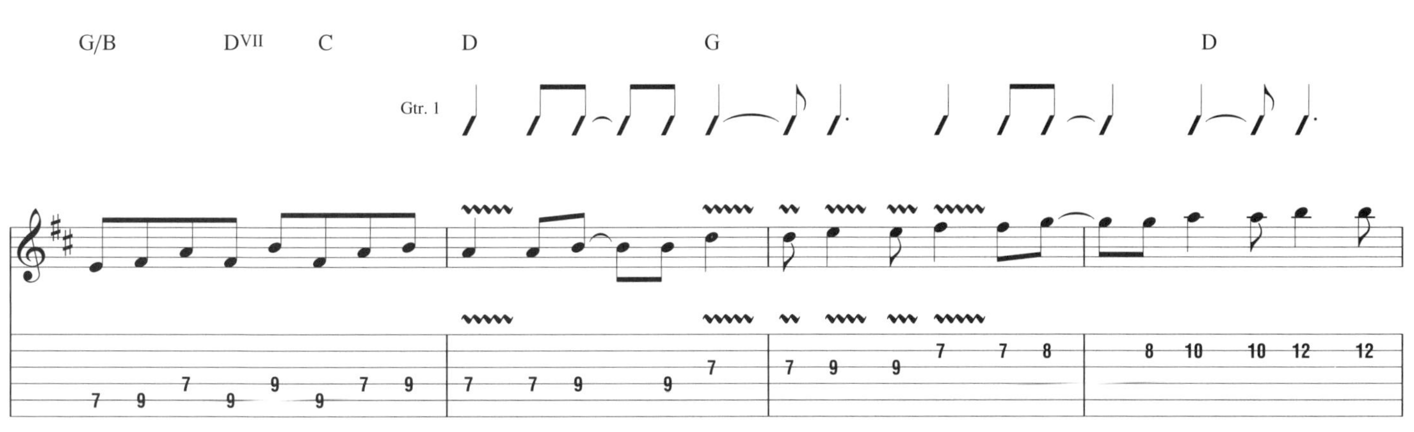
G/B D^VII C D G D
Gtr. 1

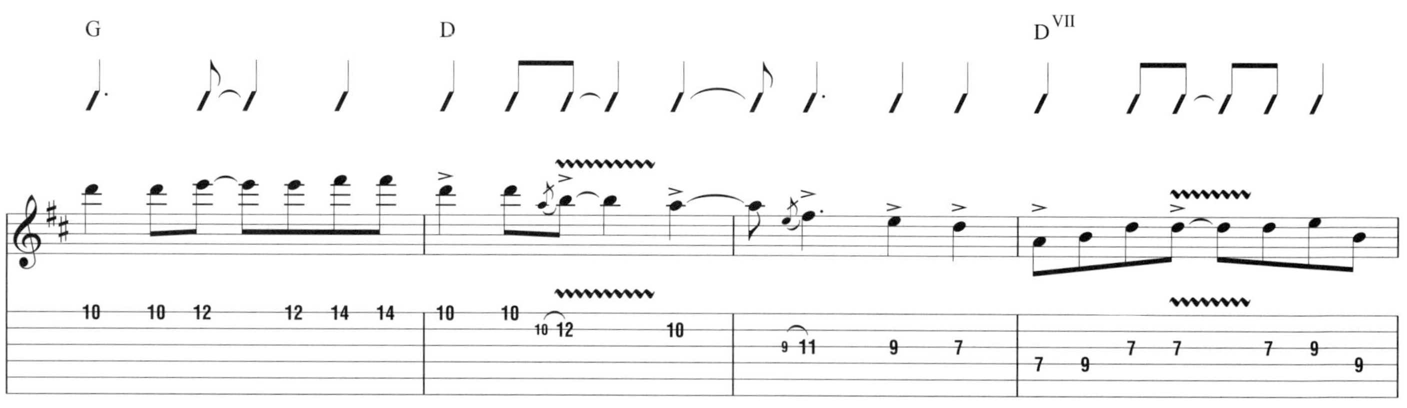
G
D
D VII
10 10 12 12 14 14
10 10 10 12 10
9 11 9 7
7 9 7 7 7 9 9

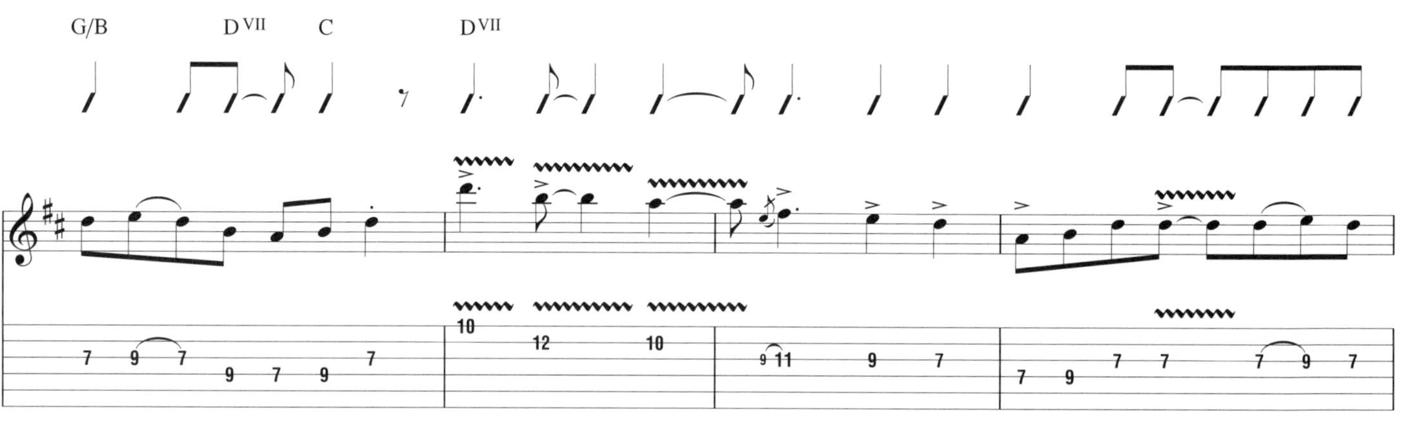
G/B
D VII
C
D VII
7 9 7 9 7 9 7
10 12 10
9 11 9 7
7 9 7 7 7 9 7

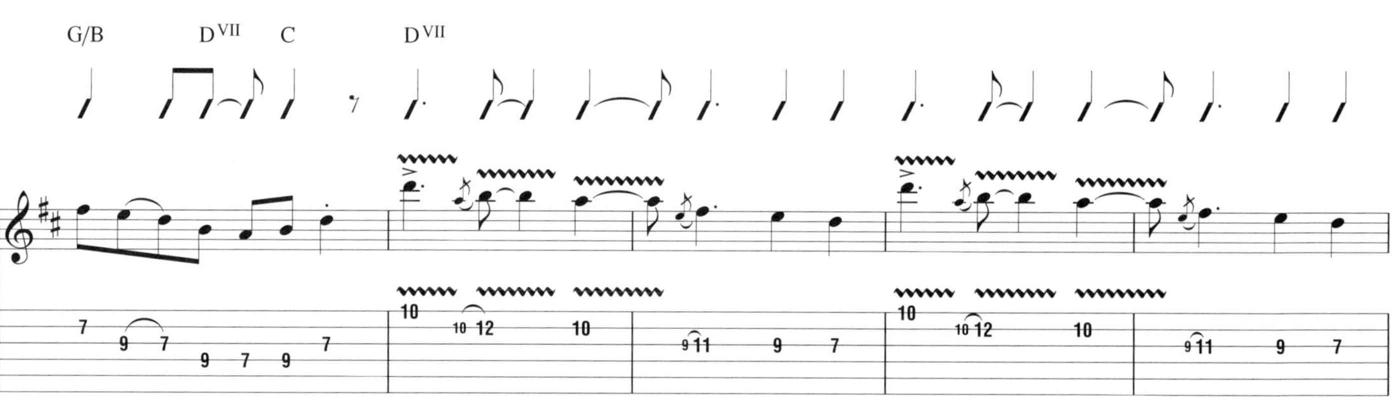
G/B
D VII
C
D VII
7 9 7 9 7 9 7
10 10 12 10
9 11 9 7
10 10 12 10
9 11 9 7

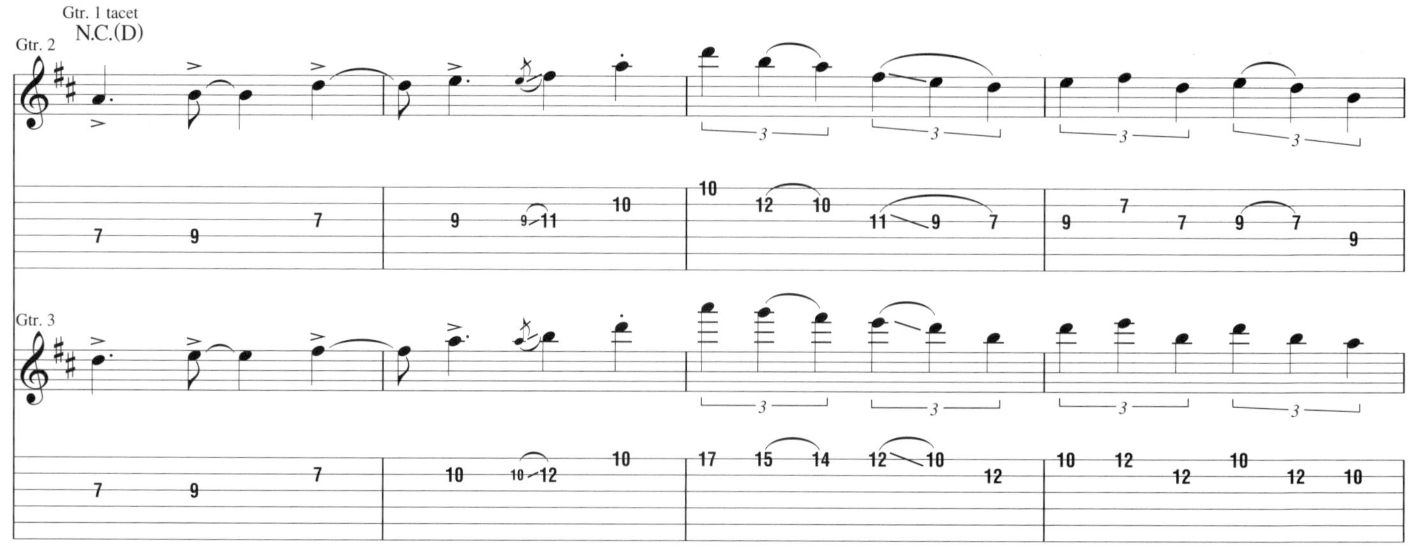
Gtr. 1 tacet
N.C.(D)
Gtr. 2
3
7 9 7
9 9 11 10
10 12 10 11 9 7
9 7 7 9 7 9
Gtr. 3
10 12 10 12 10 17 15 14 12 10 12 10 12 12 10 12 10
7 9 7

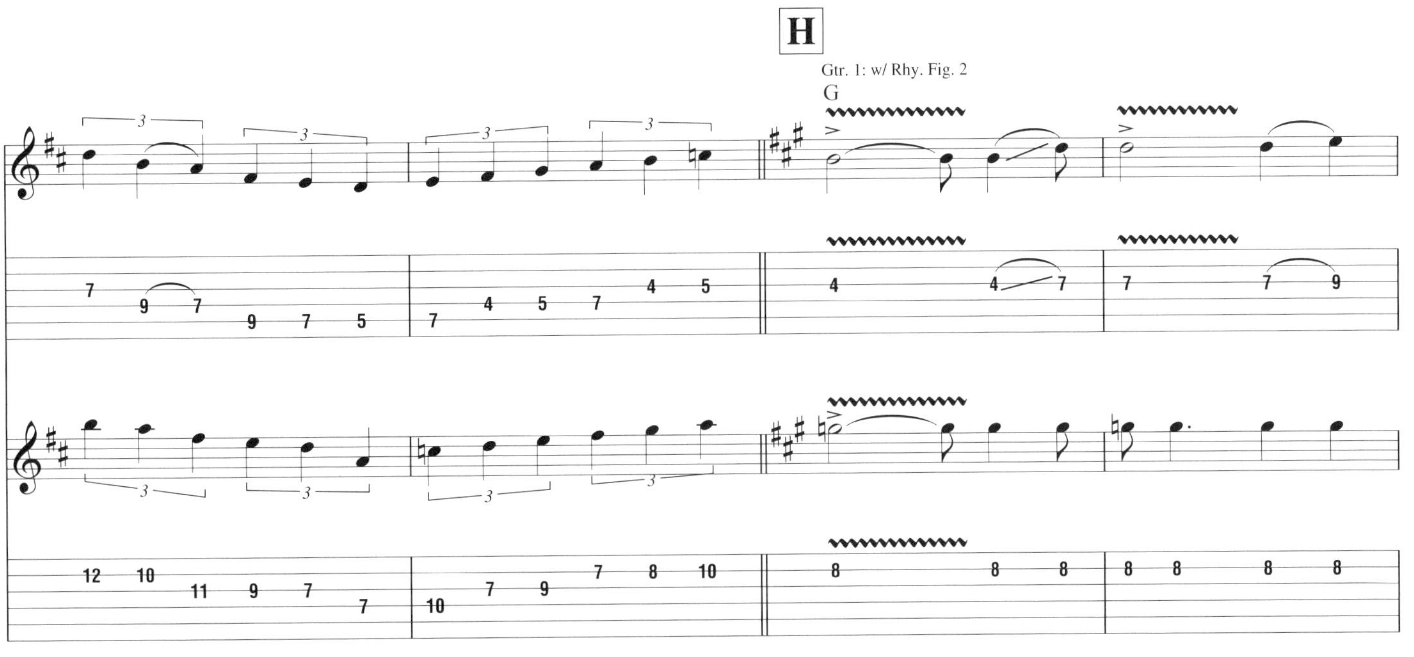

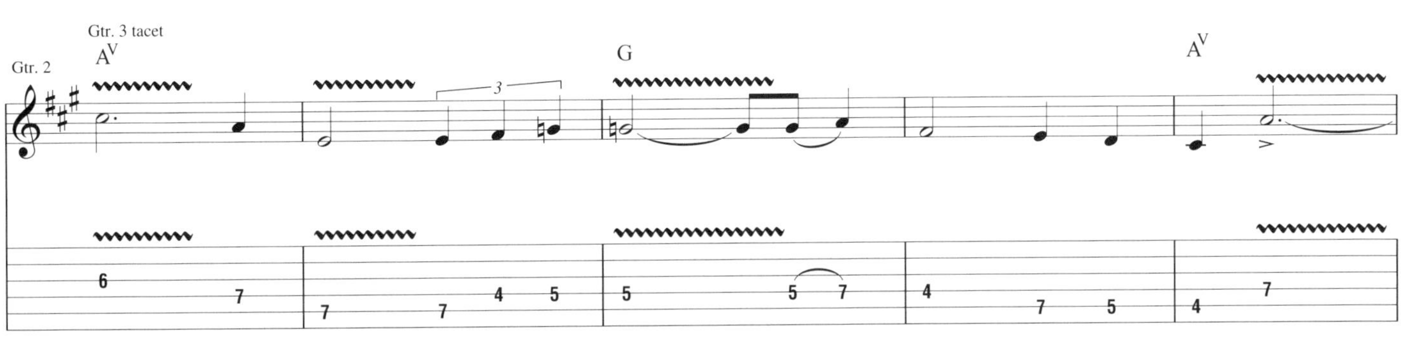

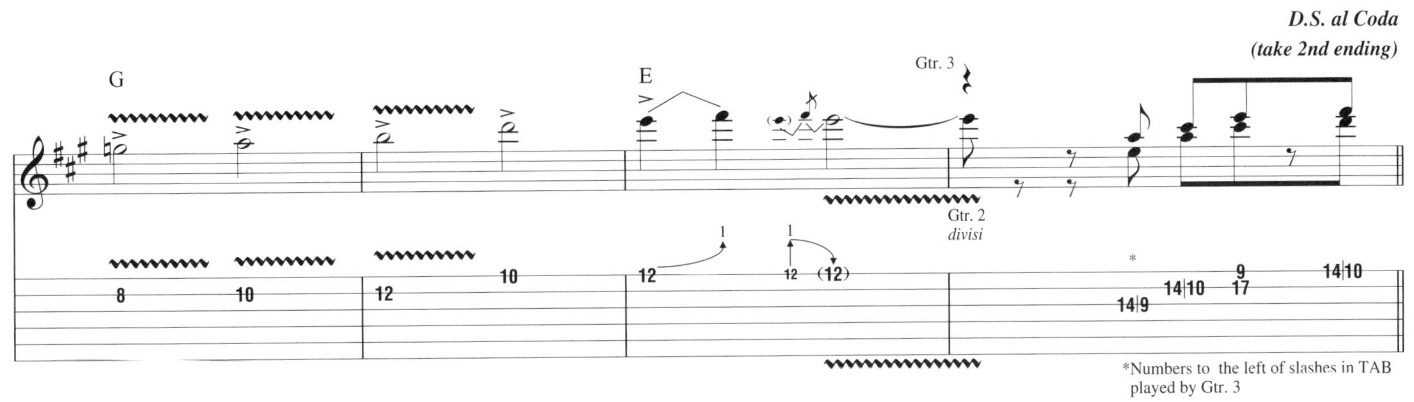

*Numbers to the left of slashes in TAB played by Gtr. 3

Coda

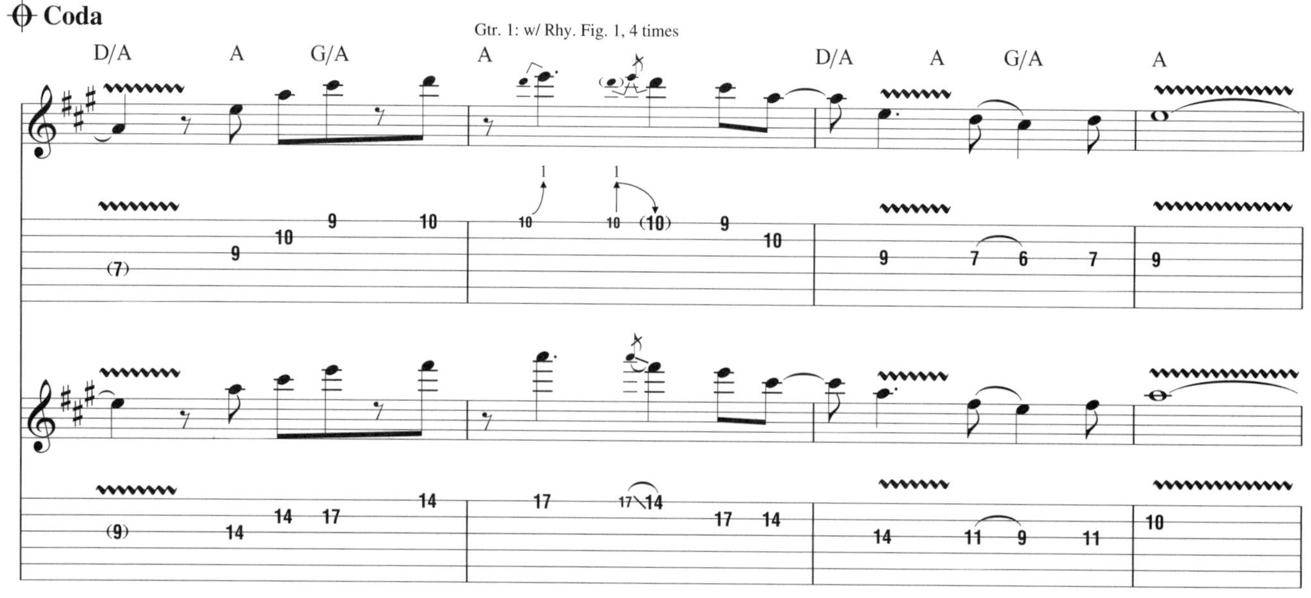
Gtr. 1: w/ Rhy. Fig. 1, 4 times
D/A
A
G/A
A
D/A
A
G/A
A

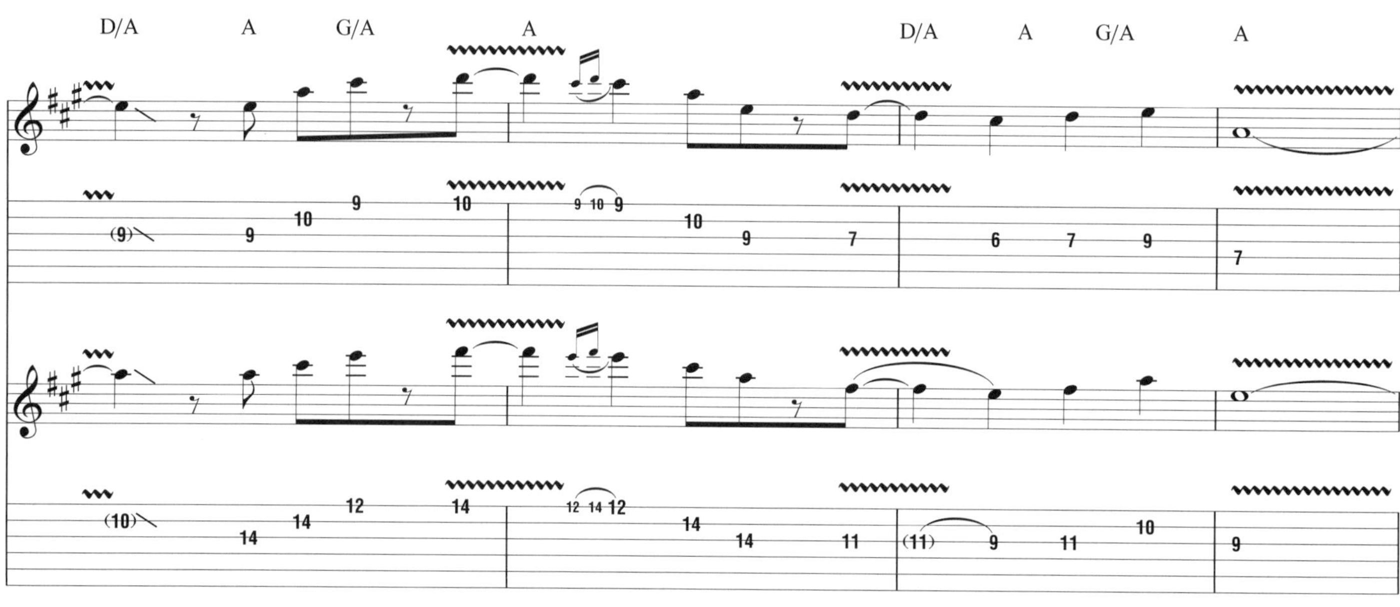
D/A
A
G/A
A
D/A
A
G/A
A

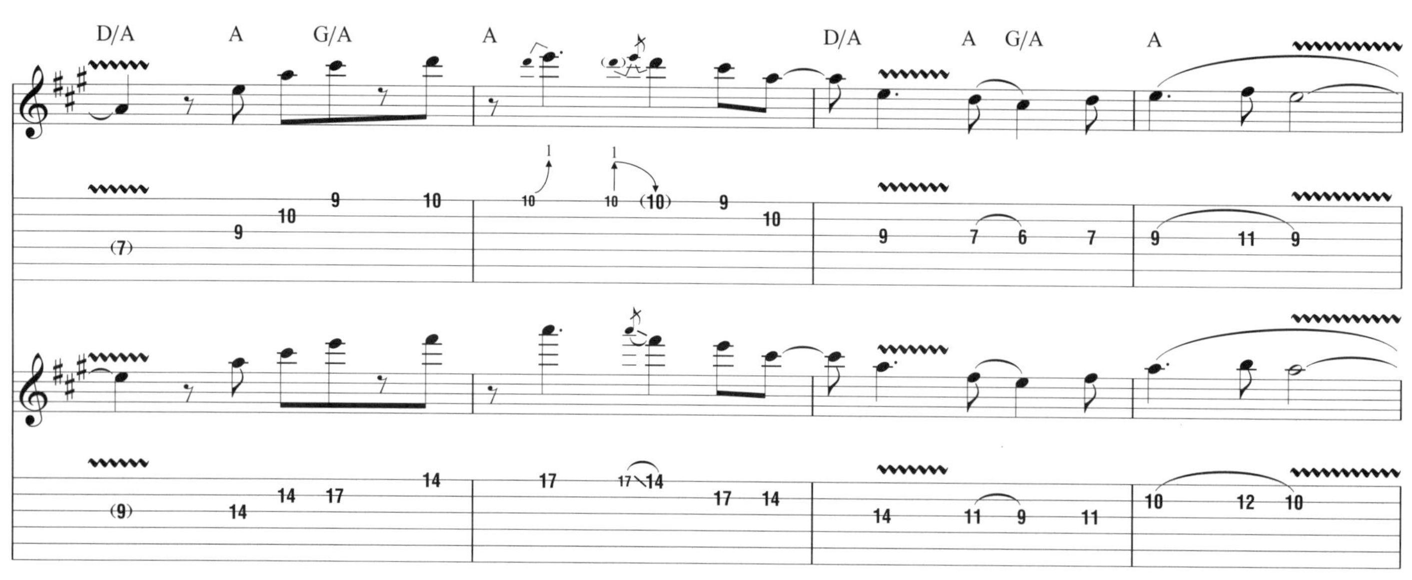
D/A
A
G/A
A
D/A
A
G/A
A

D/A A G/A A D/A A G/A A D/A A G/A
I
Free time
G
Gtr. 1
Gtr. 2
A V
8va

Just Like a Woman

By B.B. King

*Gtr. 2 (clean); composite arrangement
**Chord symbols reflect basic harmony.

C
Gtr. 2 tacet
D
G7
Gtr. 1
C7
G7
Voc. Fig. 1
End Voc. Fig. 1
Just like a wom - an.
Just like a wom - an.
D7
C7
G7
D
D7
G7

Bkgd. Voc.: w/ Voc. Fig. 1

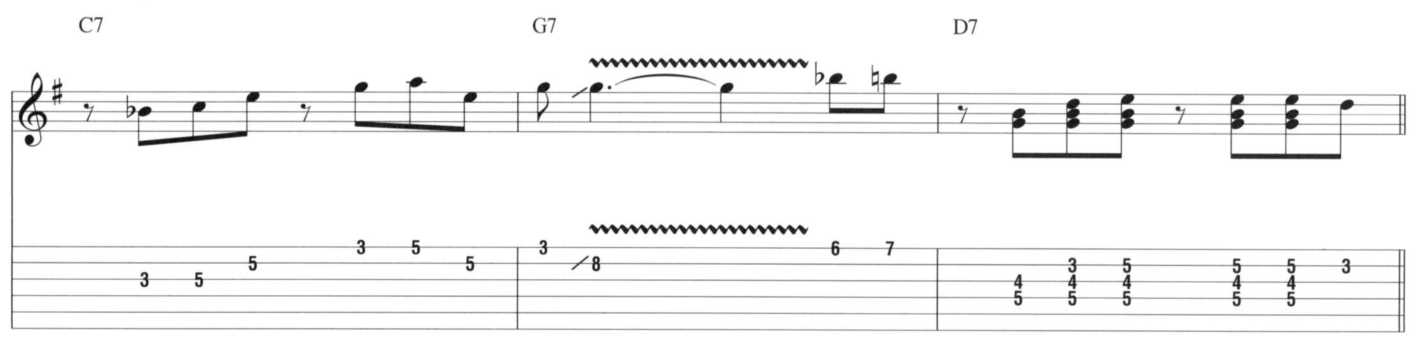

E

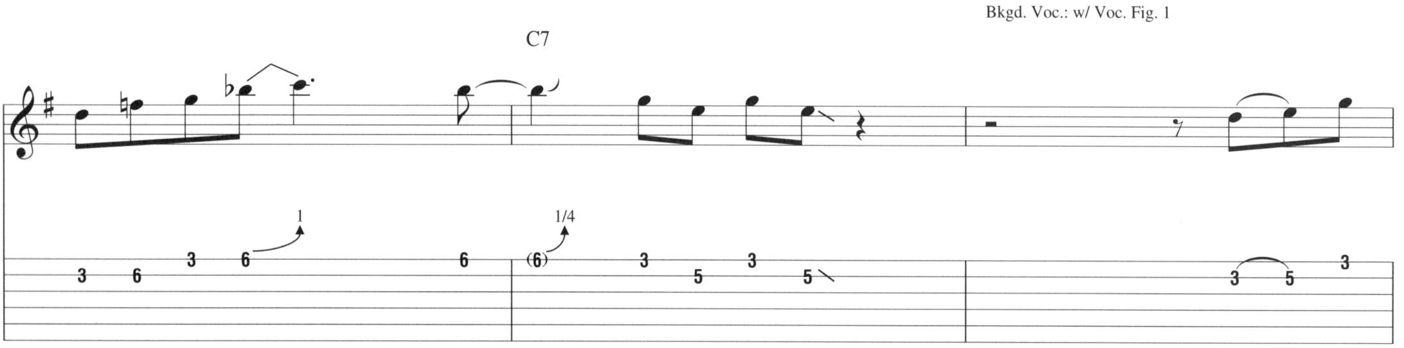

F

C7
G7
D7
G
G7
C7
rake
G7
D7
C7
G7
D7

H
G7
C7
G7
D7
C7
I
G7
D7
G7
p
mp
mf
C7
1/4

G7

D7
C7
G7
D7
f

J
G7

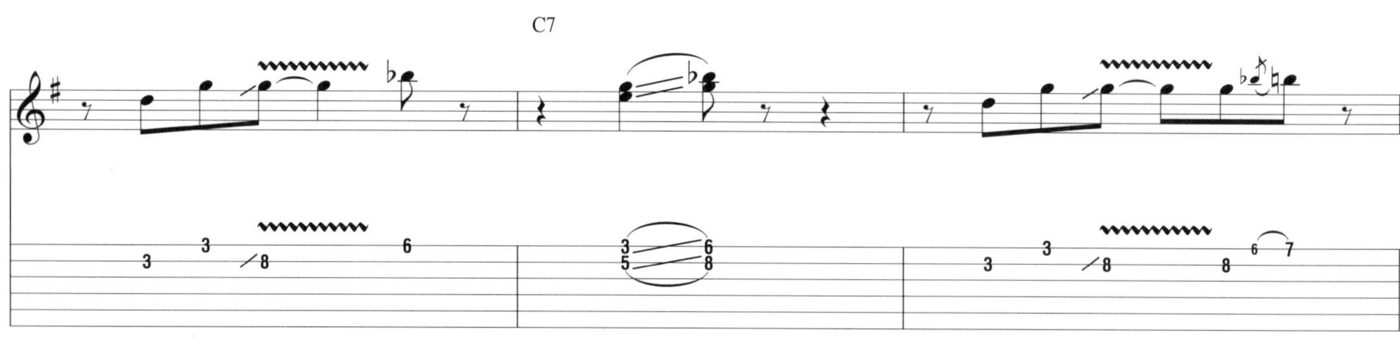
C7

G7
D7

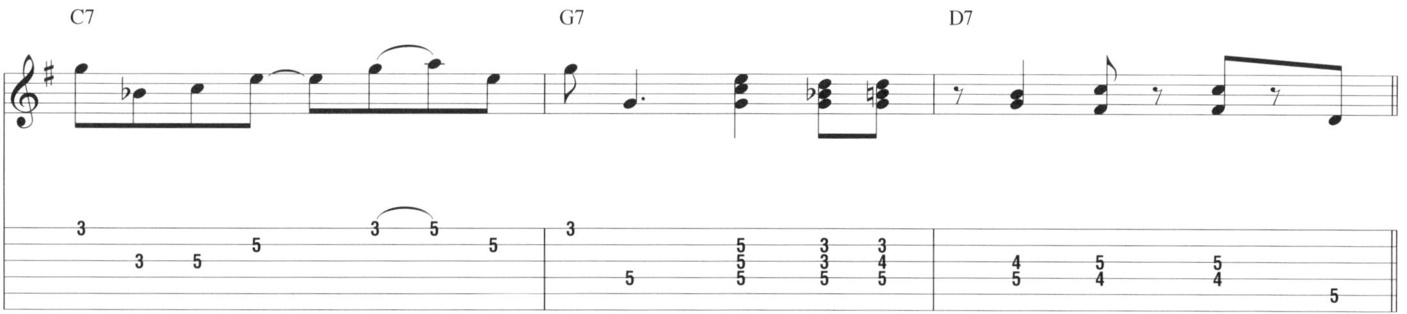
C7
G7
D7

K

G7

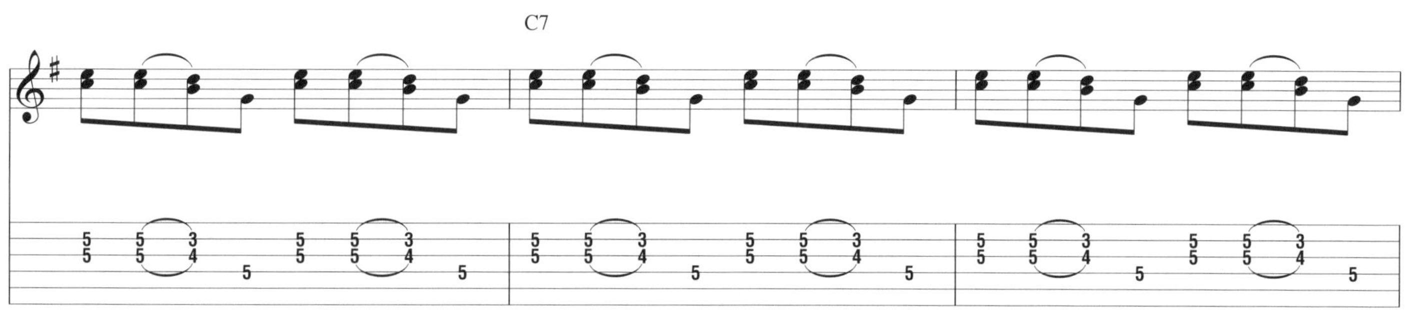
C7

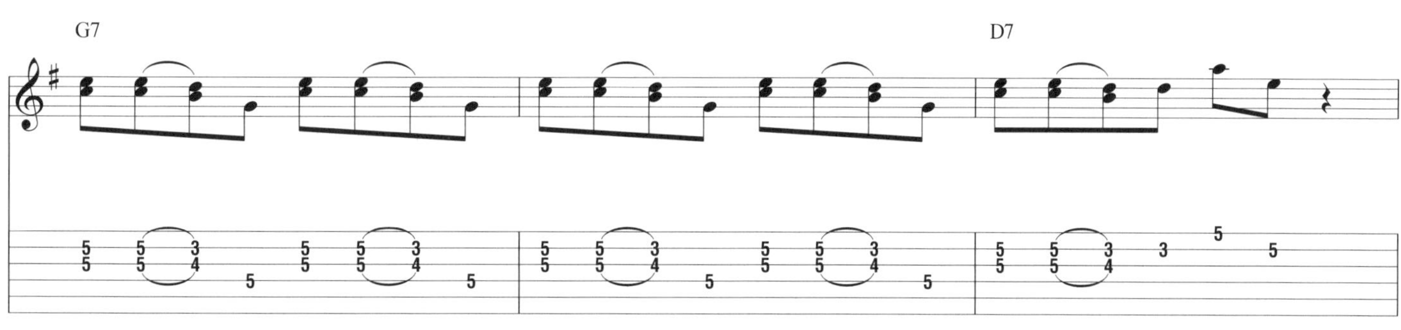
G7
D7

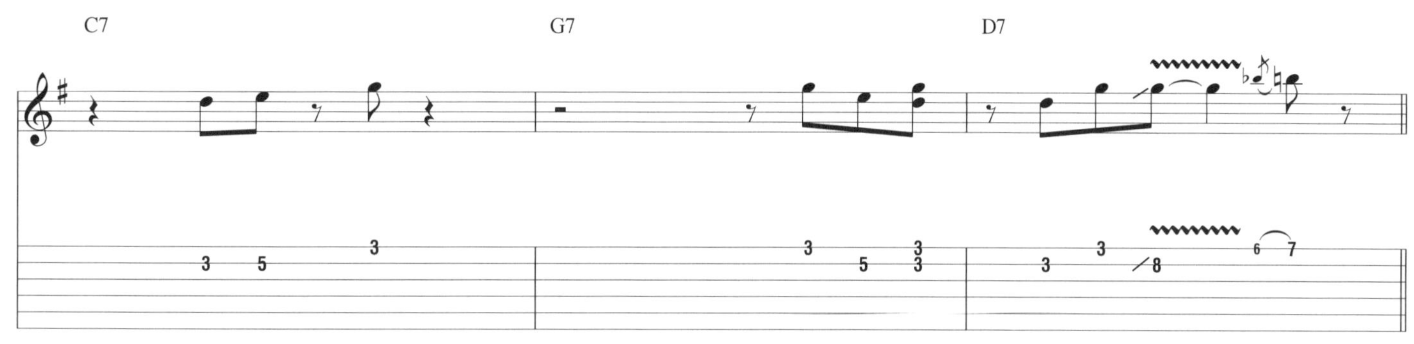
C7
G7
D7

L

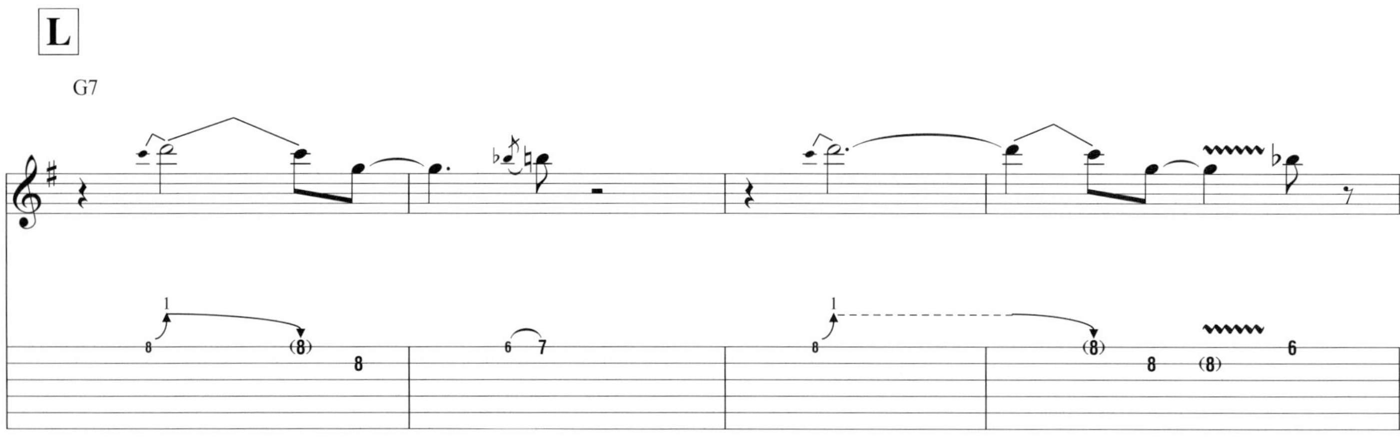
G7
1
8
(8)
8
6
7
1
8
(8)
8
(8)
6

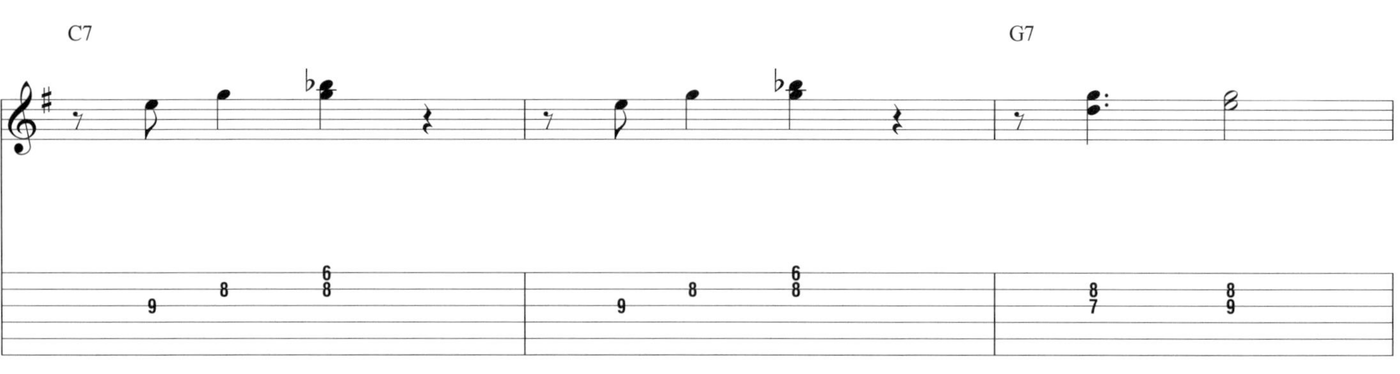
C7
G7
9
8
6
8
9
8
6
8
8
7
8
9

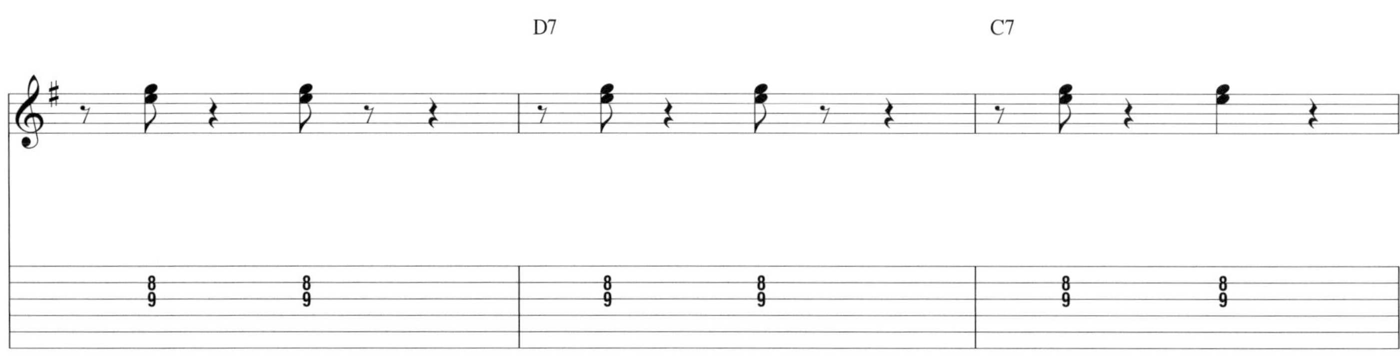
D7
C7
8
9
8
9
8
9
8
9
8
9
8
9

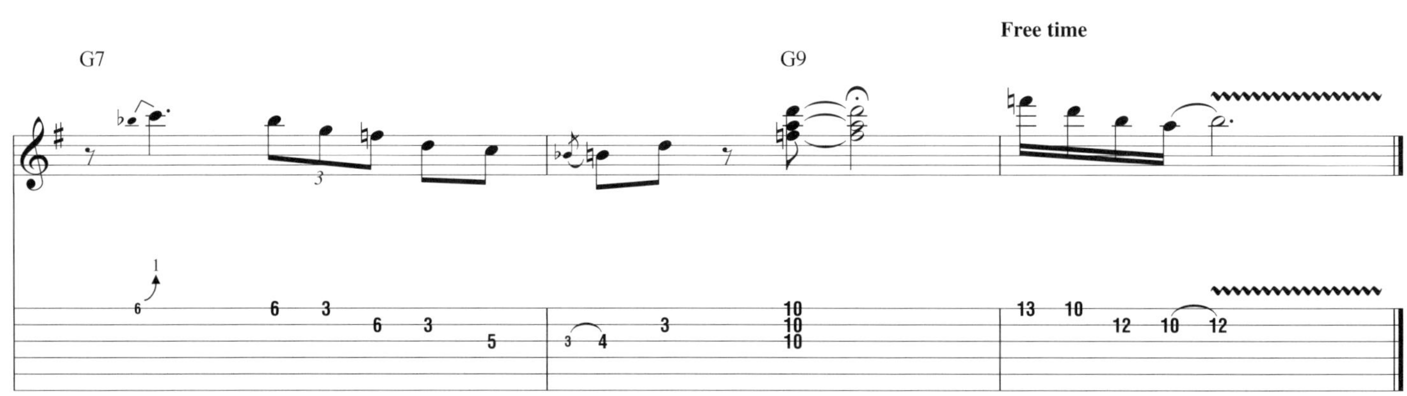
Free time
G7
G9
3
1
6
6
3
6
3
5
3
4
3
10
10
10
13
10
12
10
12

Misirlou

By Nicolas Roubanis

E

steady gliss.

B
Gtr. 1
E
Gtr. 2 (clean)
mp

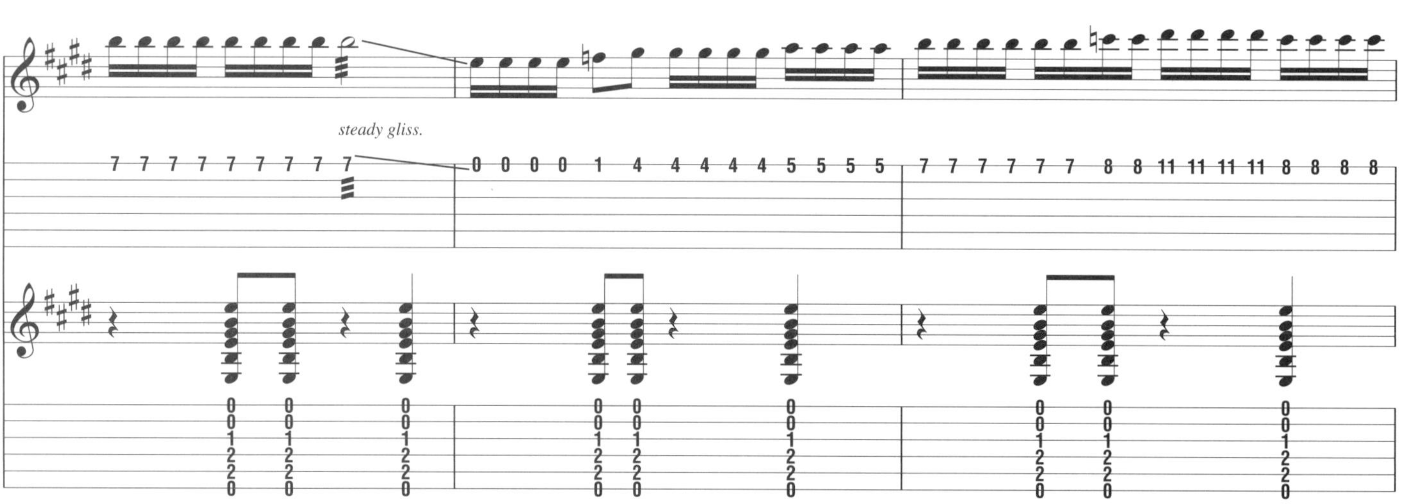
steady gliss.

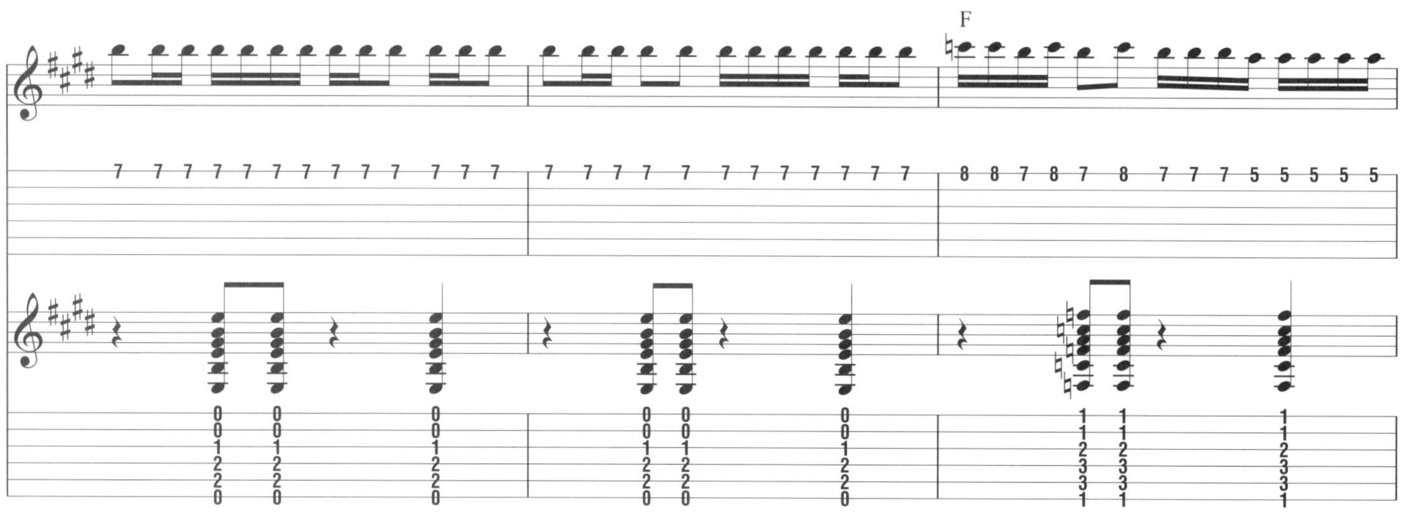
F

E
F
E
C
Gtr. 1 tacet
Am
*Gtr. 3
mf
*Trumpet arr. for gtr.
Gtr. 1
Gtr. 2
p

Gtr. 3
G
F
Gtr. 2
E
F
mp
E
F
E

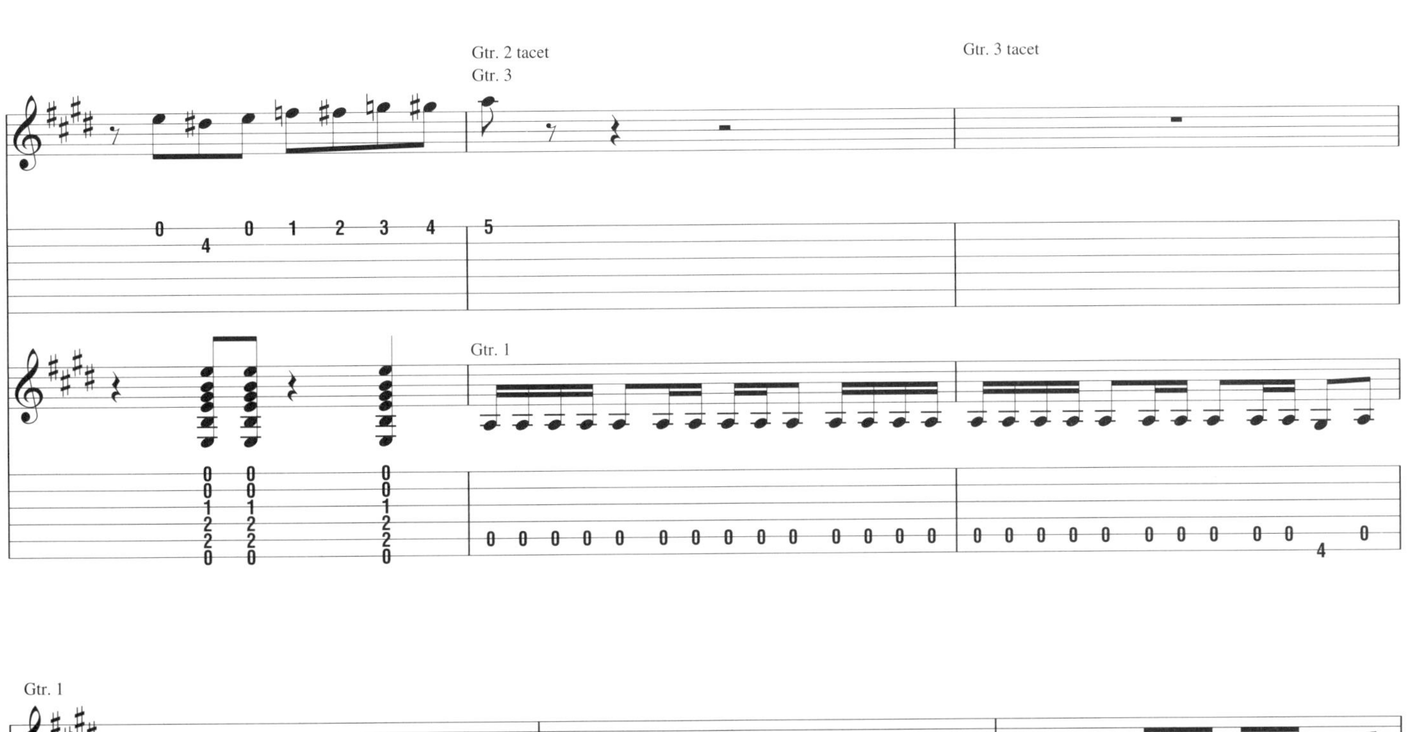
Gtr. 2 tacet
Gtr. 3
Gtr. 3 tacet
Gtr. 1

Gtr. 1

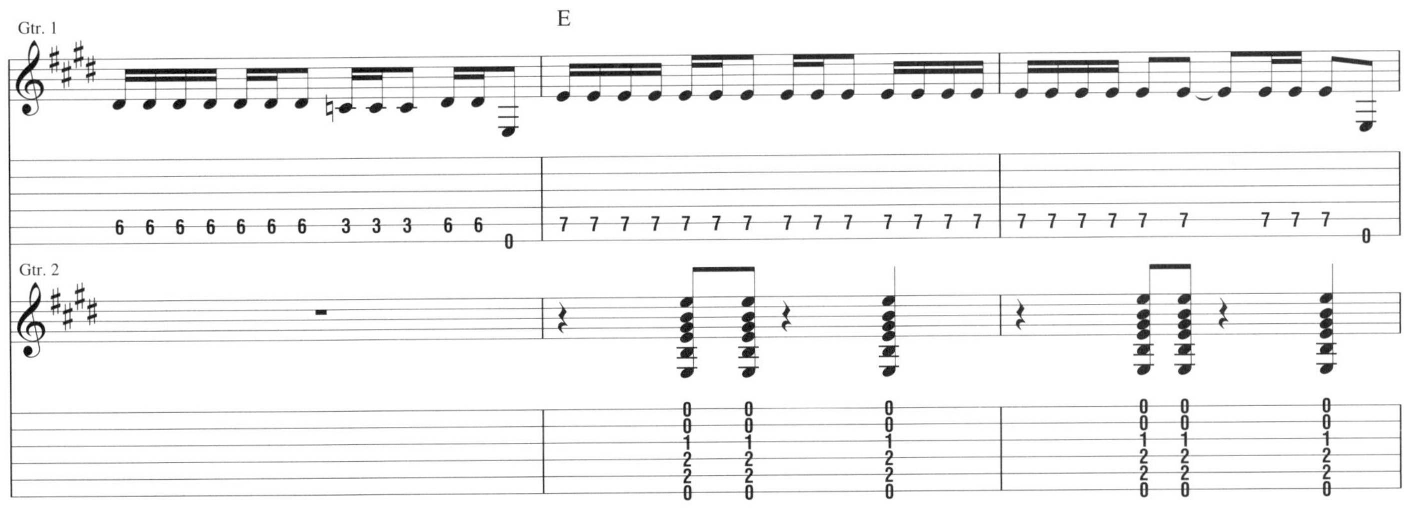
Gtr. 1
E
Gtr. 2

Dm
E

Dm
E
Play 5 times

F
E
F
E
Play 5 times and fade

Peter Gunn

Theme Song from The Television Series

By Henry Mancini

Tune Up 1/2 Step:

① = F ④ = E♭
② = C ⑤ = B♭
③ = A♭ ⑥ = F

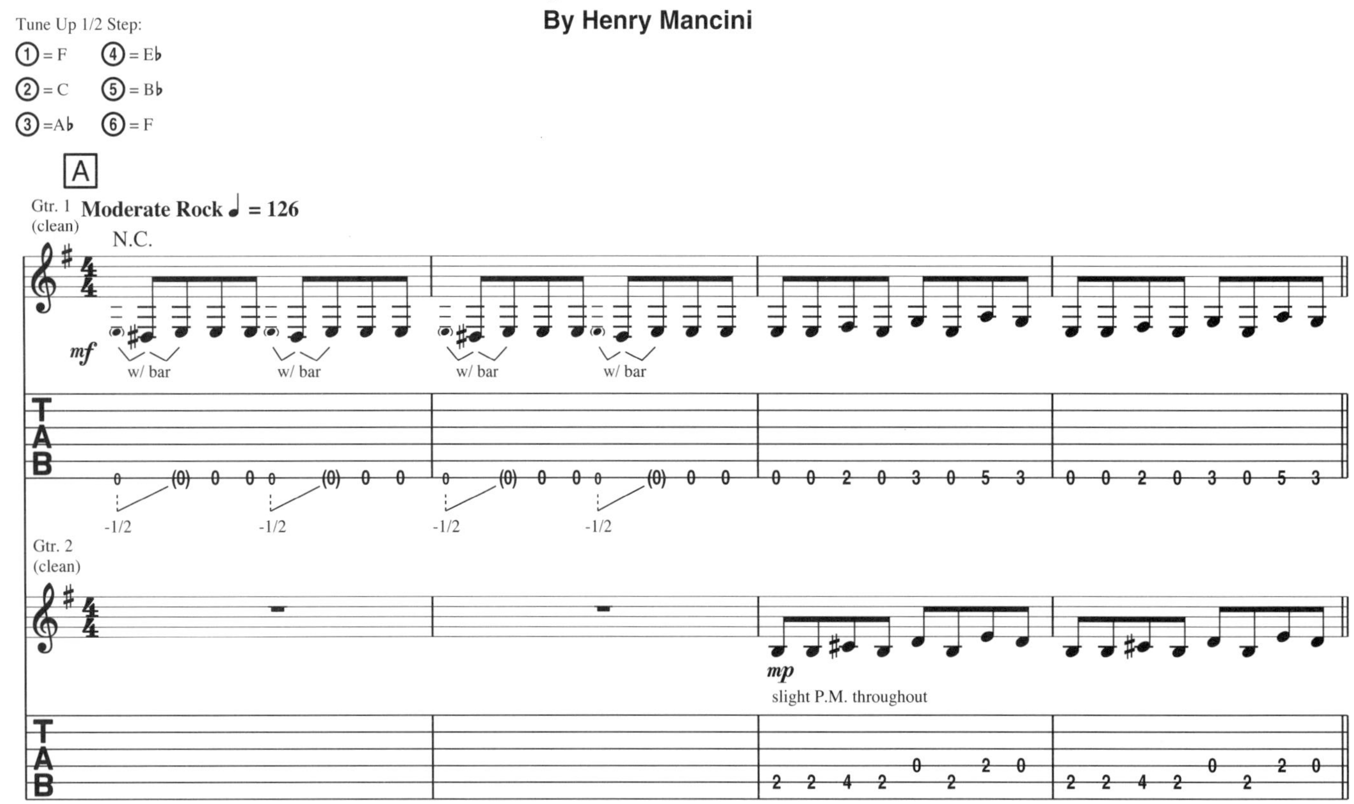

Sax
Gtr. 1
Gtr. 2
N.C.
w/ bar
w/ bar
-1/2
-1/2

C
Gtr. 1
E7(no 3rd)
play 4 times
Gtr. 2
D
N.C.
Gtr. 2 tacet
w/ bar
-1/2
Gtr. 1
Gtr. 2: w/ Riff A1, till fade
E7(no 3rd)
E
E7(no 3rd)
Play 5 Times and Fade

Pipeline

By Bob Spickard and Brian Carman

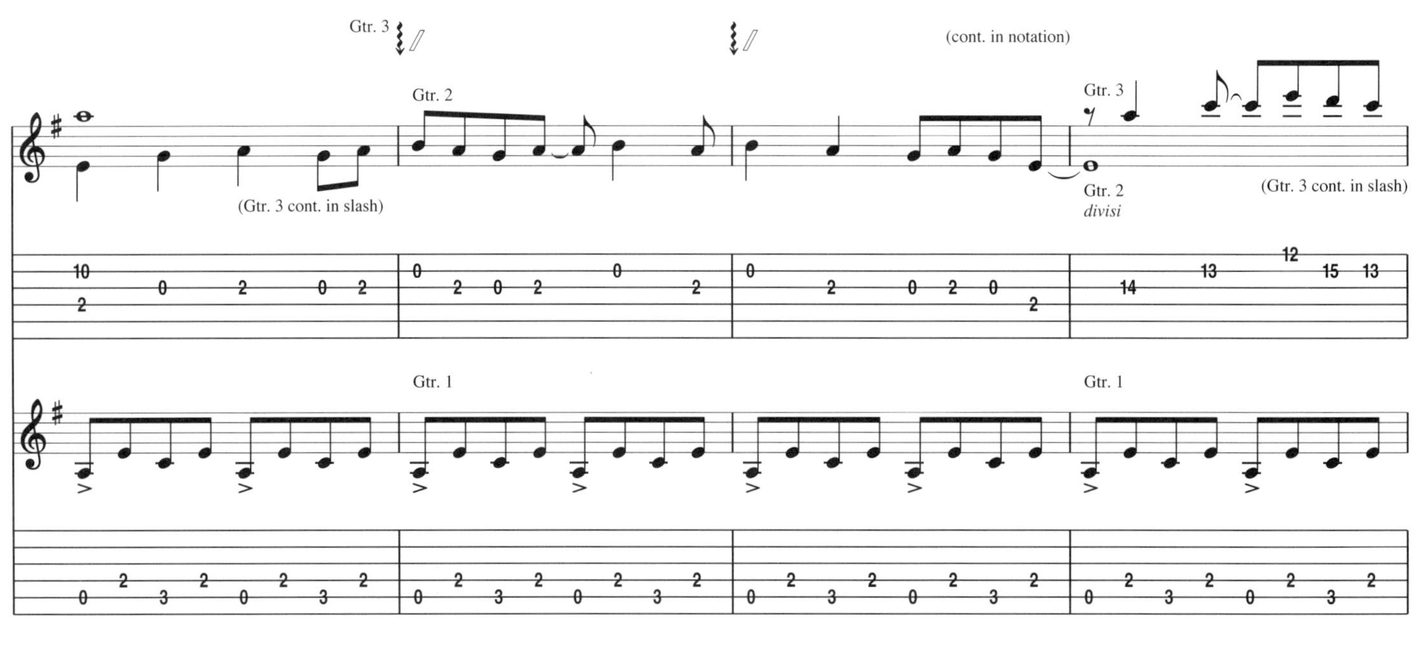
Am
Am
Gtr. 3
(cont. in notation)
Gtr. 2
Gtr. 3
(Gtr. 3 cont. in slash)
Gtr. 2
divisi
(Gtr. 3 cont. in slash)
Gtr. 1
Gtr. 1

B
C
B
Gtr. 3
Gtr. 2
Gtr. 1

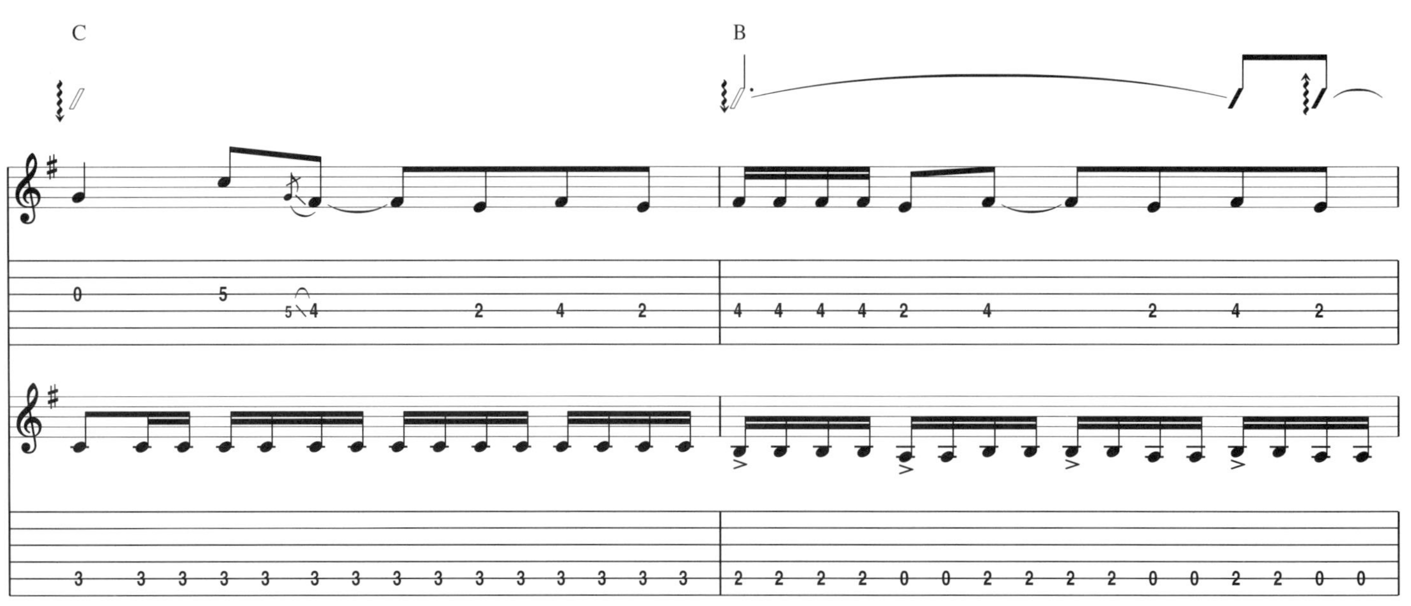
C
B

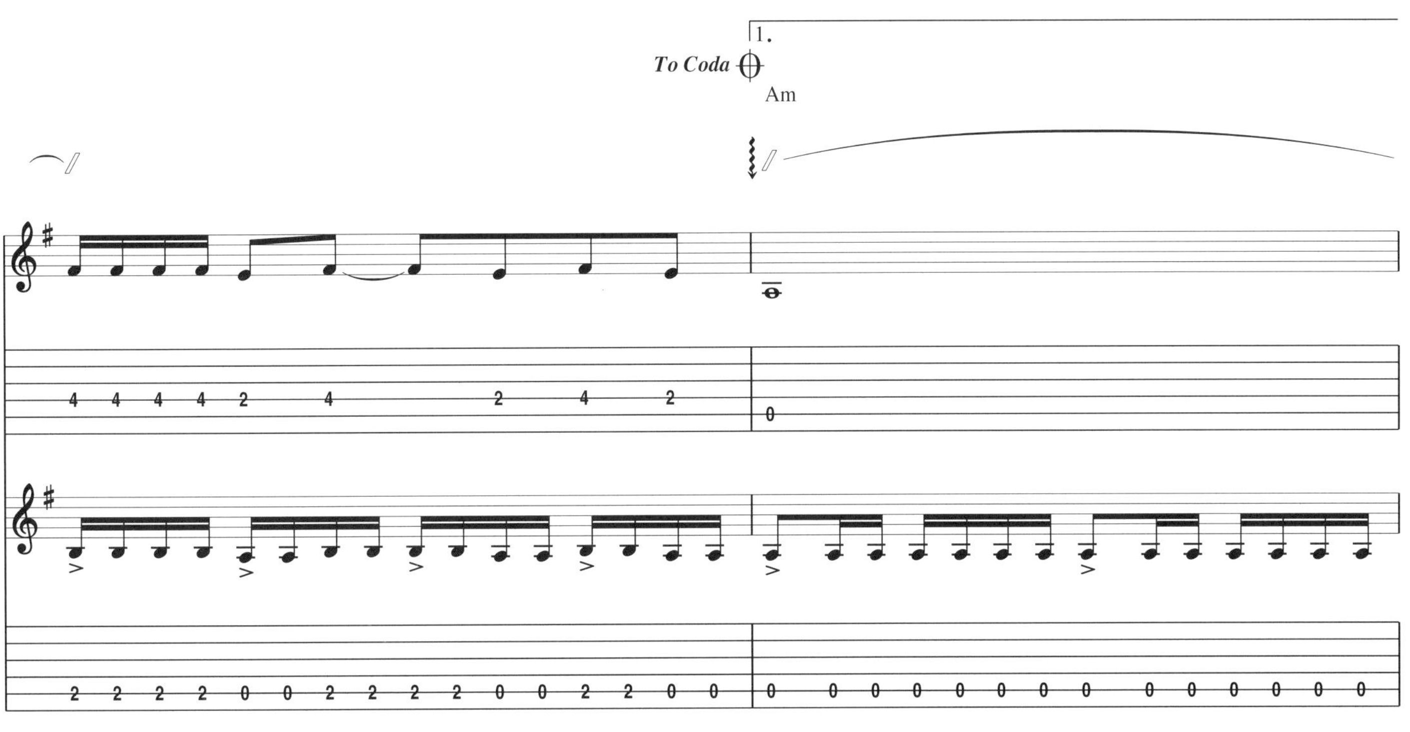
To Coda
1.
Am

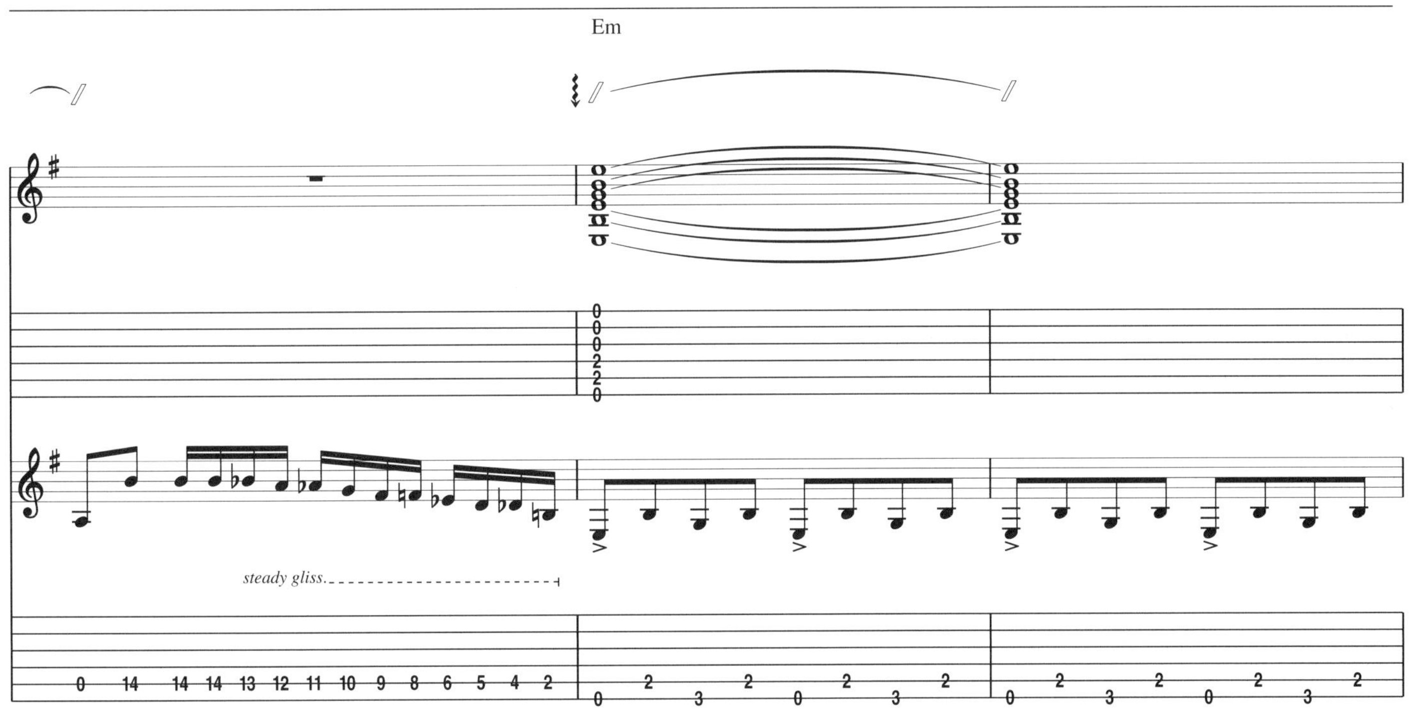
Em
steady gliss.

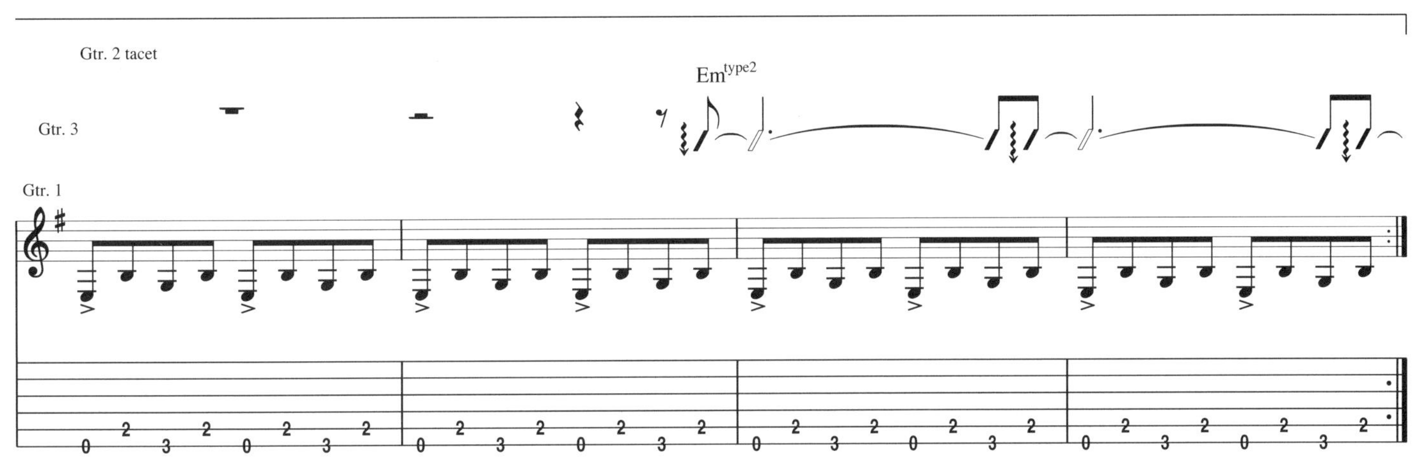
Gtr. 2 tacet
Gtr. 3
Em type2
Gtr. 1

2.
C Bridge
Gtr. 2 tacet
Am
G
Gtr. 3
mp
tremolo off
Gtr. 1
*Played ahead of the beat.
F
G

Am
G
F

Em
let ring
(cont. in slash)
steady gliss.
D Interlude
Gtr. 3
Gtr. 1
D.S. al Coda
Em type2
w/ amp tremolo
Coda
Am
B
1
19fr
Em type2
steady gliss.
steady gliss.

Ramrod

By Al Casey

*Capo II
A
Bright Rock ♩ = 165
† B
**(A)
Gtr. 1 (clean)
mf
Gtr. 2 (clean)
mf
*Recorded in key of A, sped up to key of B♭ to add Sax., sped up to key of B for final mix. Capo II to match recording.
**Symbols in parentheses represent chord names respective to capoed guitar.
Symbols above reflect actual sounding chord. Capoed fret is "0" in TAB.
† Chord symbols reflect basic tonality.
B
B
(A)
simile on repeats
Rhy. Fig. 1
simile on repeats
E
(D)
B
(A)

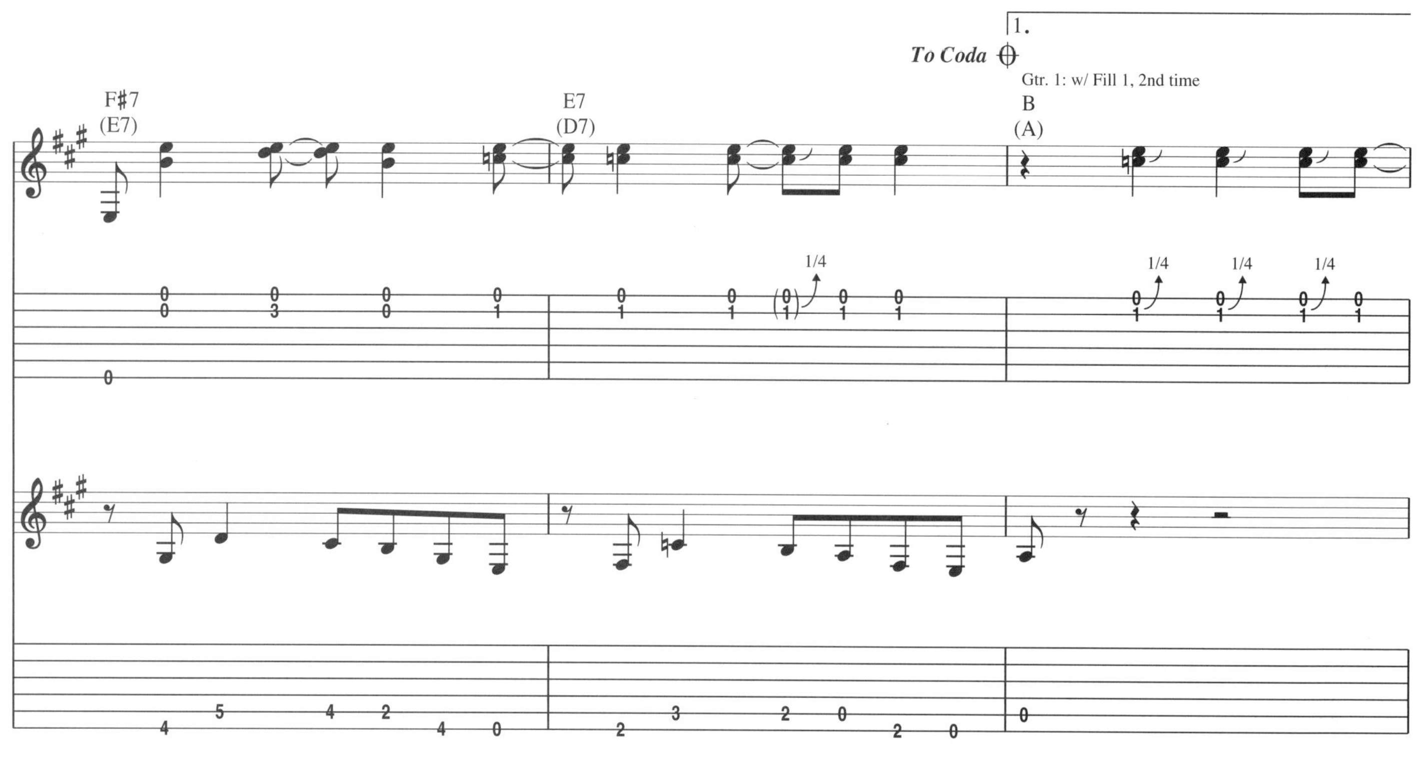
1.
To Coda
Gtr. 1: w/ Fill 1, 2nd time
F#7
(E7)
E7
(D7)
B
(A)

2.
B
(A)
End Rhy. Fig. 1

Fill 1
Gtr. 1

C
Gtr. 2: w/ Rhy. Fig. 1, simile
B7
(A7)
Gtr. 1

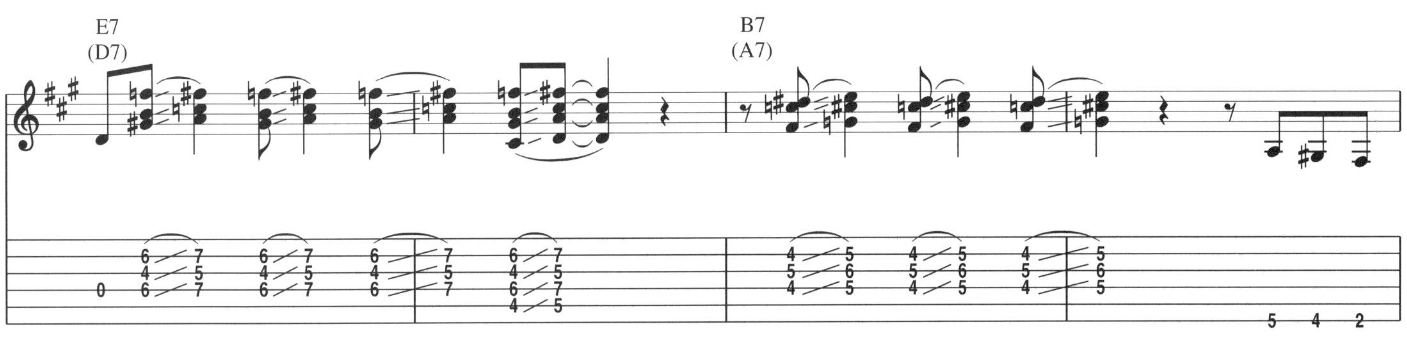
E7
(D7)
B7
(A7)

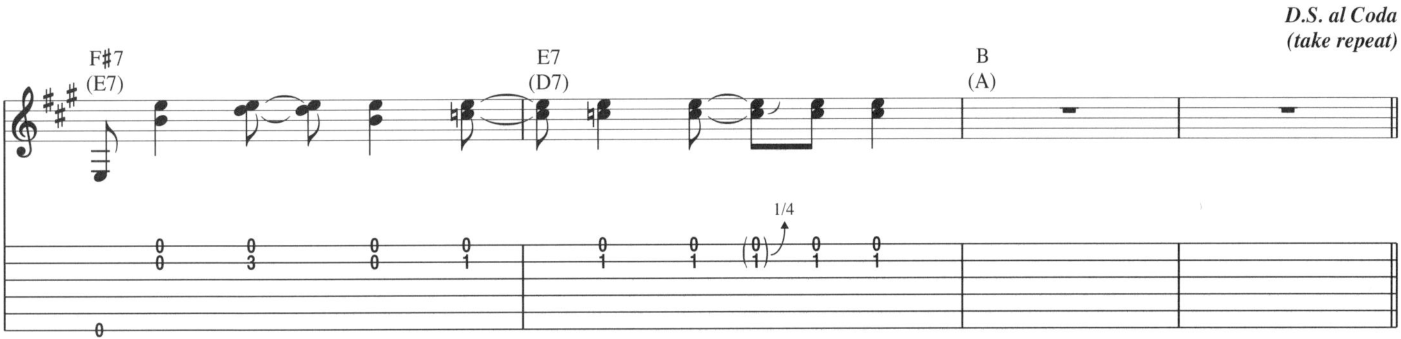
D.S. al Coda
(take repeat)
F#7
(E7)
E7
(D7)
B
(A)
1/4

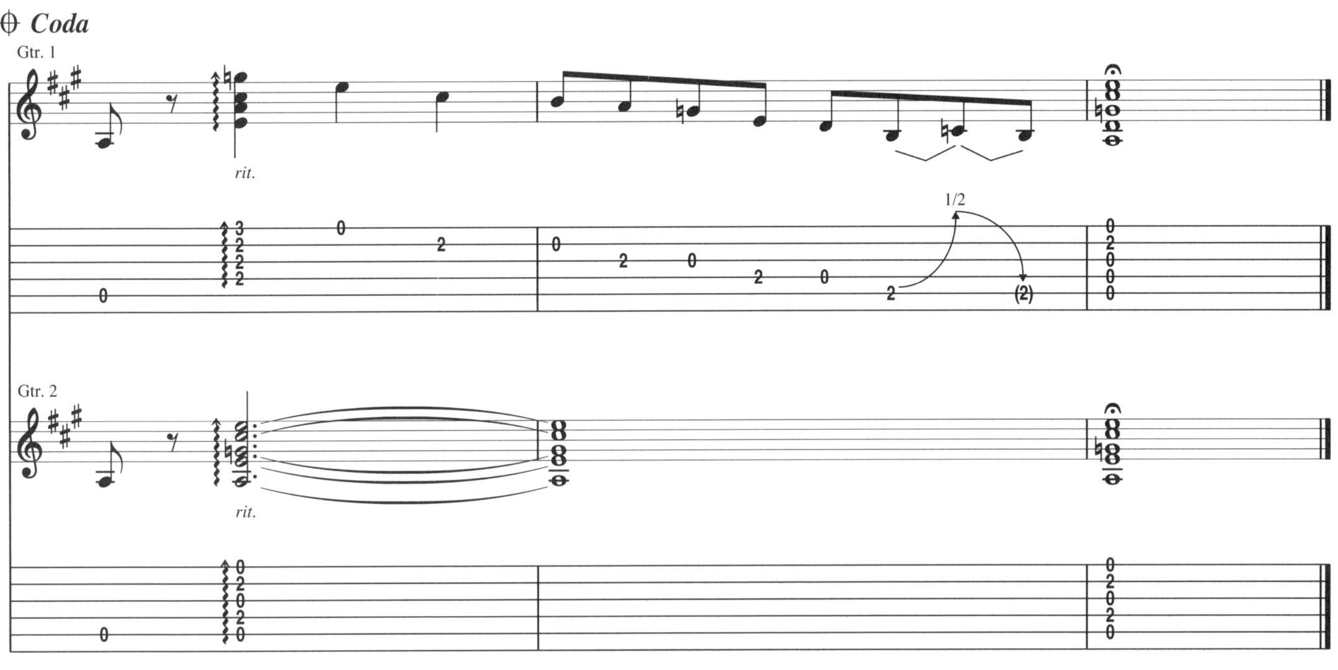
Coda
Gtr. 1
rit.
1/2
Gtr. 2
rit.

Raunchy

By William Justis and Sidney Manker

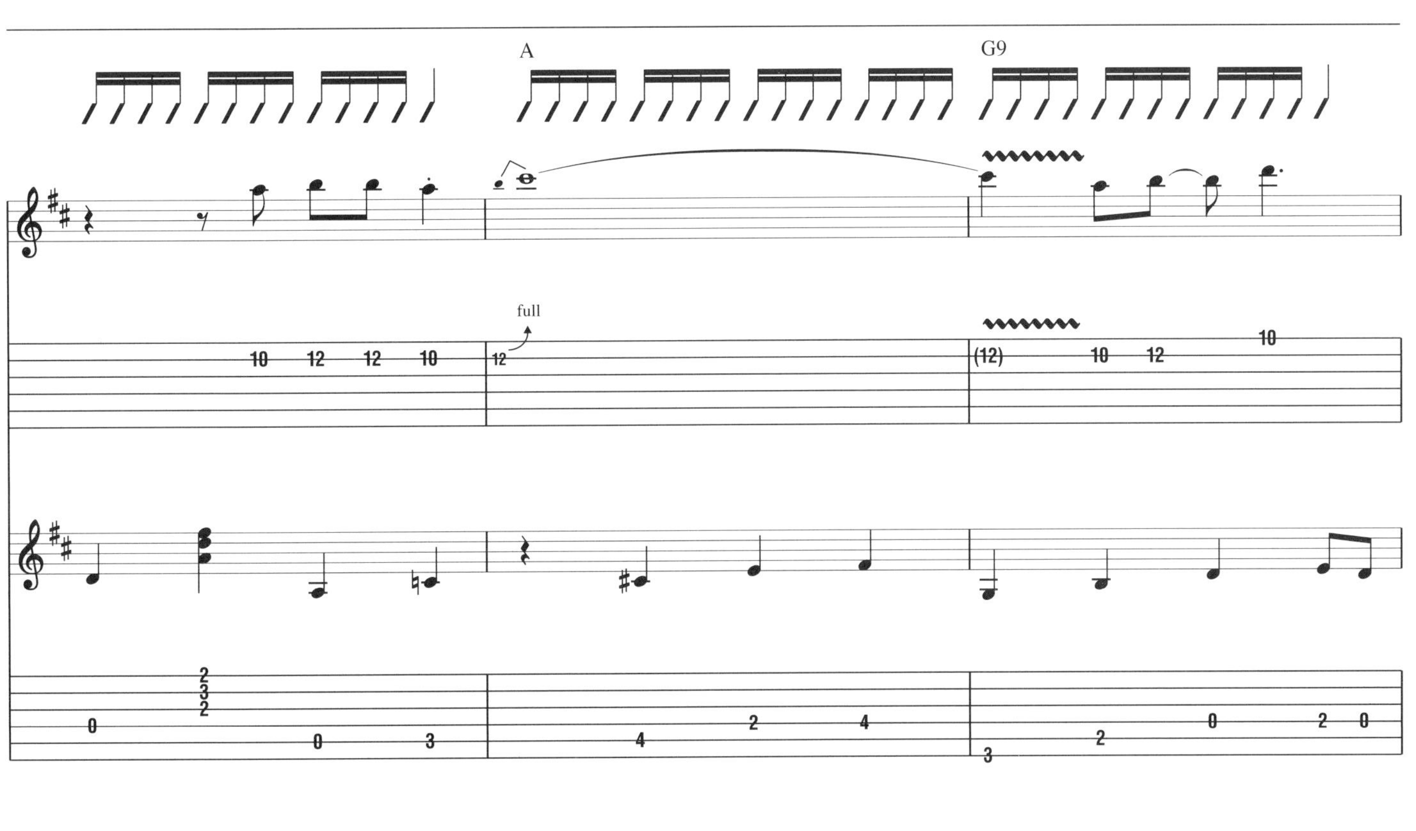
A
G9
full

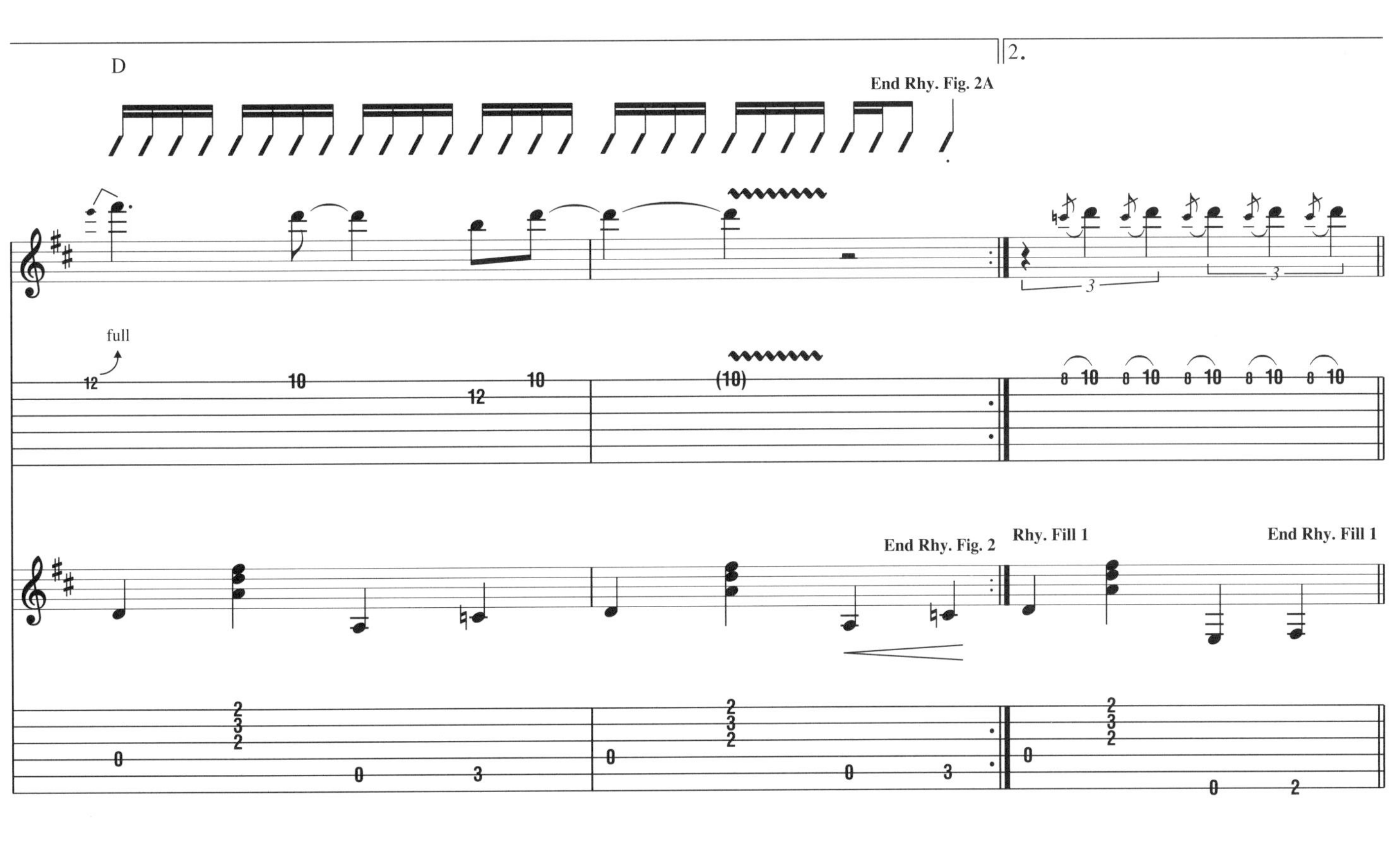
D
2.
End Rhy. Fig. 2A
full
End Rhy. Fig. 2
Rhy. Fill 1
End Rhy. Fill 1

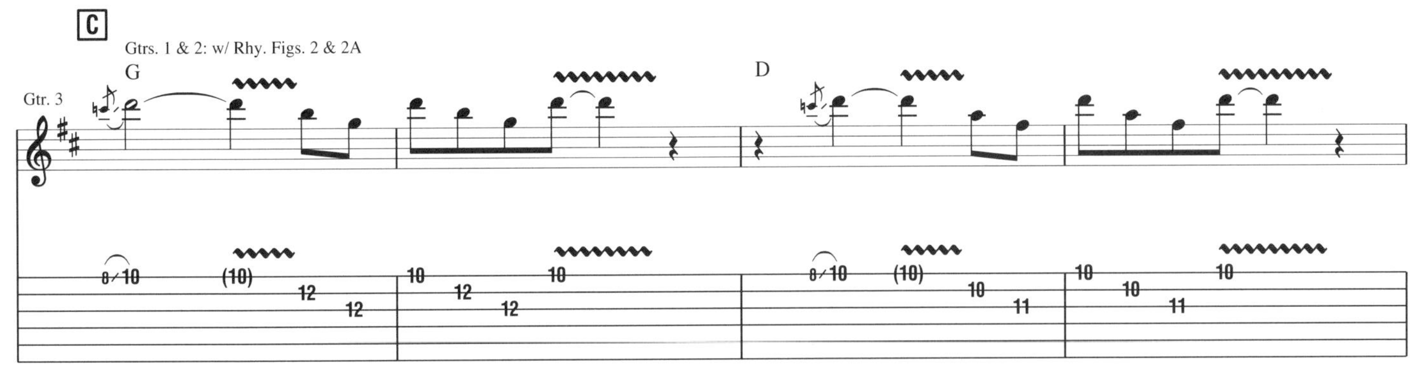
C
Gtrs. 1 & 2: w/ Rhy. Figs. 2 & 2A
G
Gtr. 3
D

A
G9
D
full
full
full
full
D
Gtr. 1: w/ Rhy. Fig. 1
Gtr. 2: w/ Riff A, 2 times
Gtr. 3 tacet
D
Gtr. 4 (clean)
mf
E
Gtr. 1: w/ Rhy. Fig. 2, 1st 7 meas.
G
D
A
G9
D
Gtr. 4
D.S. al Coda
(take repeat)
Gtr. 1
divisi
Coda
Gtr. 1: w/ Rhy. Fill 1
Gtr. 3
F
Gtrs. 1 & 2: w/ Rhy. Figs. 2 & 2A
G
D
A
G
Gtr. 1: w/ Rhy. Fig. 1, 1st 4 meas., 2 times
Gtr. 2: w/ Riff A, 2 times
Play 2 Times and Fade
G9
D
D

Rawhide

By Link Wray and Milt Grant

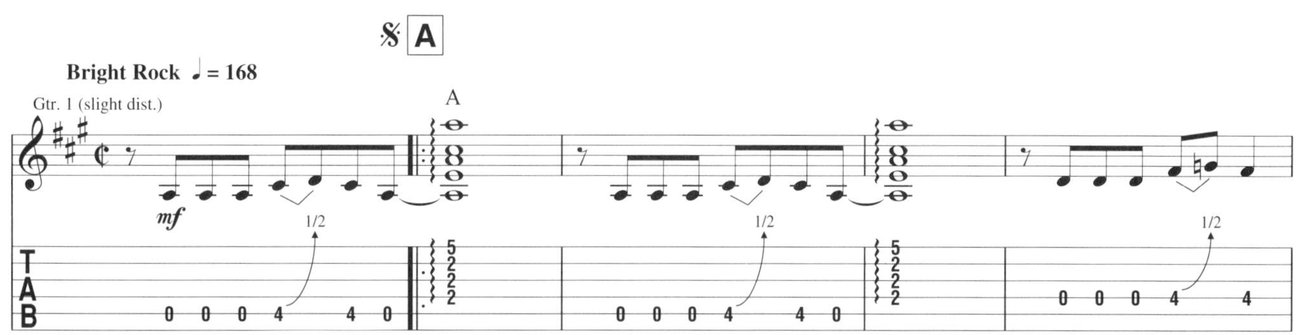

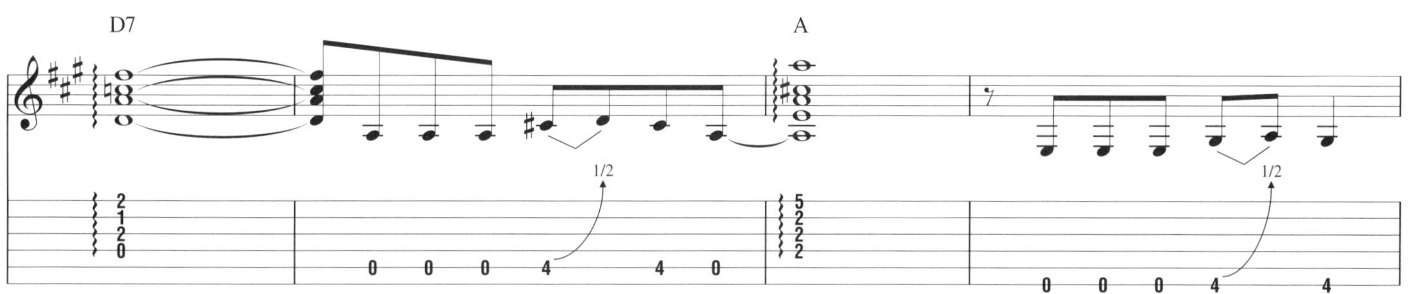

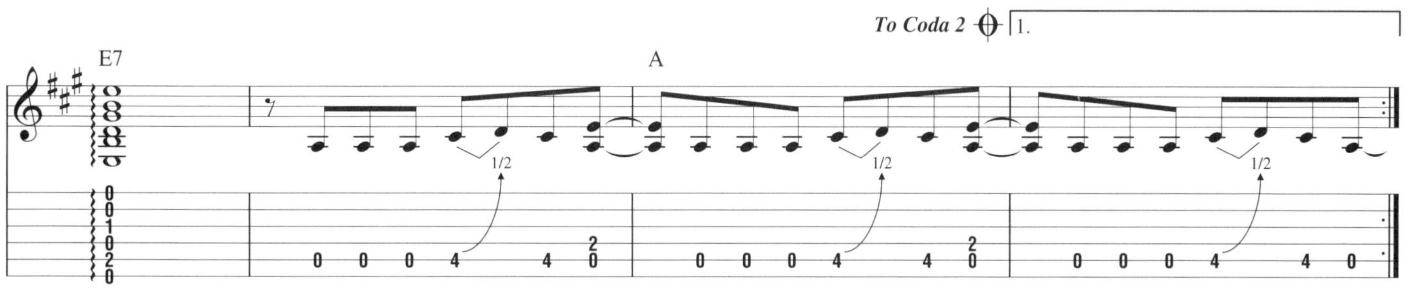

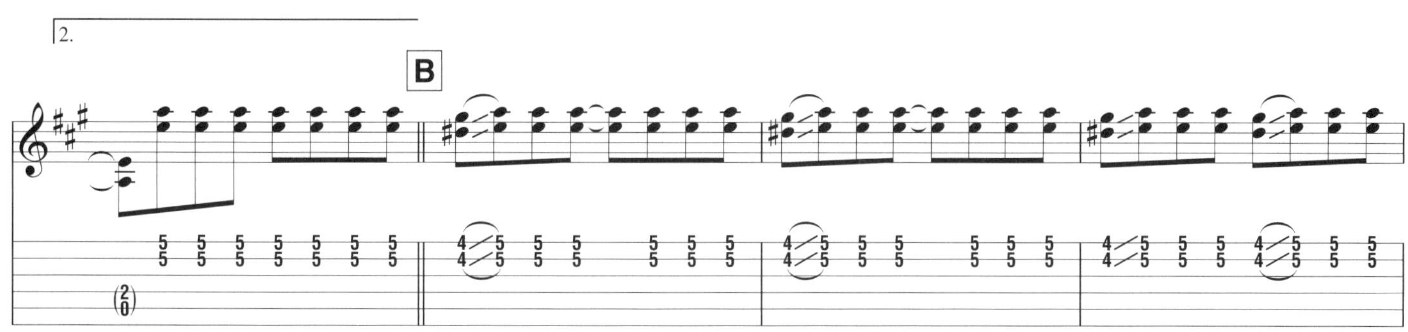

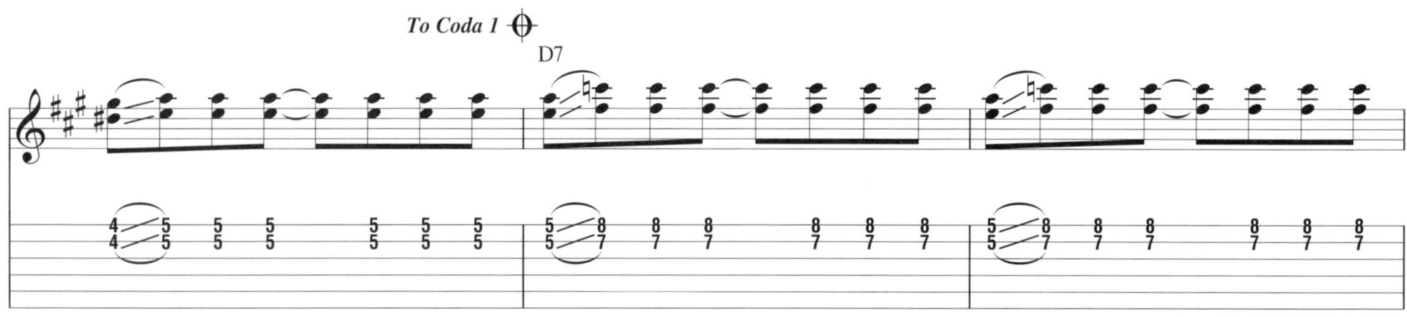
To Coda 1
D7

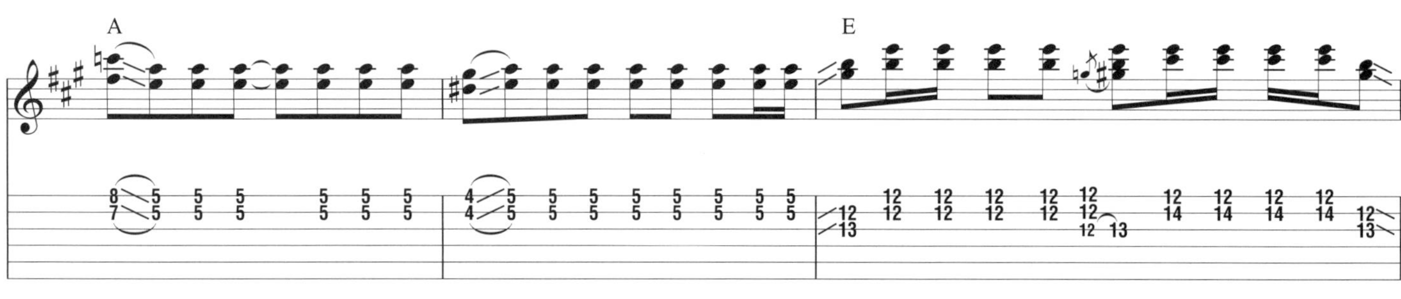
A
E

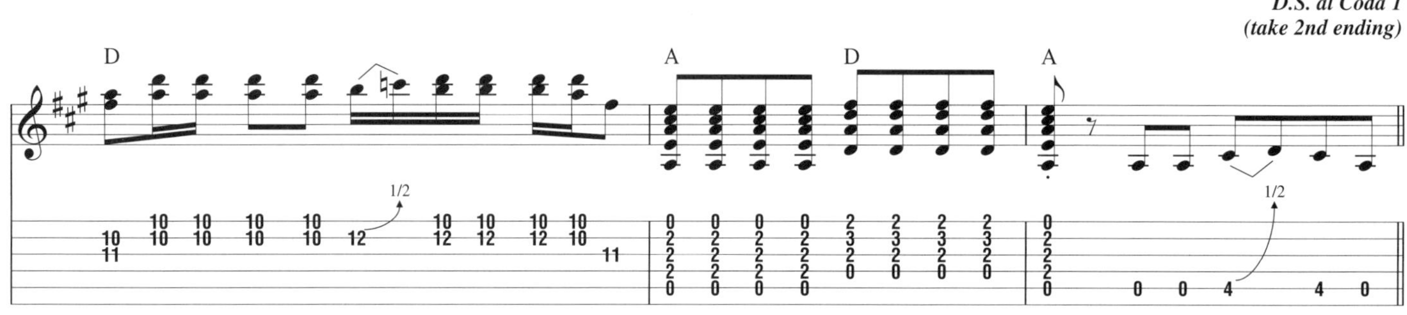
D.S. al Coda 1
(take 2nd ending)
D
A
D
A
1/2
1/2

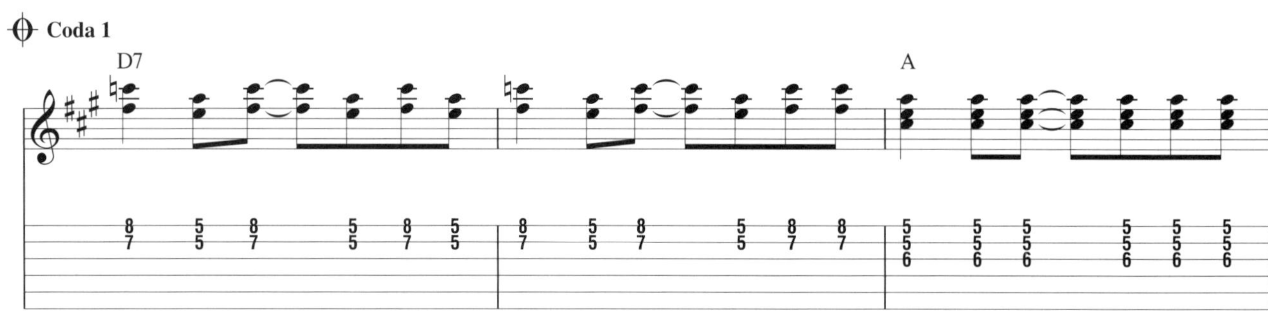
Coda 1
D7
A

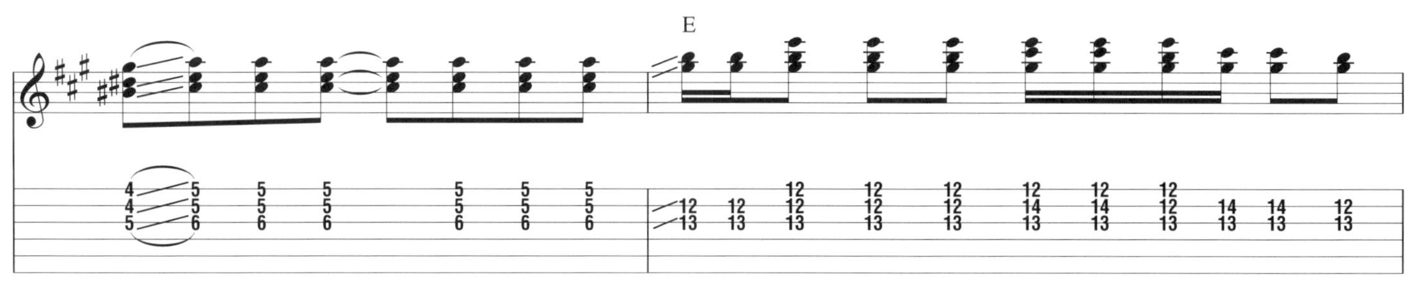
E

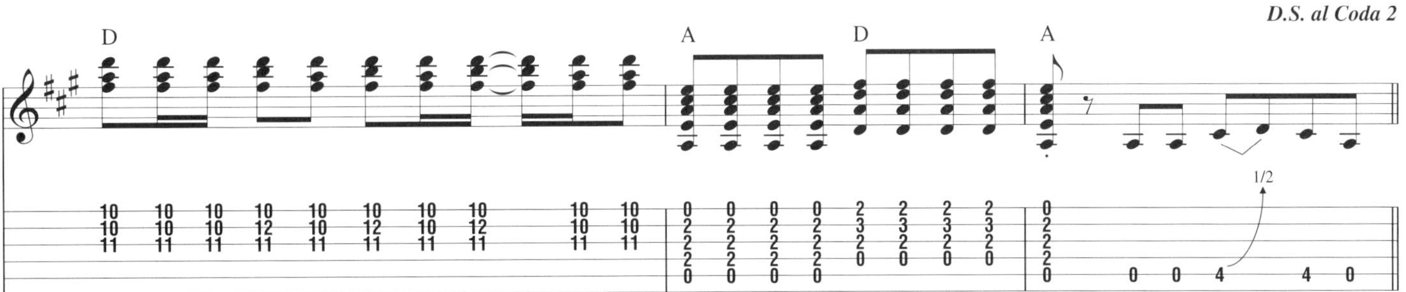
D.S. al Coda 2
D
A
D
A
1/2

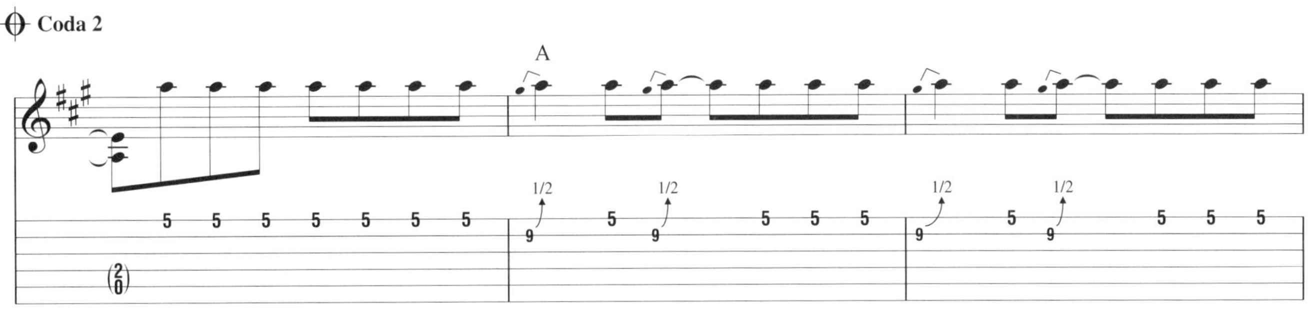
Coda 2
A
1/2

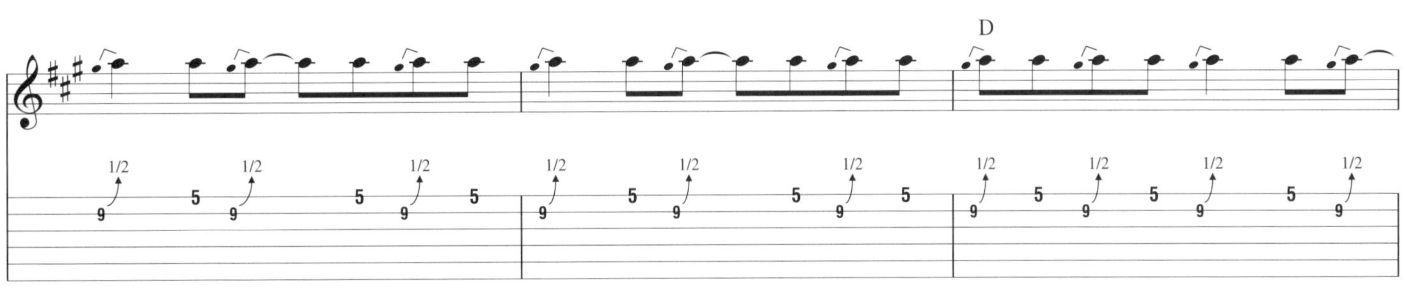
D
1/2

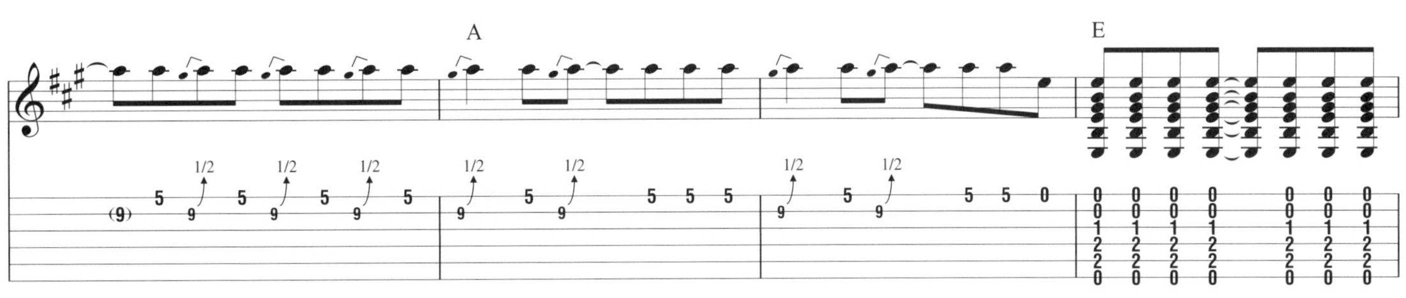
A
E
1/2

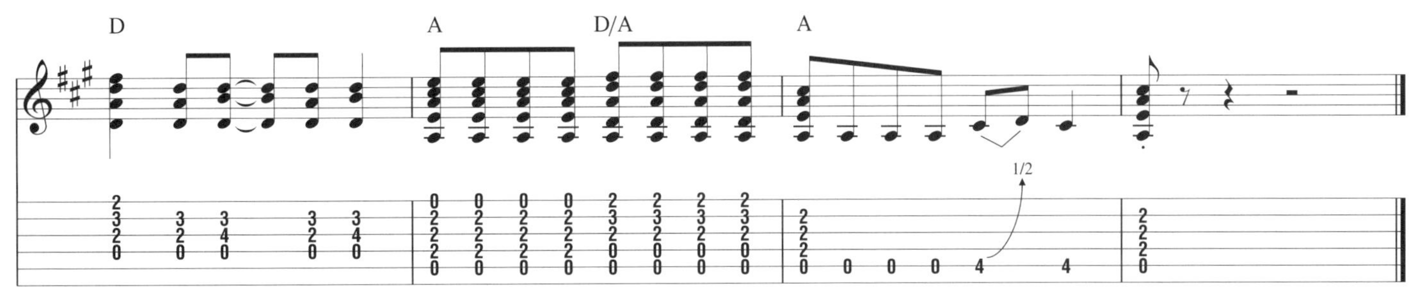
D
A
D/A
A
1/2

Rebel 'Rouser

By Duane Eddy and Lee Hazlewood

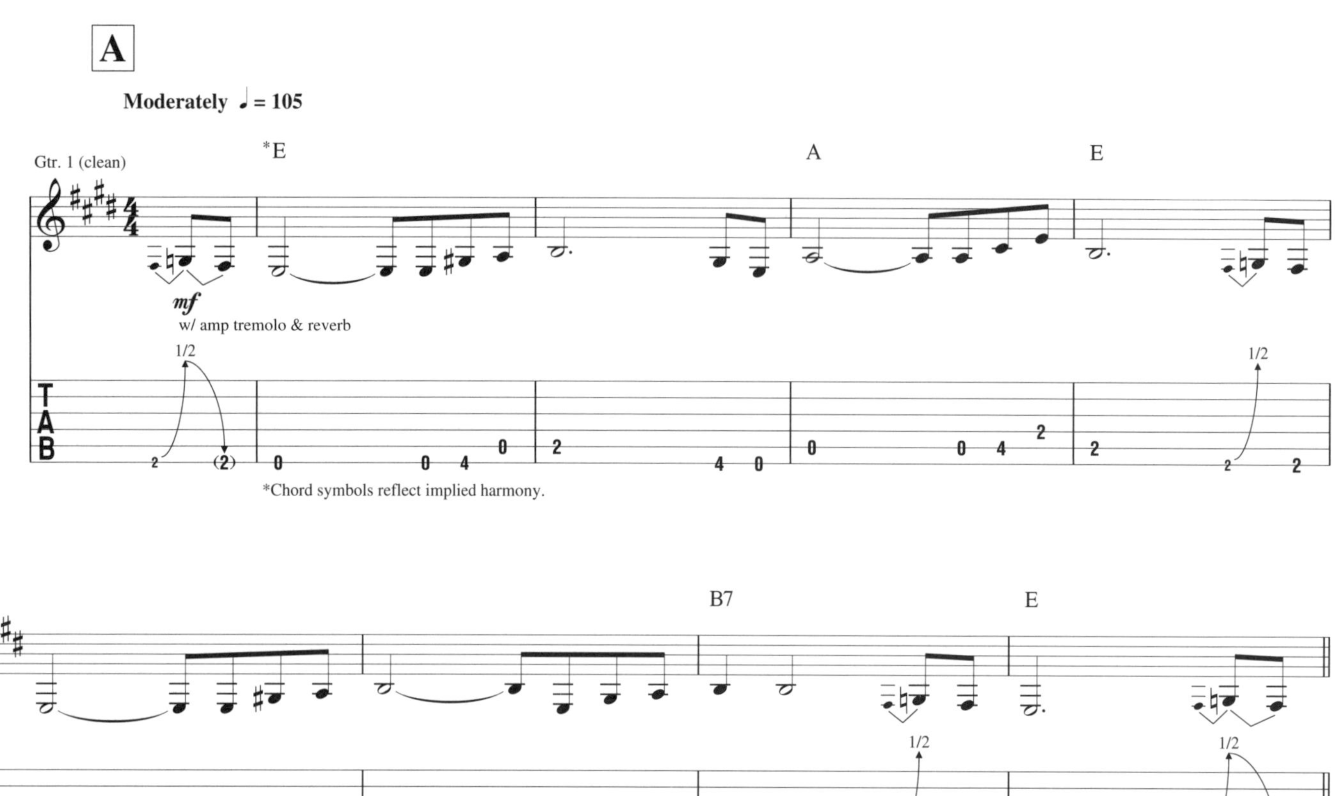

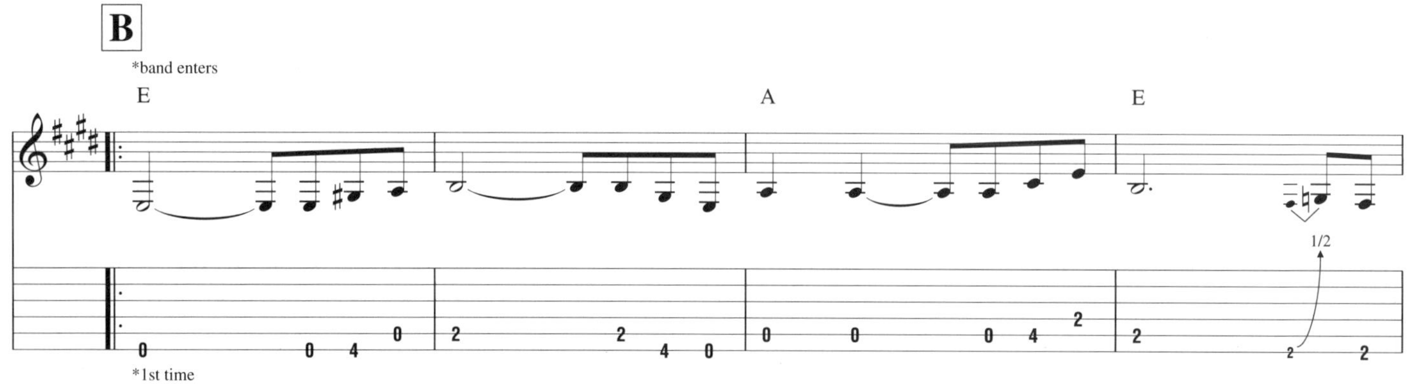

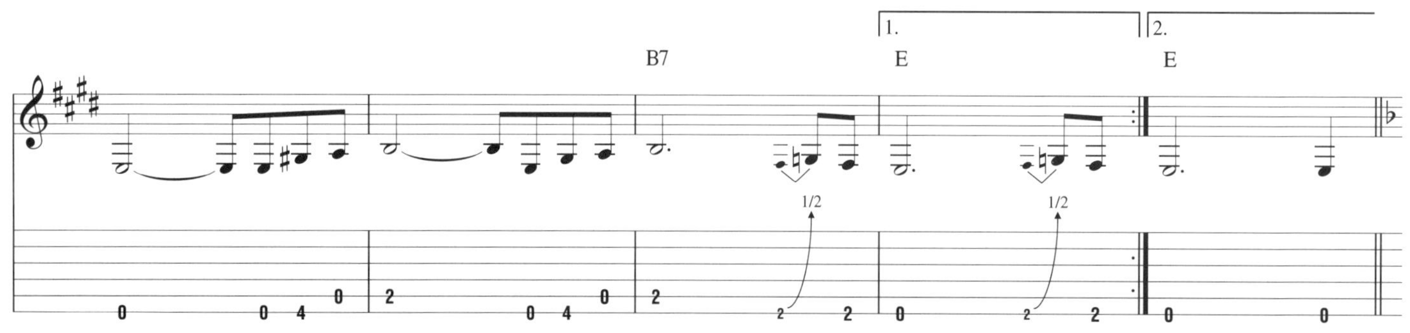

C
F
B♭
F
C7
F
D
F♯
B
F♯
C♯7
F♯
E
G
C
G
Play 3 times & fade
D7
G

Tune Down 1/2 Step:
① = E♭ ④ = D♭
② = B♭ ⑤ = A♭
③ = G♭ ⑥ = E♭

Red River Rock

Written by Tom King, Ira Mack and Fred Mendelsohn

* Organ arr. for gtr. ** Chord symbols reflect basic tonality.

1.
2.
To Coda
C
G
C
Riff A
G
End Riff A
G
B
Gtr. 1 tacet
Gtr. 2
C
F
full
C
G
1/2
F
Gtr. 1: w/ Riff A, simile
C
D.S. al Coda
(take repeat)
G
Coda
Gtr. 2: w/ Rhy. Fig. 1
C
Begin Fade
Fade Out
Gtr. 1
8va

(Ghost) Riders in the Sky
(A Cowboy Legend)
from RIDERS IN THE SKY
By Stan Jones

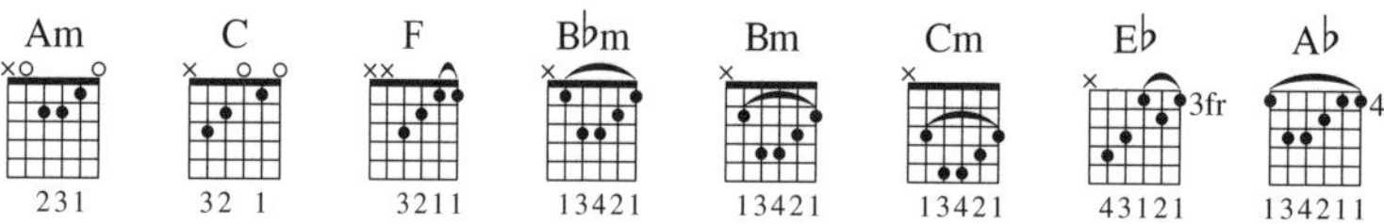

*Tune down 1/4 step

Moderately 𝅗𝅥 = 114

*Recording sounds 1/4 step lower than standard due to slower tape speed on playback.

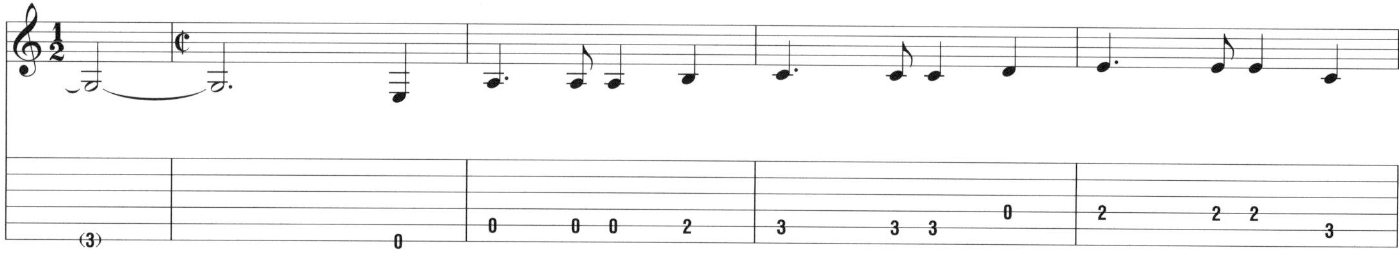

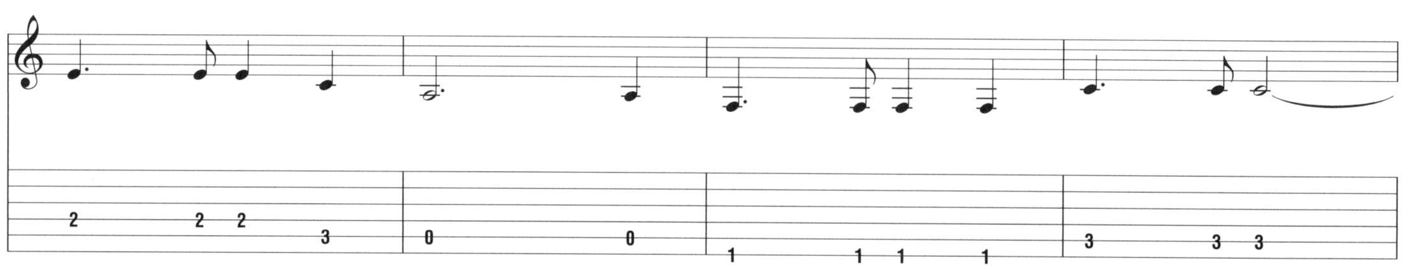

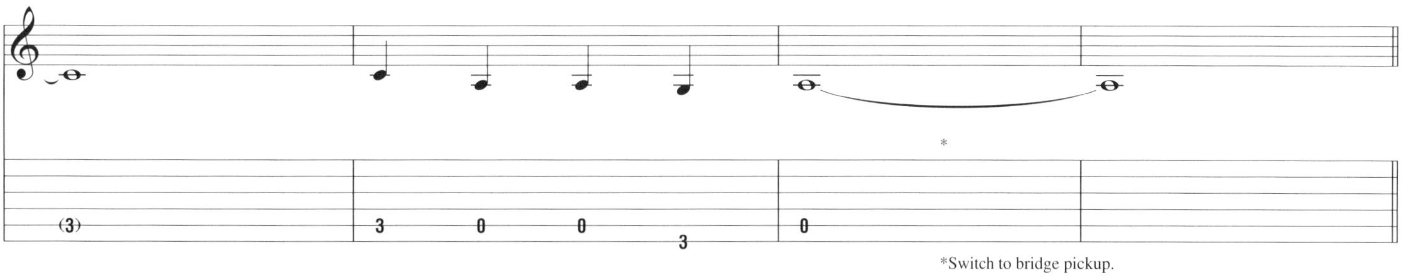

*Switch to bridge pickup.

*Chord symbols reflect overall harmony.

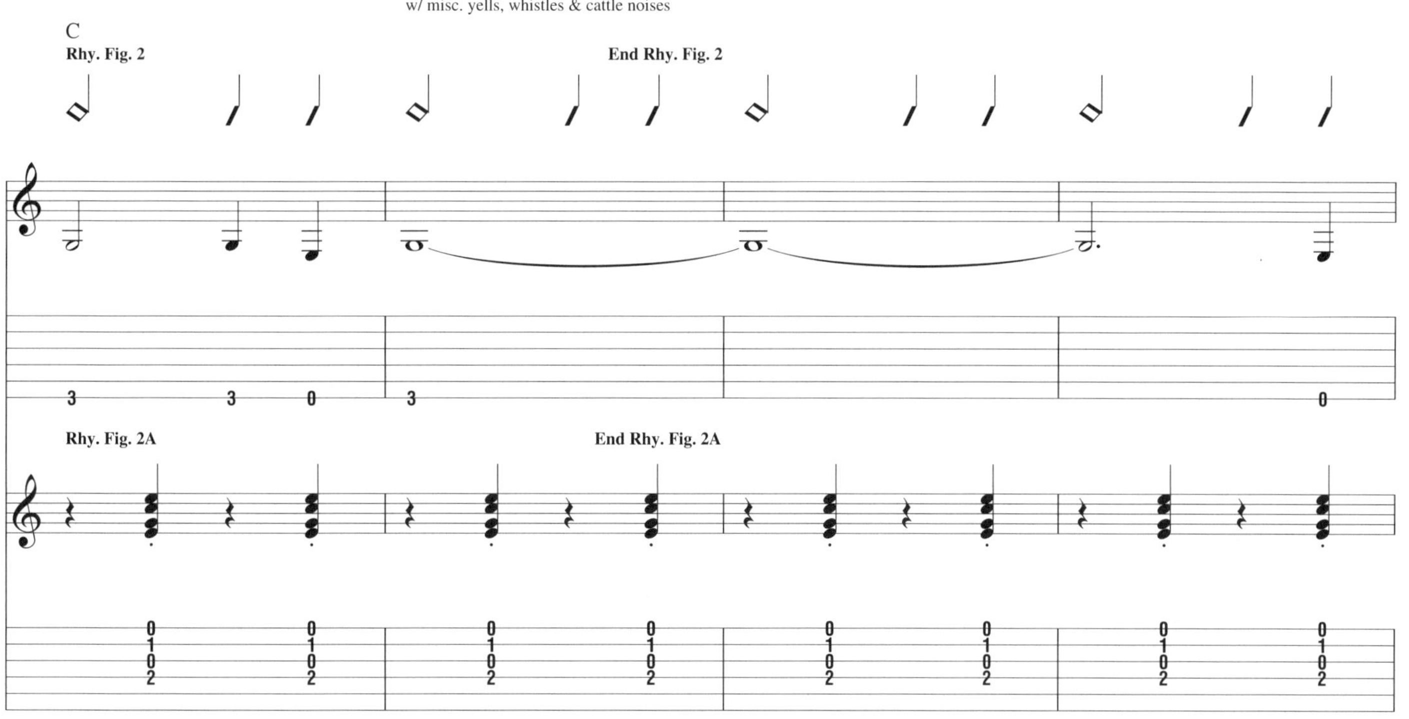

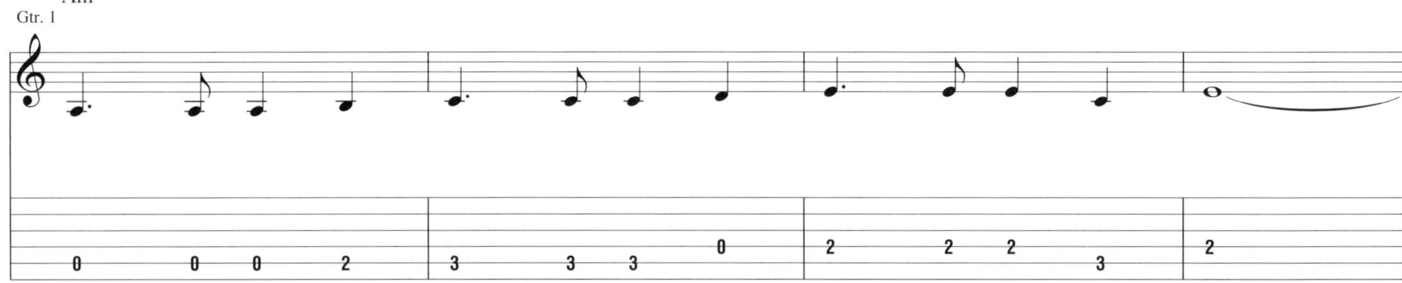
Gtrs. 2 & 3: w/ Rhy. Figs. 1 & 1A (4 times)
Am
Gtr. 1

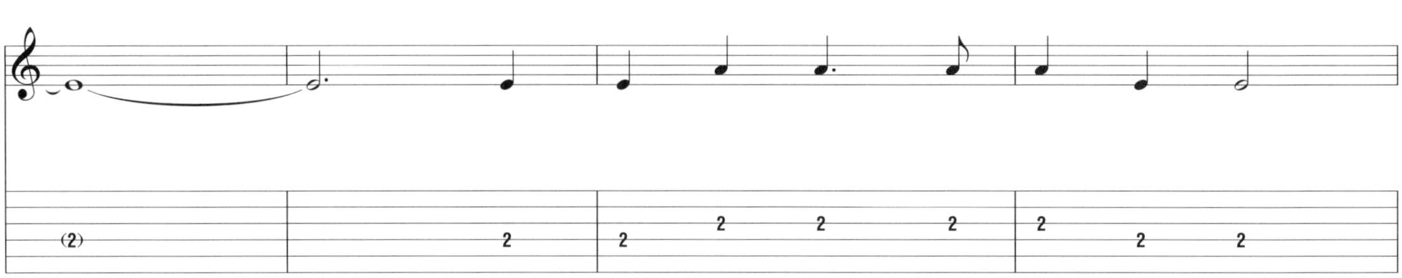

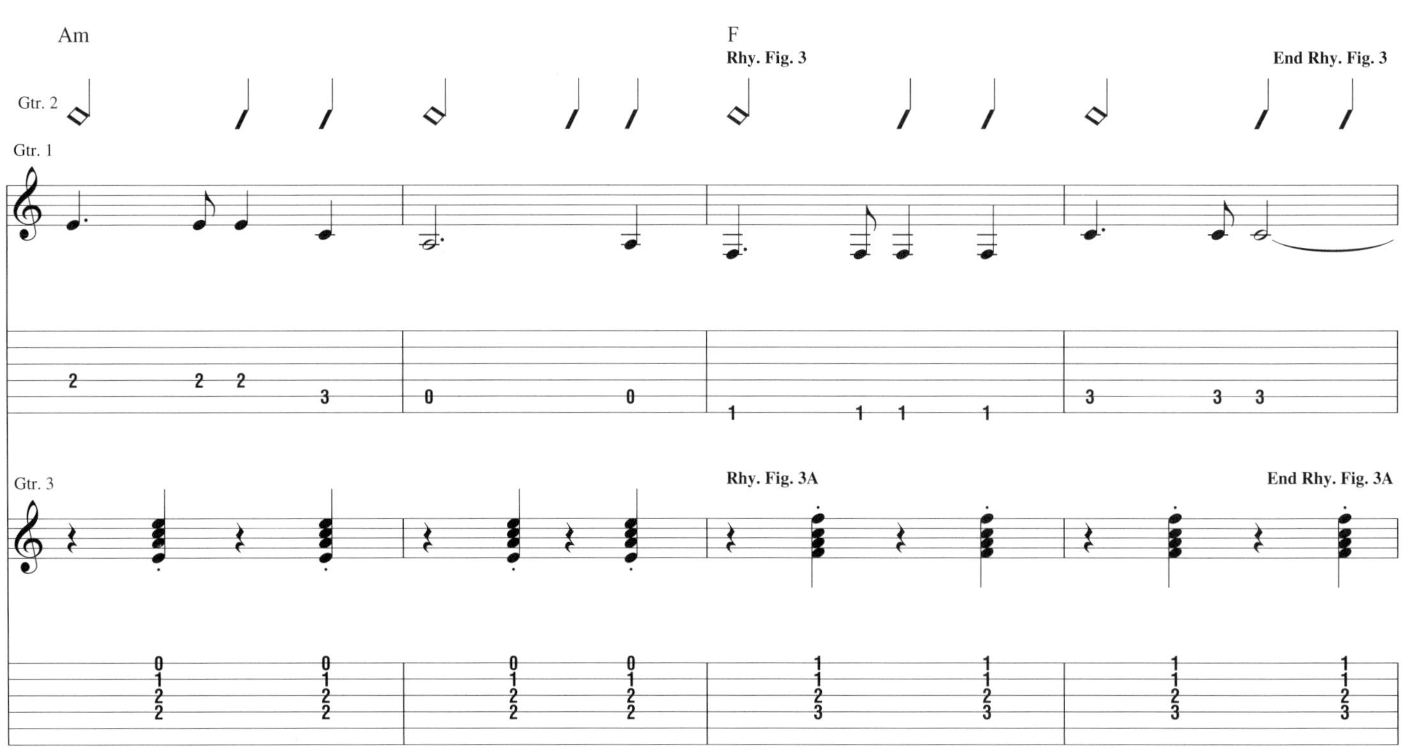
Am
F
Rhy. Fig. 3
End Rhy. Fig. 3
Gtr. 2
Gtr. 1
Gtr. 3
Rhy. Fig. 3A
End Rhy. Fig. 3A

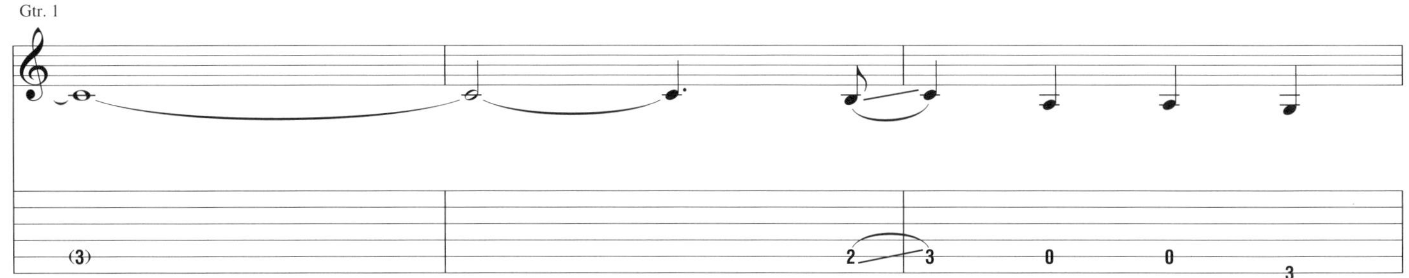
Gtrs. 2 & 3: w/ Rhy. Figs. 3 & 3A (1 1/2 times)
Gtr. 1

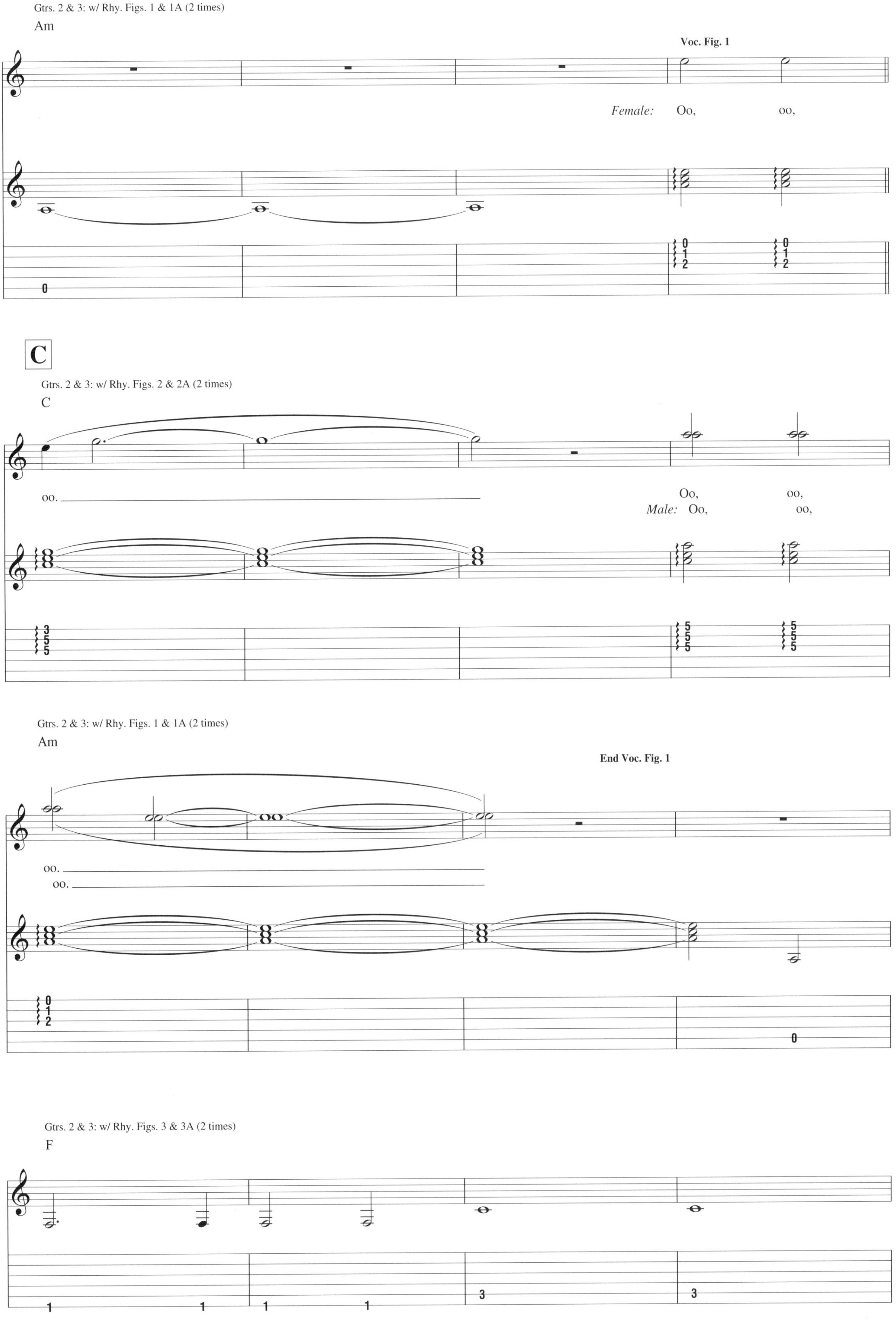

Gtrs. 2 & 3: w/ Rhy. Figs. 1 & 1A (2 times)

Am

Voc. Fig. 1

Female: Oo, oo,

C

Gtrs. 2 & 3: w/ Rhy. Figs. 2 & 2A (2 times)

C

oo. ______

Oo, oo,

Male: Oo, oo,

Gtrs. 2 & 3: w/ Rhy. Figs. 1 & 1A (2 times)

Am

End Voc. Fig. 1

oo. ______

oo. ______

Gtrs. 2 & 3: w/ Rhy. Figs. 3 & 3A (2 times)

F

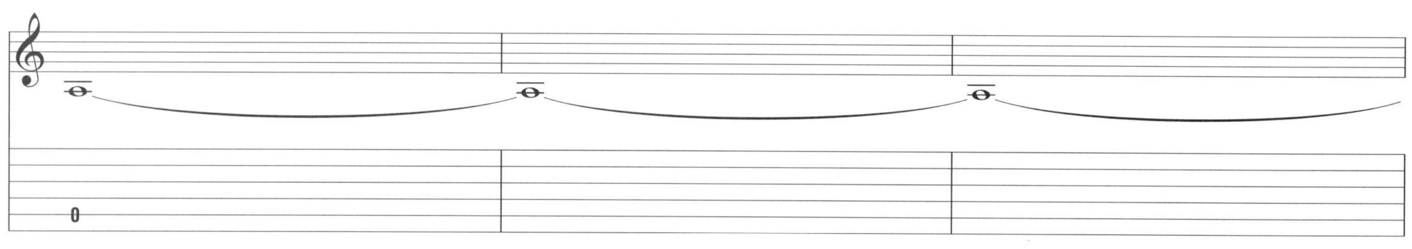

Gtrs. 2 & 3: w/ Rhy. Figs. 1 & 1A (2 times)
Am

D
Gtrs. 2 & 3: w/ Rhy. Figs. 1 & 1A
Am
Gtrs. 2 & 3: w/ Rhy. Figs. 2 & 2A (2 1/2 times)
C
*Gtr. 4
mf
*Saxophone arr. for gtr.
Gtr. 1
Riff A
End Riff A
Riff B
End Riff B
P.M.

P.M.

Gtr. 1: w/ Riff A
Gtrs. 2 & 3: w/ Rhy. Figs. 1 & 1A
Am
Gtr. 1: w/ Riff B (2 1/2 times)
Gtrs. 2 & 3: w/ Rhy. Figs. 2 & 2A (2 1/2 times)
C
Gtr. 4

Gtr. 1: w/ Riff A
Gtrs. 2 & 3: w/ Rhy. Figs. 1 & 1A (2 times)
Am

Gtrs. 2 & 3: w/ Rhy. Figs. 3 & 3A (2 1/2 times)
F
Gtr. 4
Gtr. 1
P.M.

P.M.

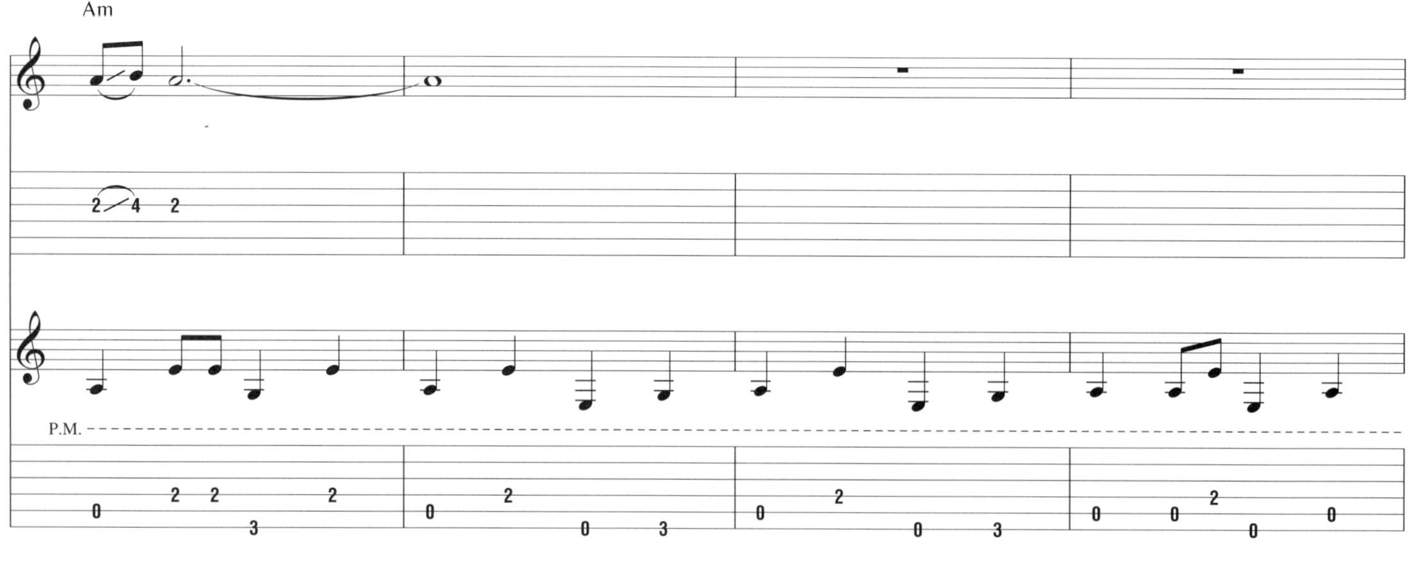
Gtrs. 2 & 3: w/ Rhy. Figs. 1 & 1A (2 times)
Gtr. 4 tacet
Am
P.M.

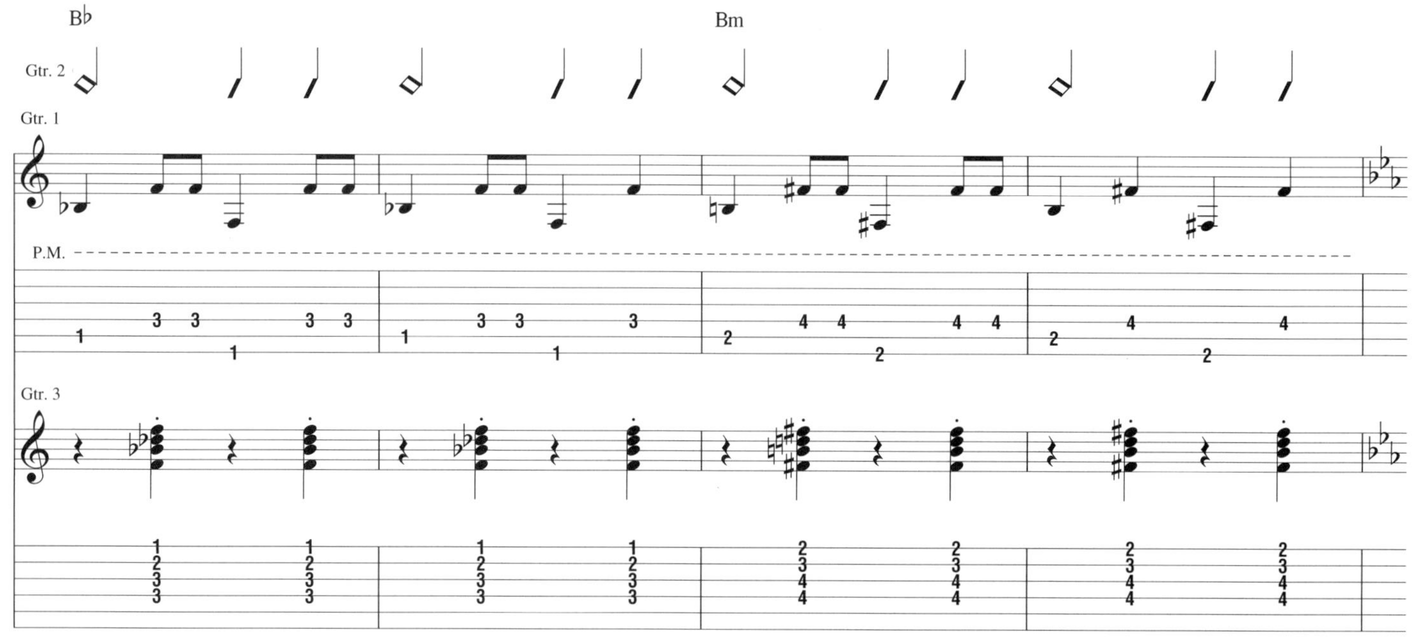
B♭
Bm
Gtr. 2
Gtr. 1
P.M.
Gtr. 3

E

Cm
Cm
Rhy. Fig. 4
End Rhy. Fig. 4
P.M.
Rhy. Fig. 4A
End Rhy. Fig. 4A

E♭
Oo.

Gtrs. 2 & 3: w/ Rhy. Figs. 4 & 4A (5 times)
Cm
Gtr. 1

A♭
Gtr. 2
Gtr. 1
Gtr. 3
Cm
Bm
P.M.
B♭m
P.M.

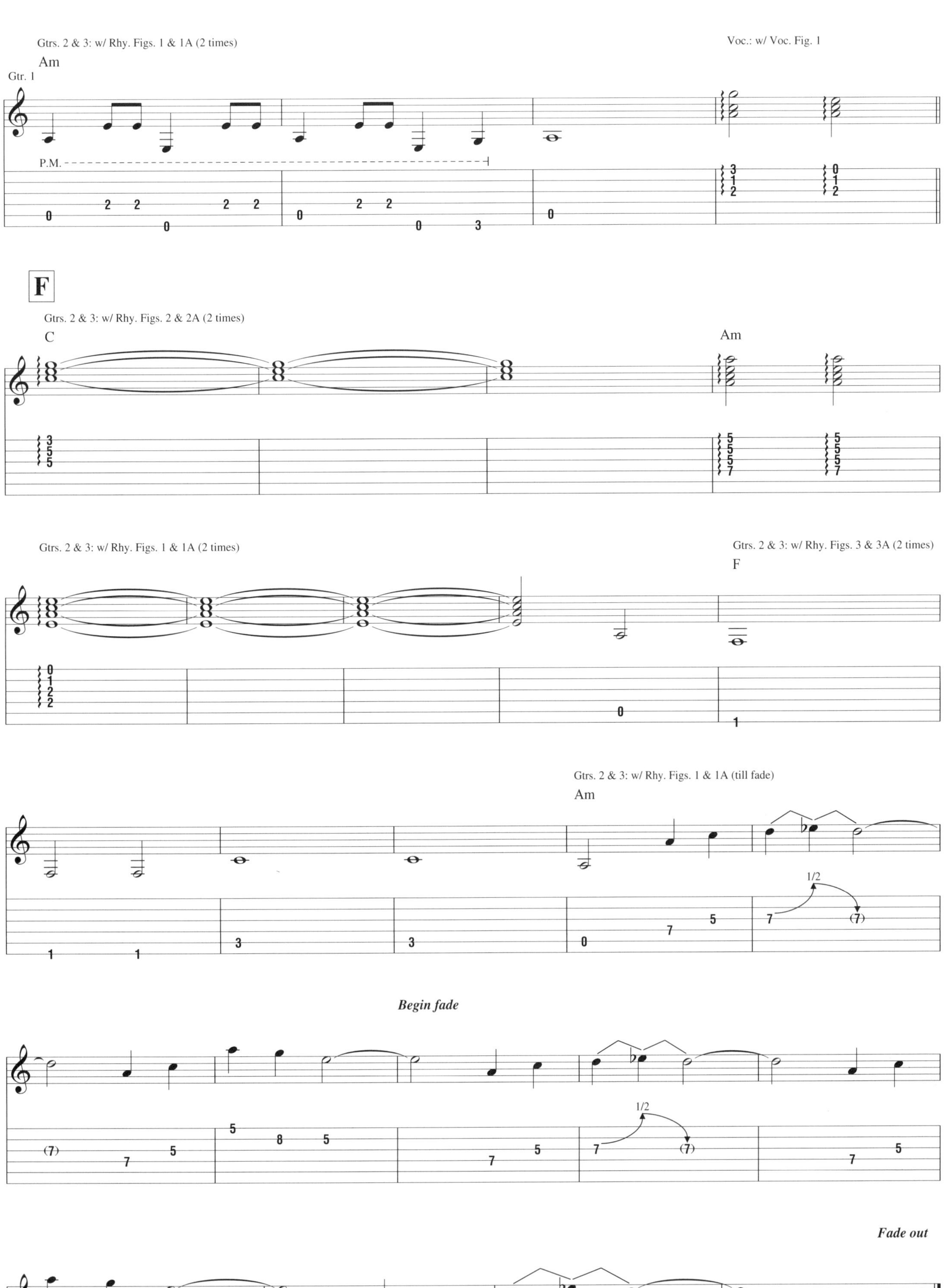
Gtrs. 2 & 3: w/ Rhy. Figs. 1 & 1A (2 times)
Voc.: w/ Voc. Fig. 1
Am
Gtr. 1
P.M.
F
Gtrs. 2 & 3: w/ Rhy. Figs. 2 & 2A (2 times)
C
Am
Gtrs. 2 & 3: w/ Rhy. Figs. 1 & 1A (2 times)
Gtrs. 2 & 3: w/ Rhy. Figs. 3 & 3A (2 times)
F
Gtrs. 2 & 3: w/ Rhy. Figs. 1 & 1A (till fade)
Am
Begin fade
Fade out

Rumble

By Link Wray and Milt Grant

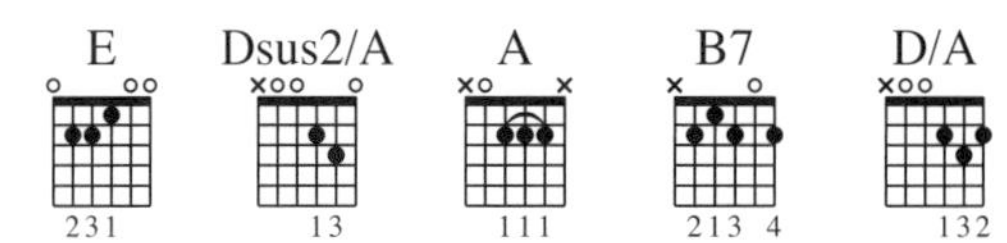

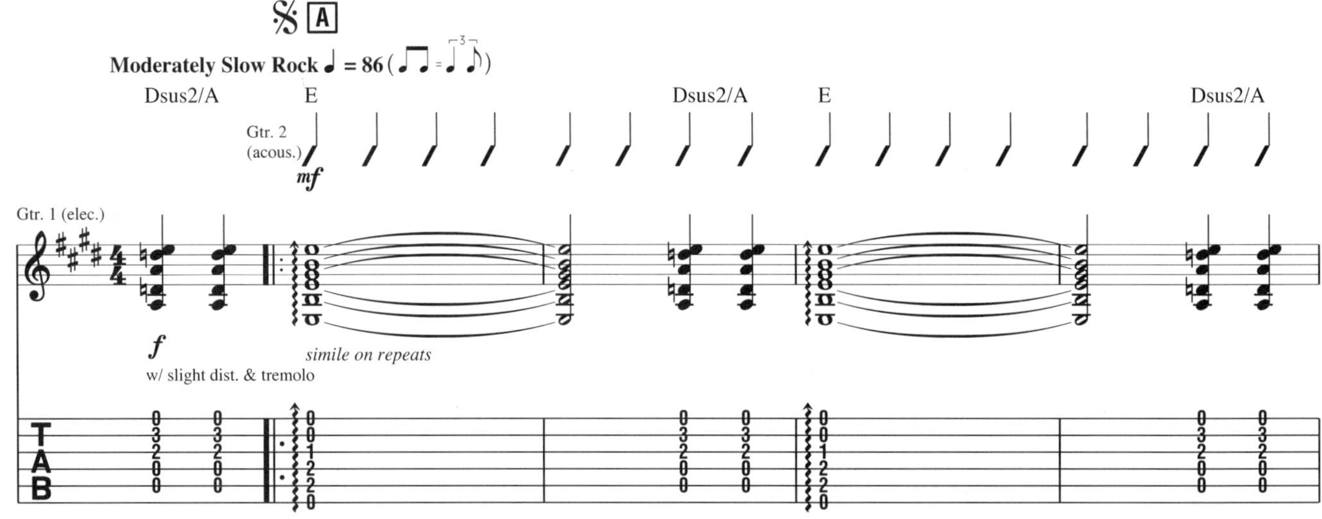

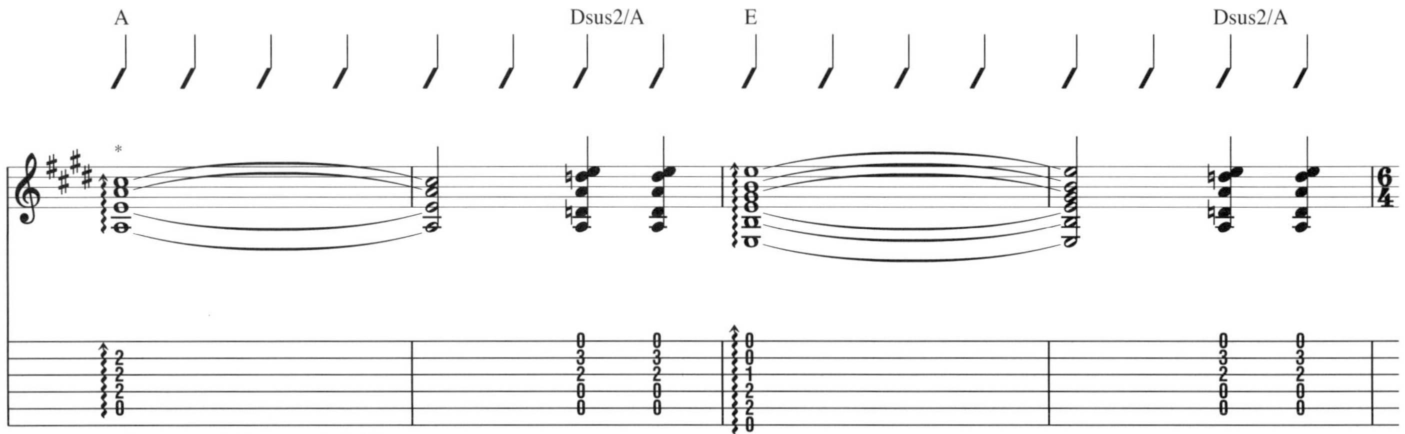

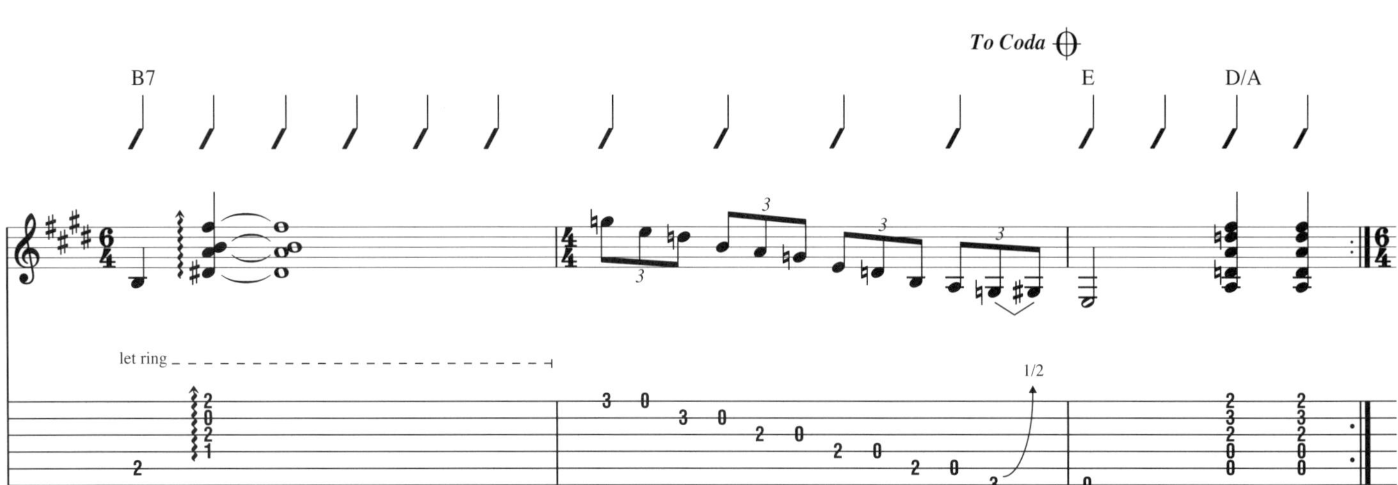

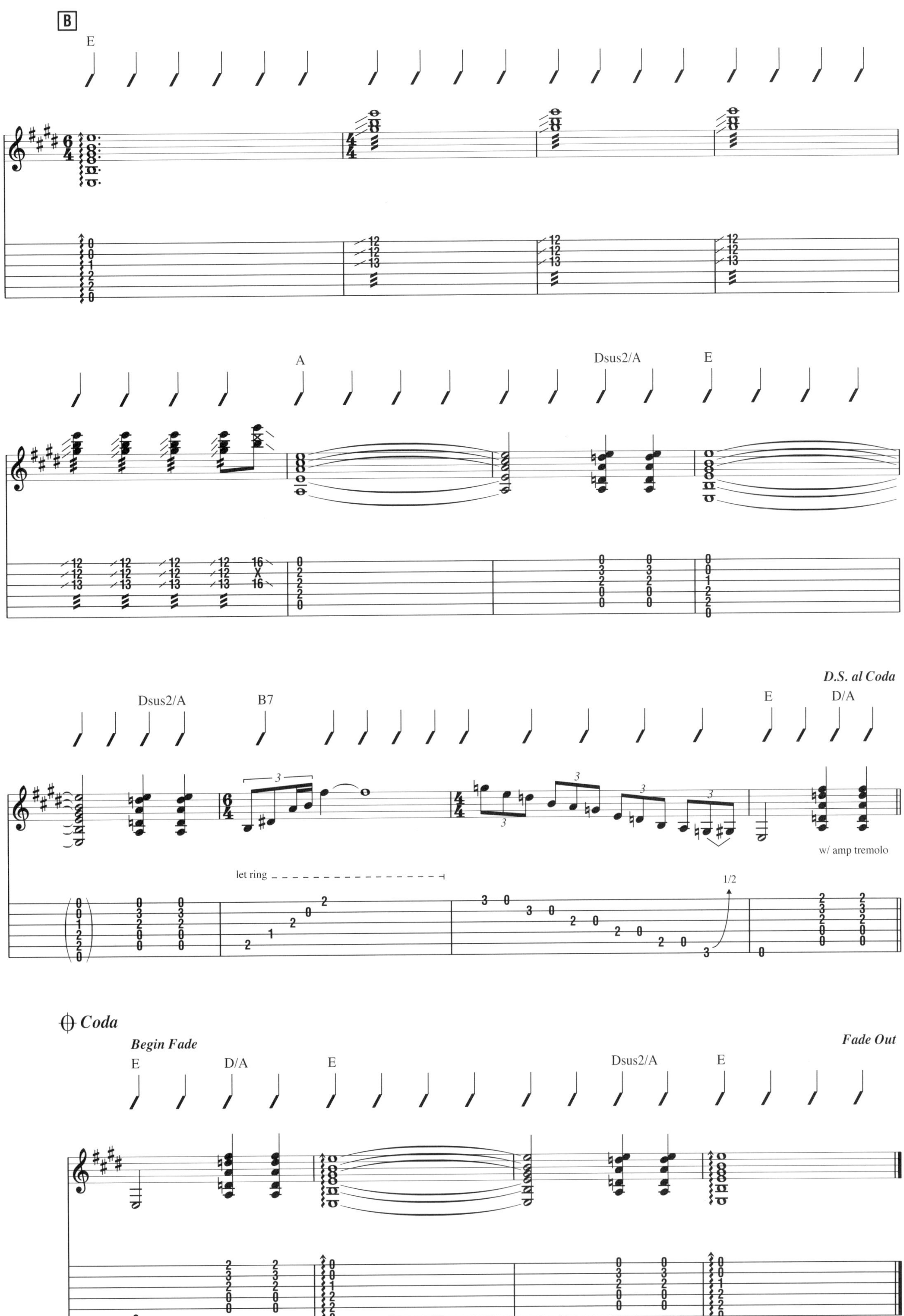
B
E
A
Dsus2/A
E
Dsus2/A
B7
let ring
D.S. al Coda
E
D/A
w/ amp tremolo
1/2
Coda
Begin Fade
E
D/A
E
Dsus2/A
E
Fade Out

San-Ho-Zay

Words and Music by Freddie King and Sonny Thompson

C
G
grad. bend
*
1/2
1/4
full
* ③ rings due to L.H. movement.
C
Gtr. 2: w/ Rhy. Fig. 2, simile
F
C
G
C
End Rhy. Fig. 2
Gtr. 1
full
1/2
let ring
1/4
1/4
1/4
1/4
grad. bend
full
full
F
C
full
1/4
1/4
G
F
C
full
full
1/2
1/4
D
Gtr. 2: w/ Rhy. Fig. 1, simile
G
C
let ring
full
full

F
C
G
F
C
E
Gtr. 2: w/ Rhy. Fig. 1, simile
G
C
let ring
F
C
grad. bend
G
F
C
F
Gtr. 2: w/ Rhy. Fig. 2, simile
G
C
let ring
P.M.
P.M.

P.M.
P.M.
P.M.
1/4
1/4
1/4
1/4
full
F
C
full
1/4
1/2
1/4
full
G
F
C
G
1/4
let ring
G
Gtr. 2: w/ Rhy. Fig. 1, 1st 10 meas., simile
C
1/4
1/4
1/4
1/4
F
C
1/4
1/4
1/4
1/4
G
F
C
D♭
C
Gtr. 2
Gtr. 1
1/4
1/4

Sleepwalk

By Santo Farina, John Farina and Ann Farina

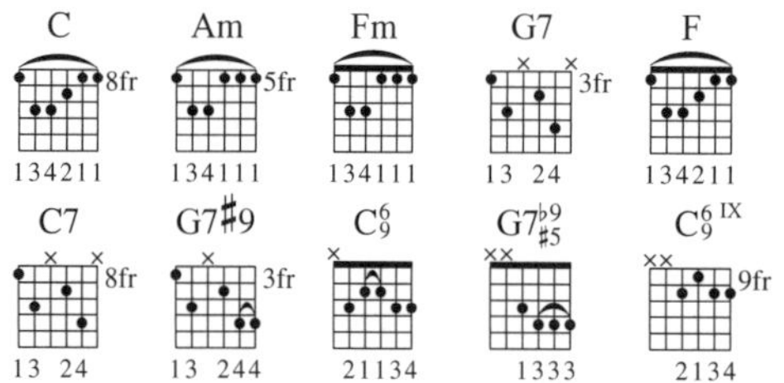

Gtr. 1: Tune up 1/2 step:
(low to high) F-B♭-E♭-A♭-C-F

*Gtr. 2: Open C6 tuning, capo I:
(low to high) G-C-E-G-A-C

*Change bottom two strings to lighter guage to facilitate higher tuning.

**Lap steel arr. for gtr. Capoed fret is "0" in tab.

***While fretting the non-parenthetical tab number, lightly touch string w/ pick hand index finger at fret indicated in parentheses, then pluck the string from behind the index finger (towards bridge).

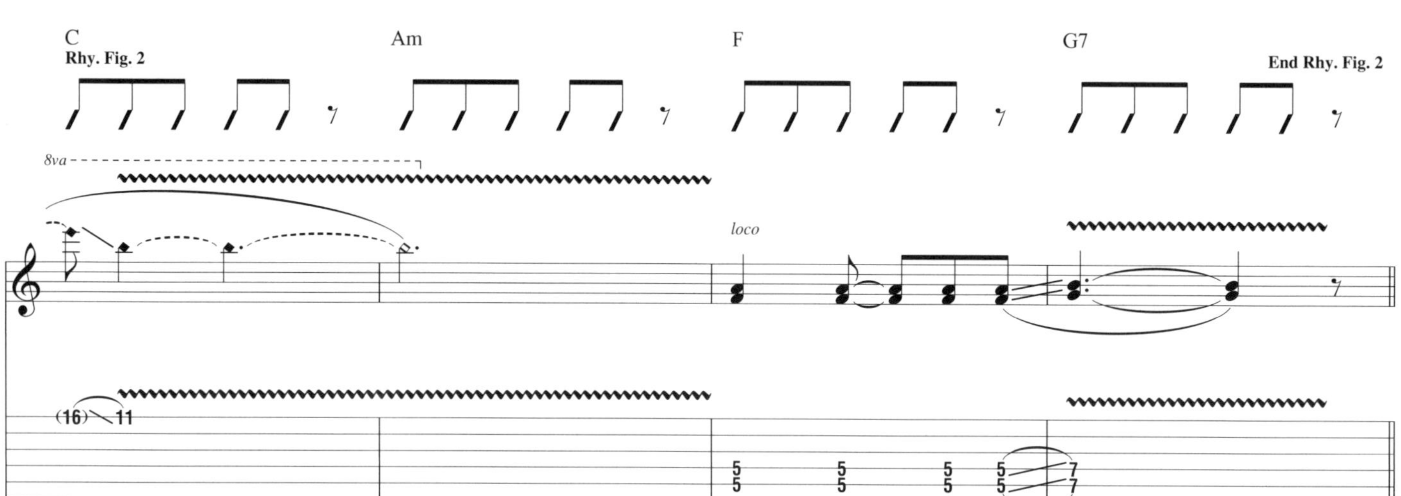

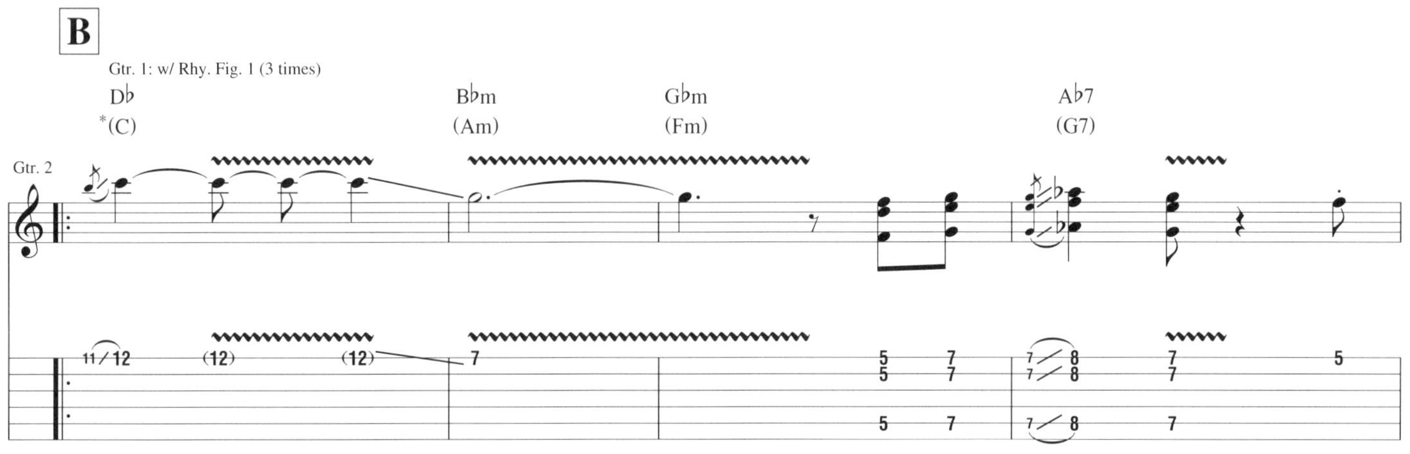

*Symbols in parentheses represent chord symbols respective to capoed gtr.
Symbols above reflect actual sounding chords.
Capoed fret is "0" in tab.

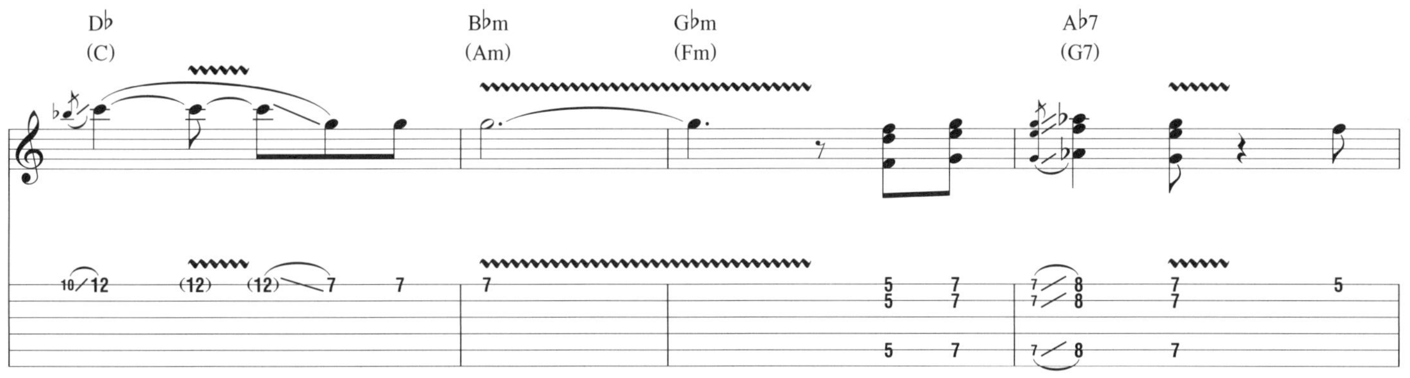

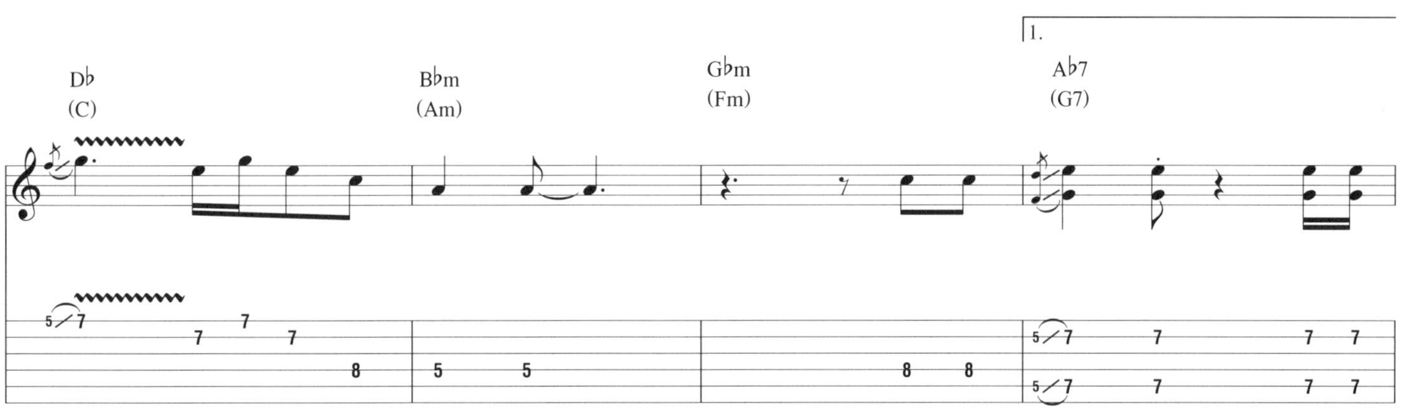

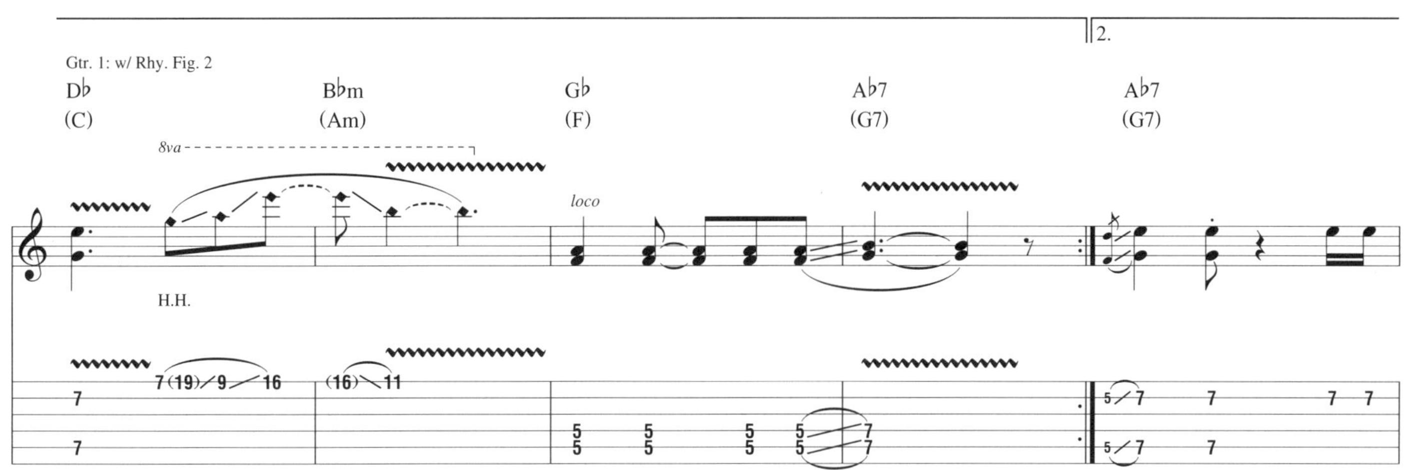

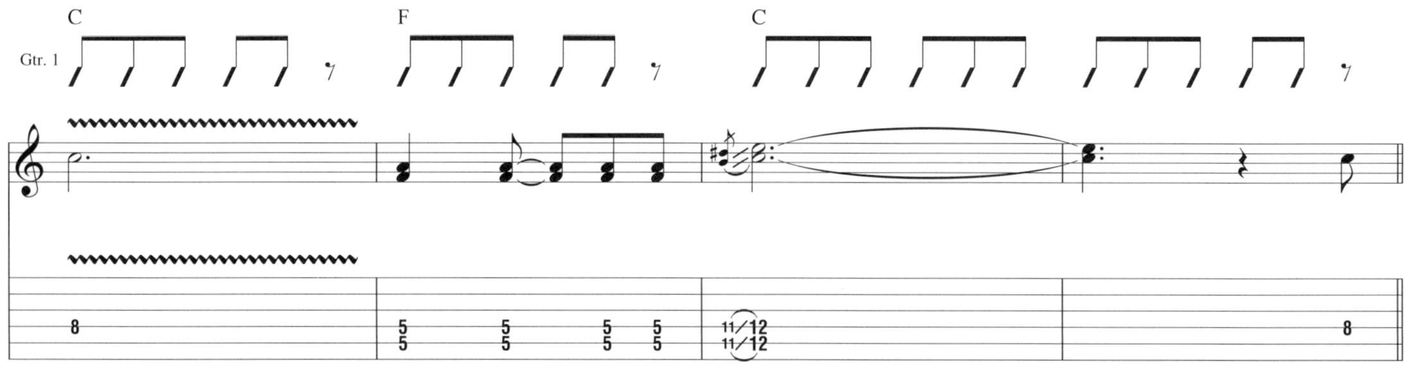
C
Gtr. 1
F
C

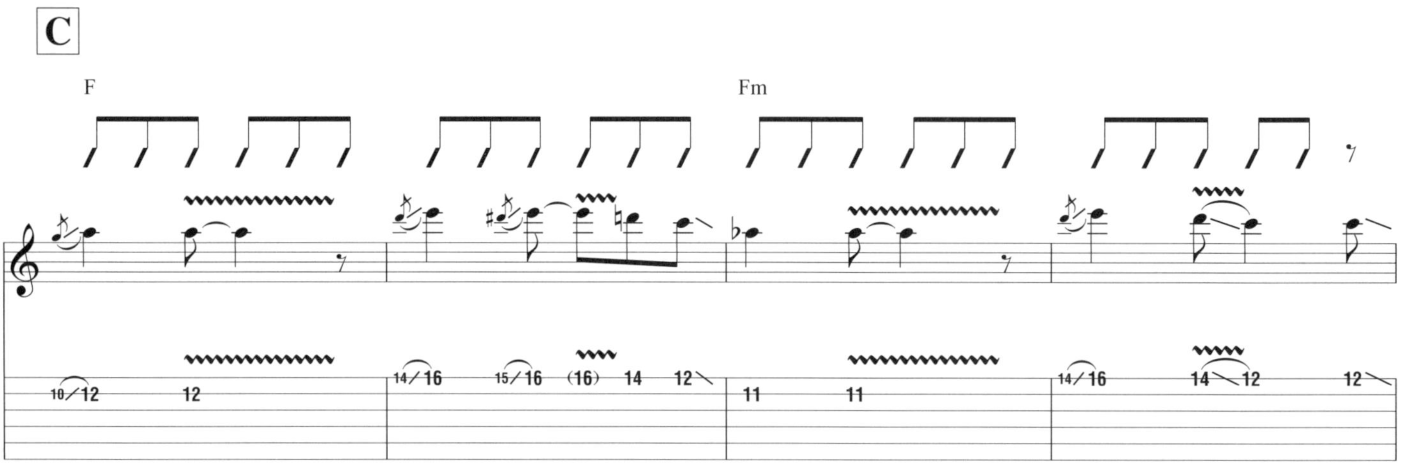
C
F
Fm

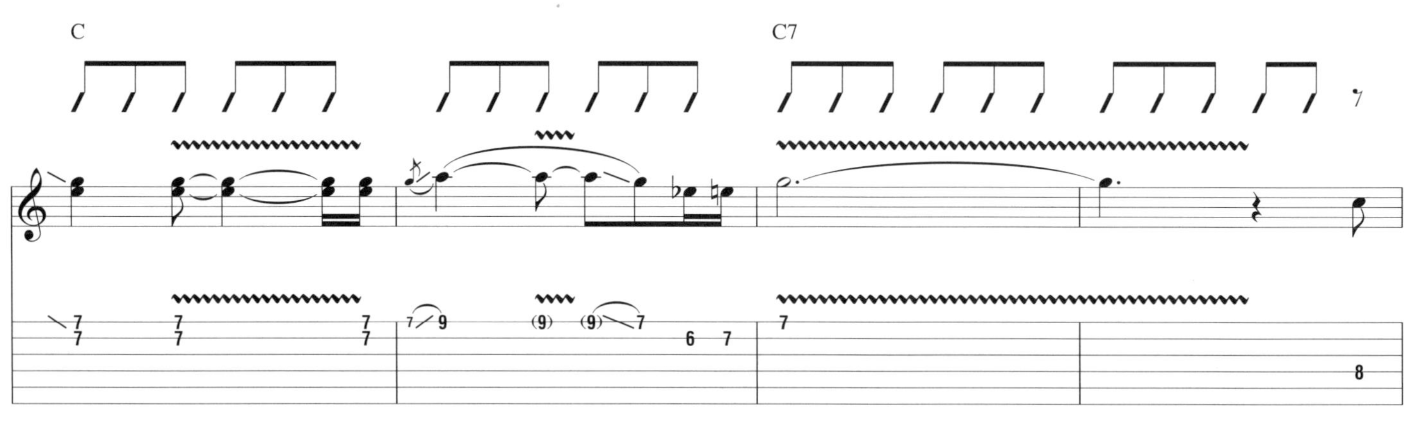
C
C7

F
Fm

G7
G7♯9
D
Gtr. 1: w/ Rhy. Fig. 1 (2 times)
D♭
(C)
B♭m
(Am)
G♭m
(Fm)
A♭7
(G7)
Gtr. 2
C
Am
Fm
Gtr. 1
rit.
Free time
G7
G7♯9
H.H.

Scuttle Buttin'

Written by Stevie Ray Vaughan

Tune down 1/2 step:
(low to high) E♭-A♭-D♭-G♭-B♭-E♭

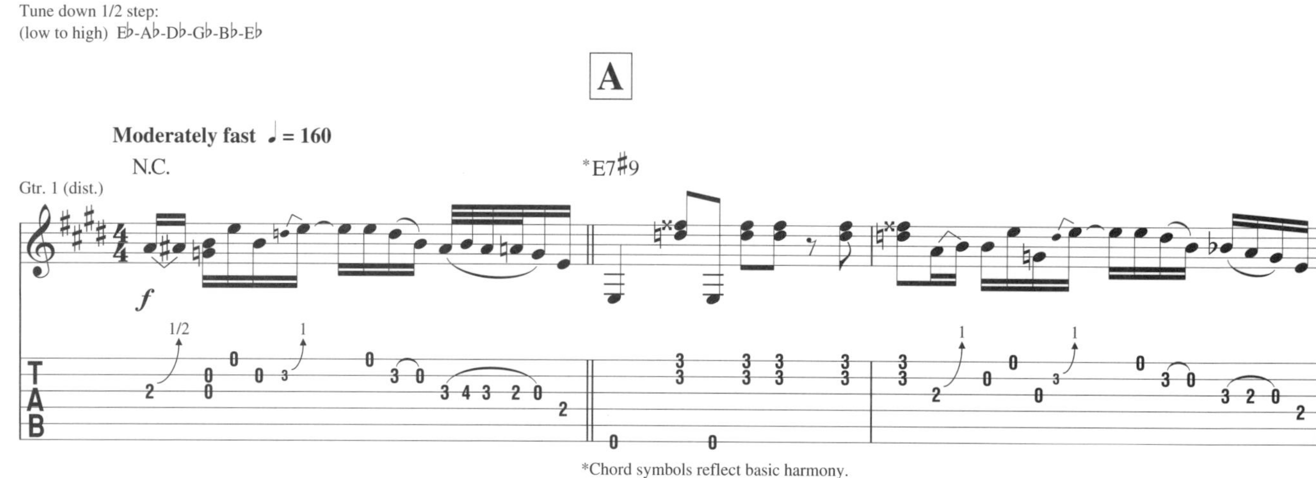

*Chord symbols reflect basic harmony.

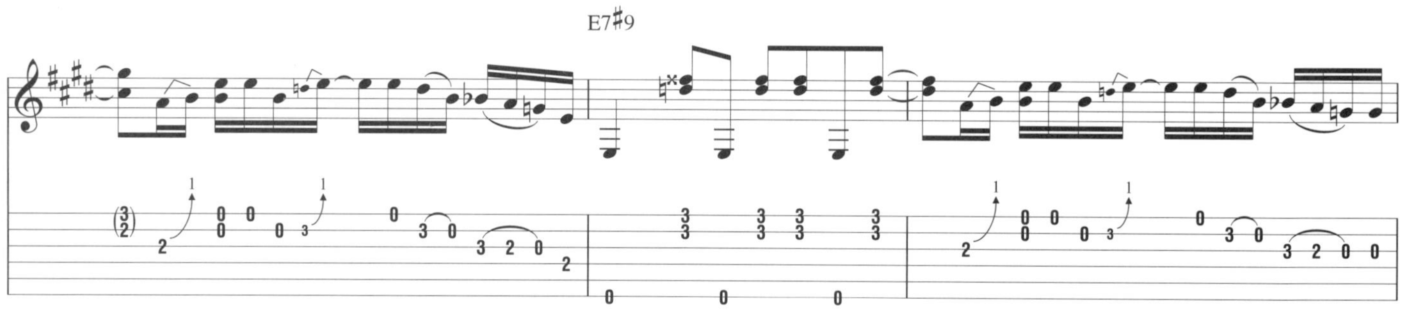

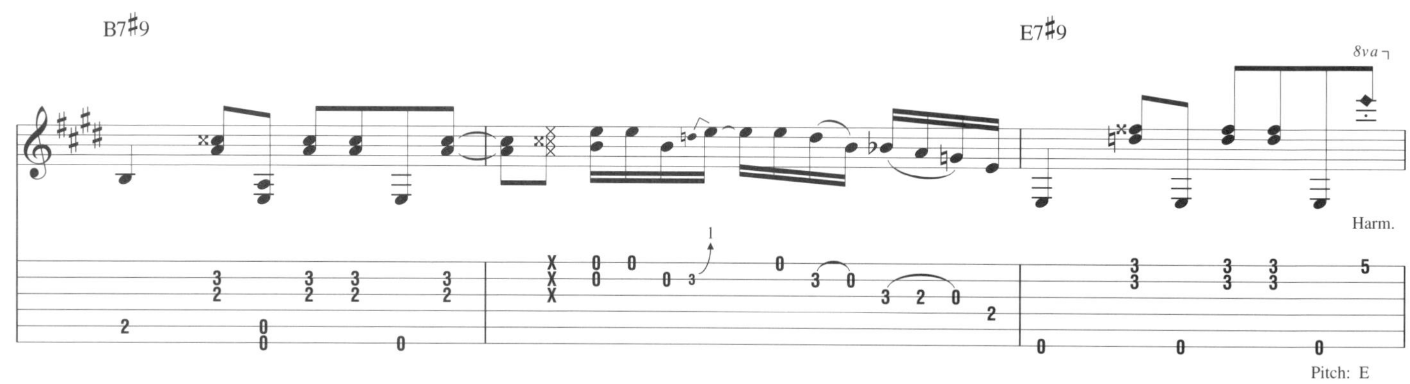

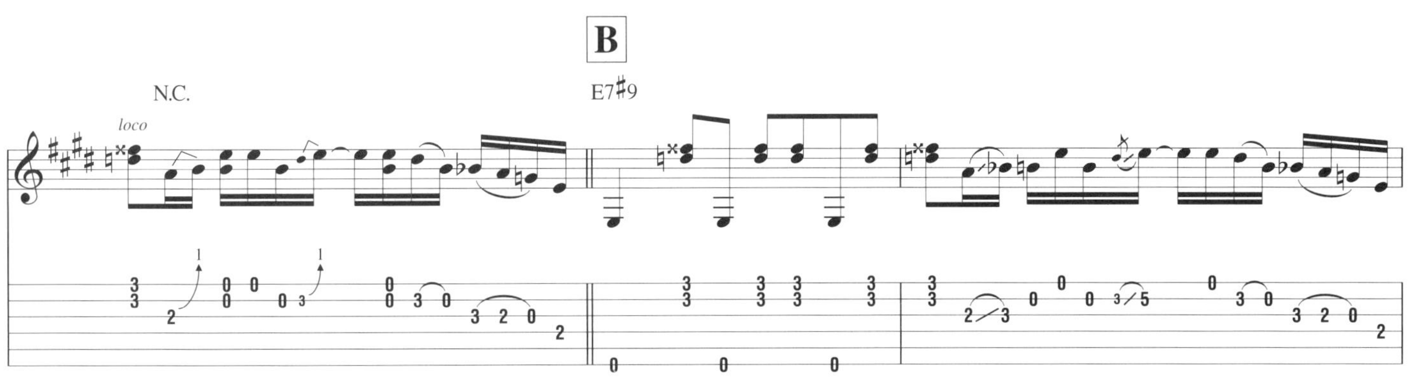
B
N.C.
loco
E7♯9

A7

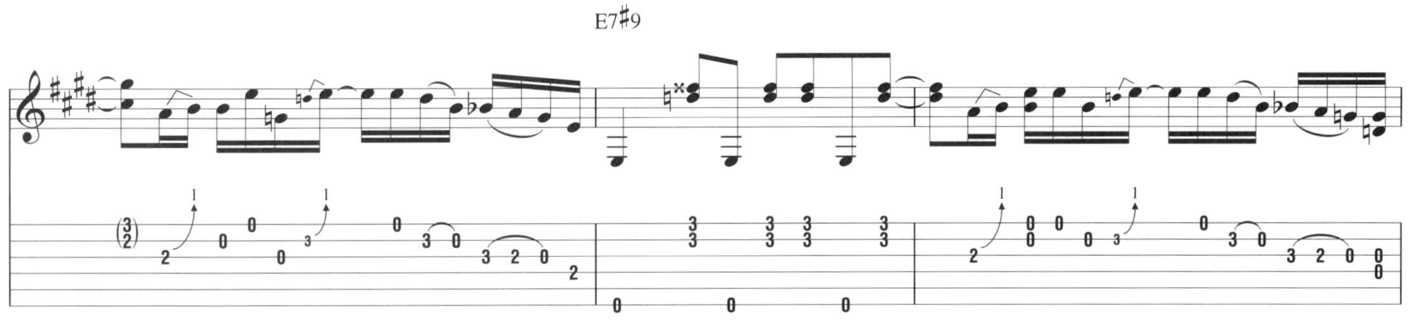
E7♯9

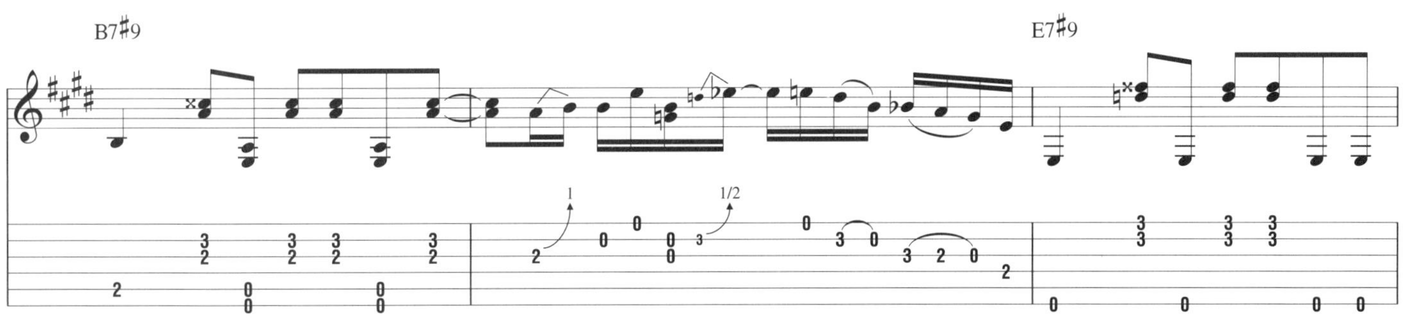
B7♯9
E7♯9

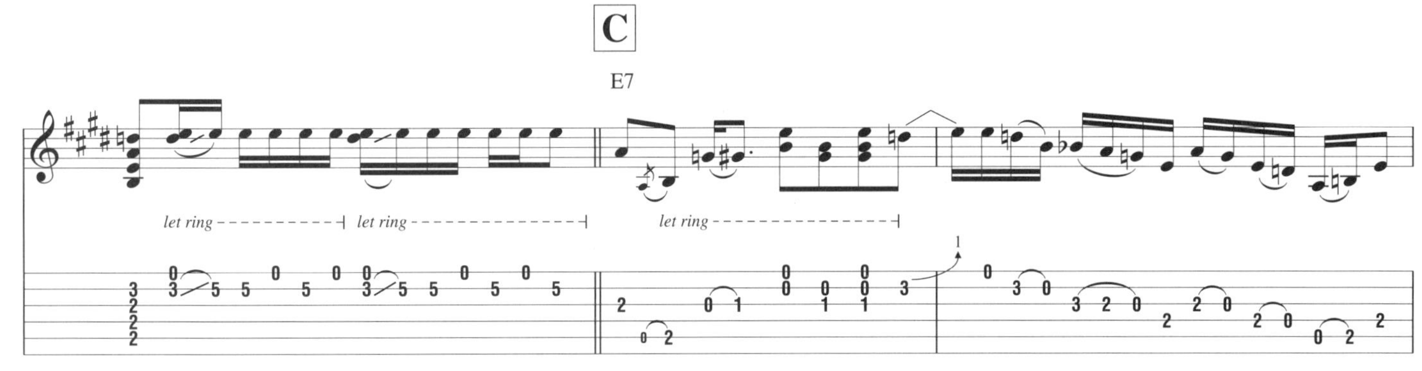
C
E7
let ring
let ring
let ring

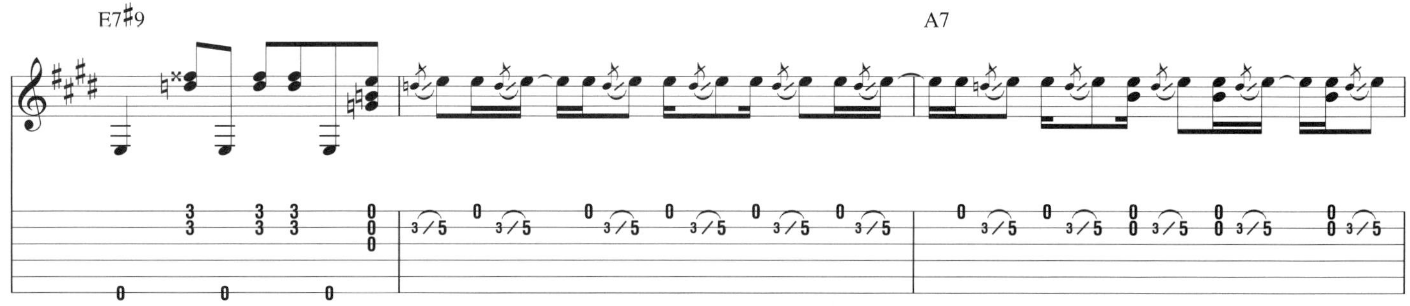
E7♯9
A7

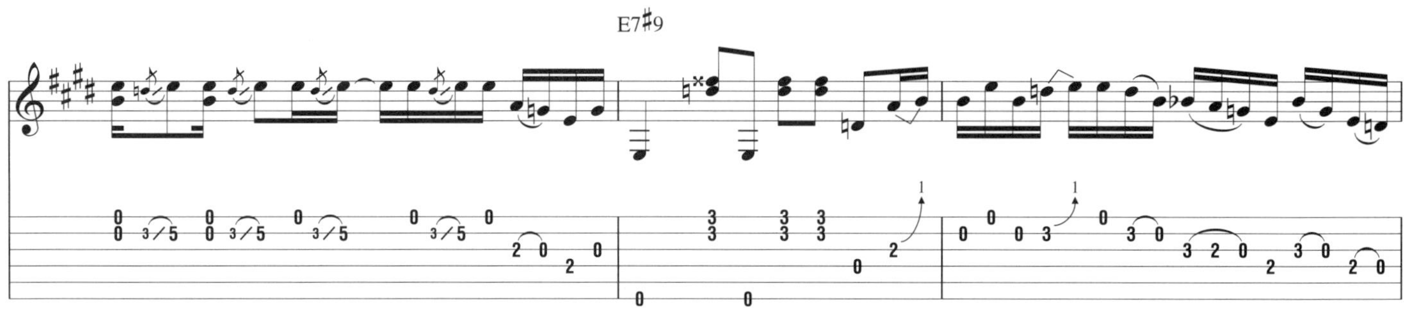
E7♯9

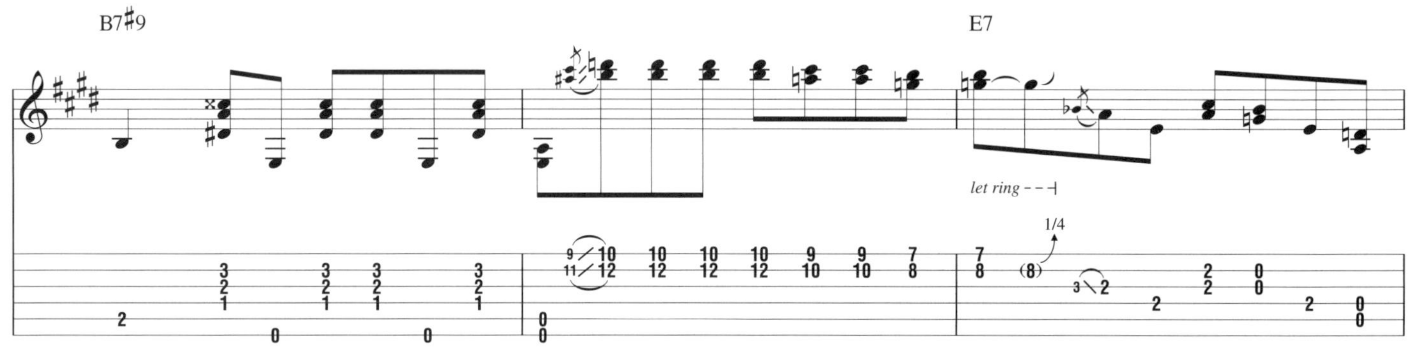
B7♯9
E7
let ring
1/4

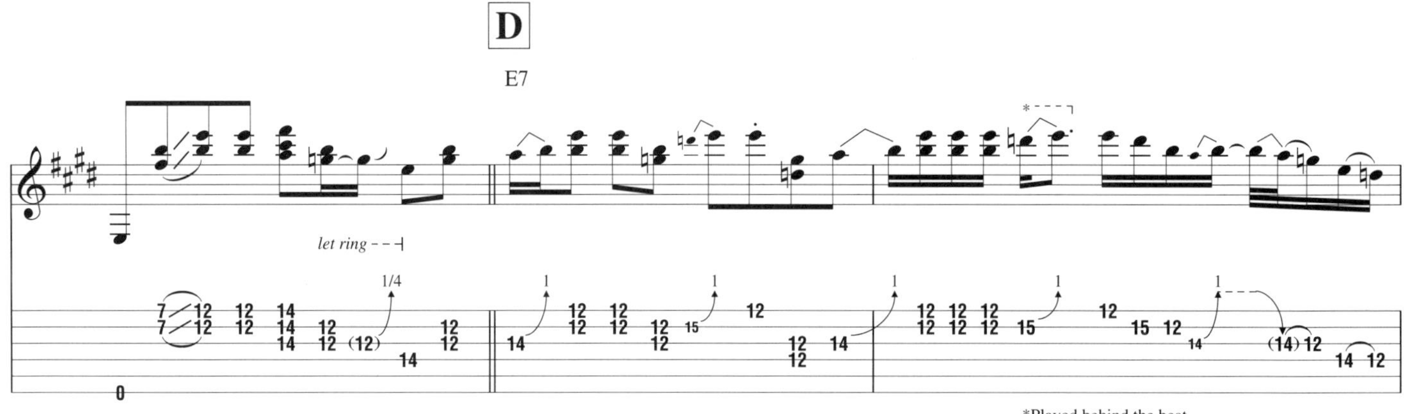
D
E7
let ring
1/4
*Played behind the beat.

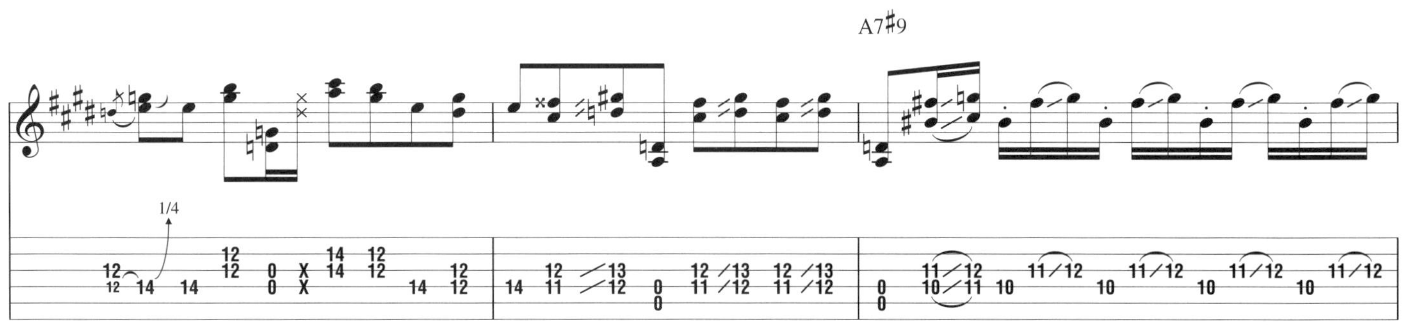
A7♯9
1/4

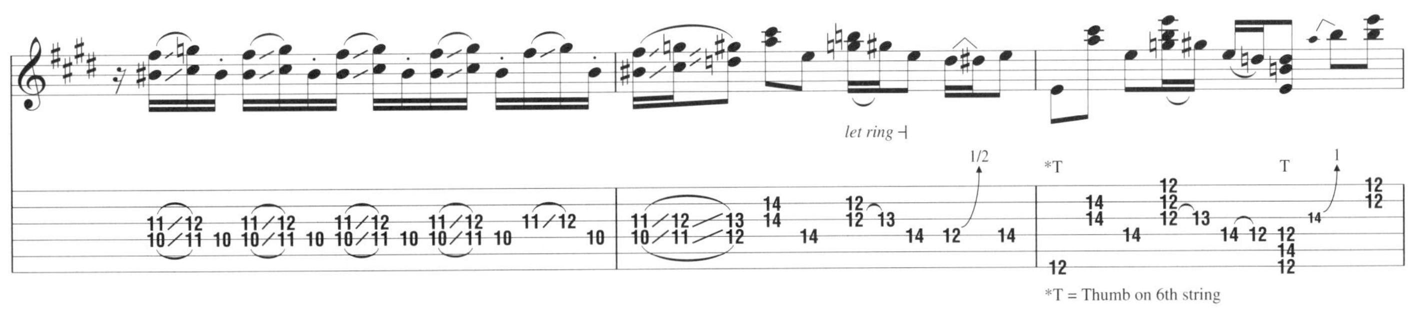
E7
let ring
*T
T
*T = Thumb on 6th string

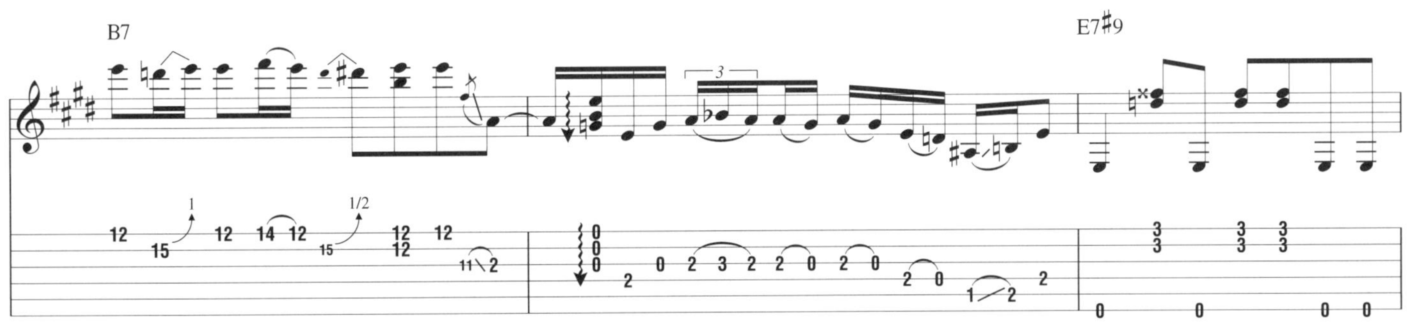
B7
E7#9

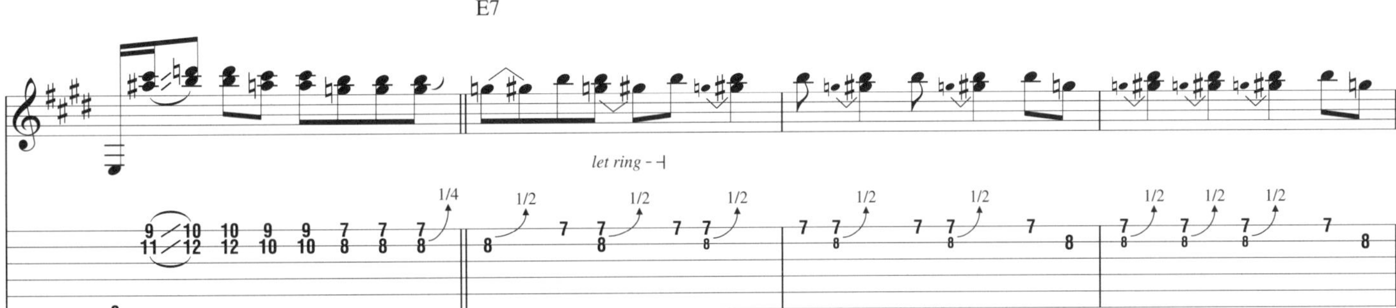
E
E7
let ring

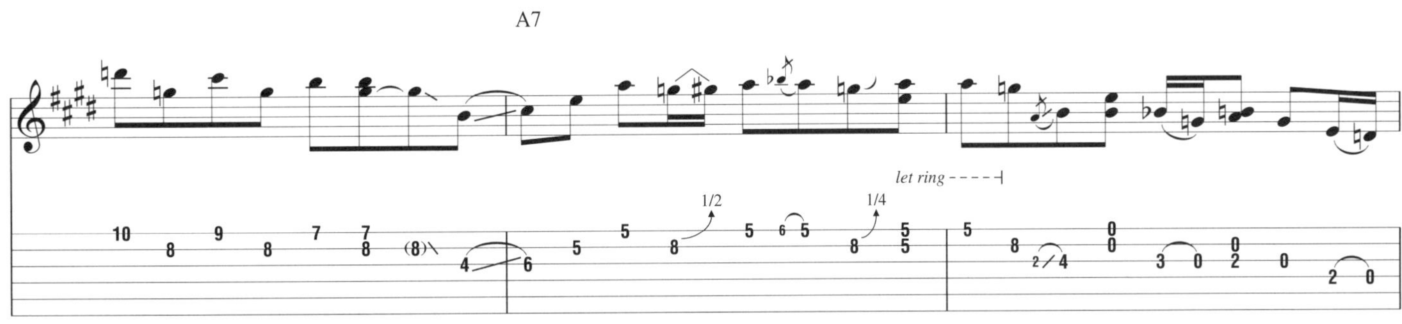
A7
let ring

E7#9
B7#9

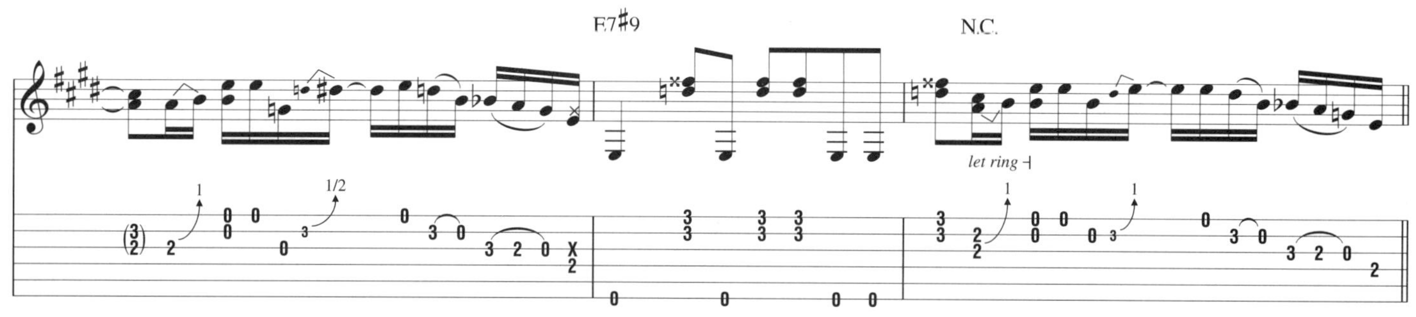

F

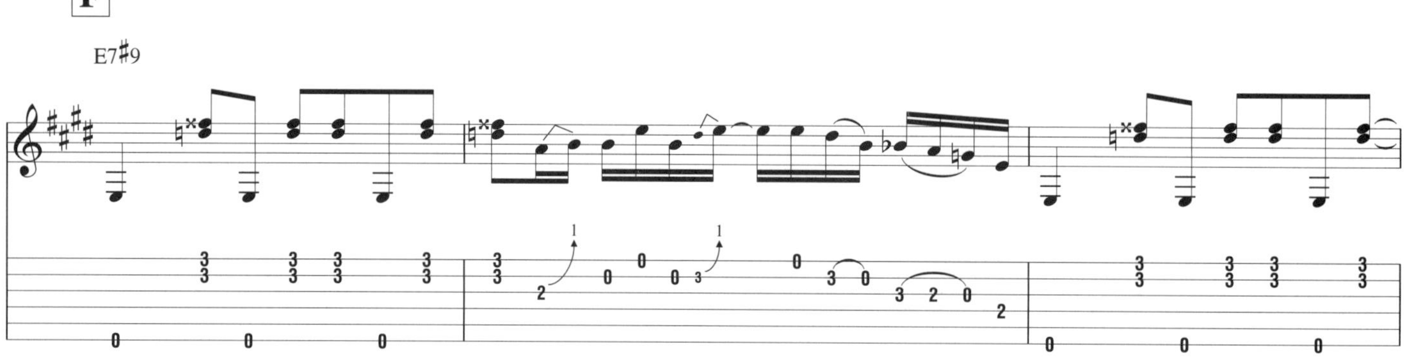

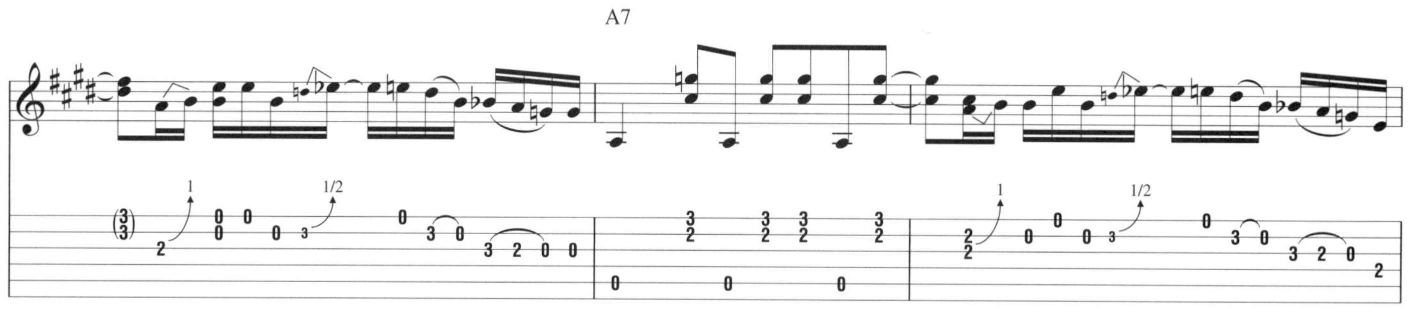

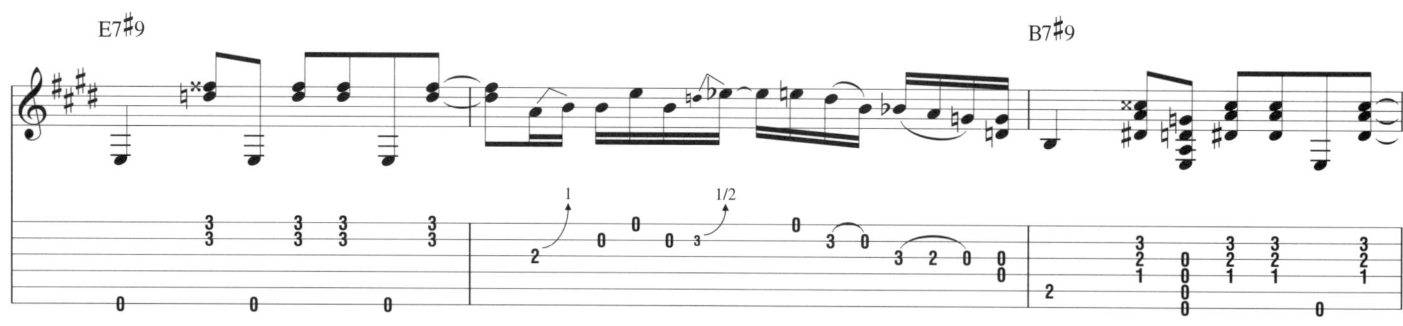

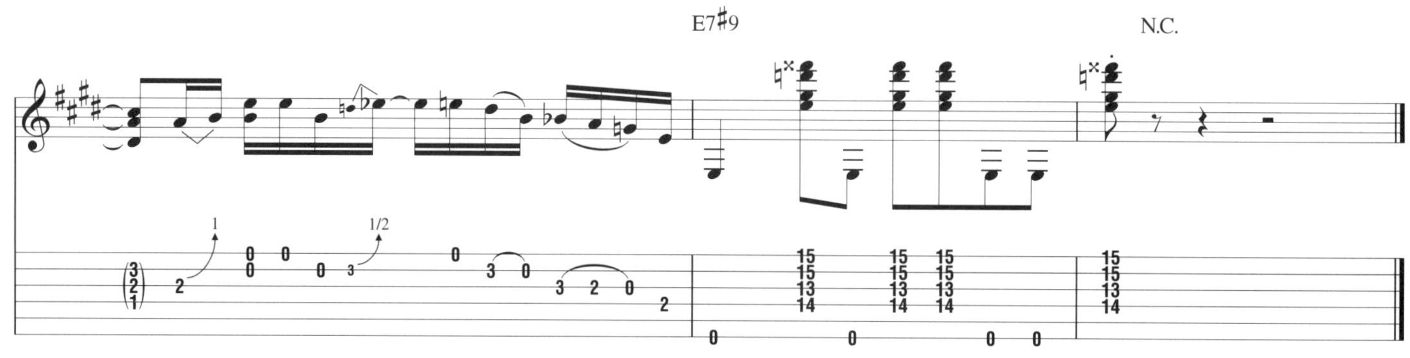

Tequila

By Chuck Rio

F
Eb/C
End Riff A
Rhy. Fill 1
End Rhy. Fill 1
Eb/Bb
Gtr. 1
mf
steady gliss.

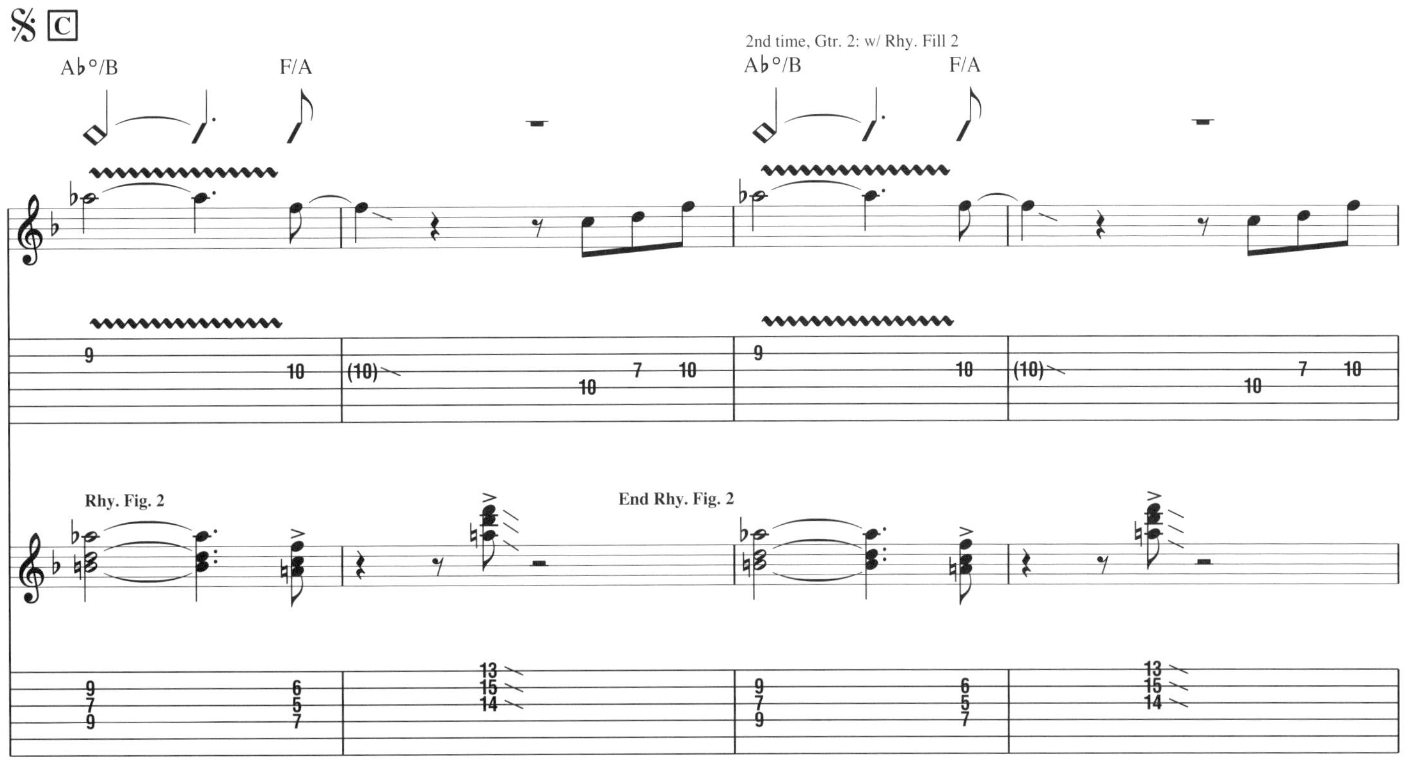
C
2nd time, Gtr. 2: w/ Rhy. Fill 2
Ab°/B
F/A
Rhy. Fig. 2
End Rhy. Fig. 2

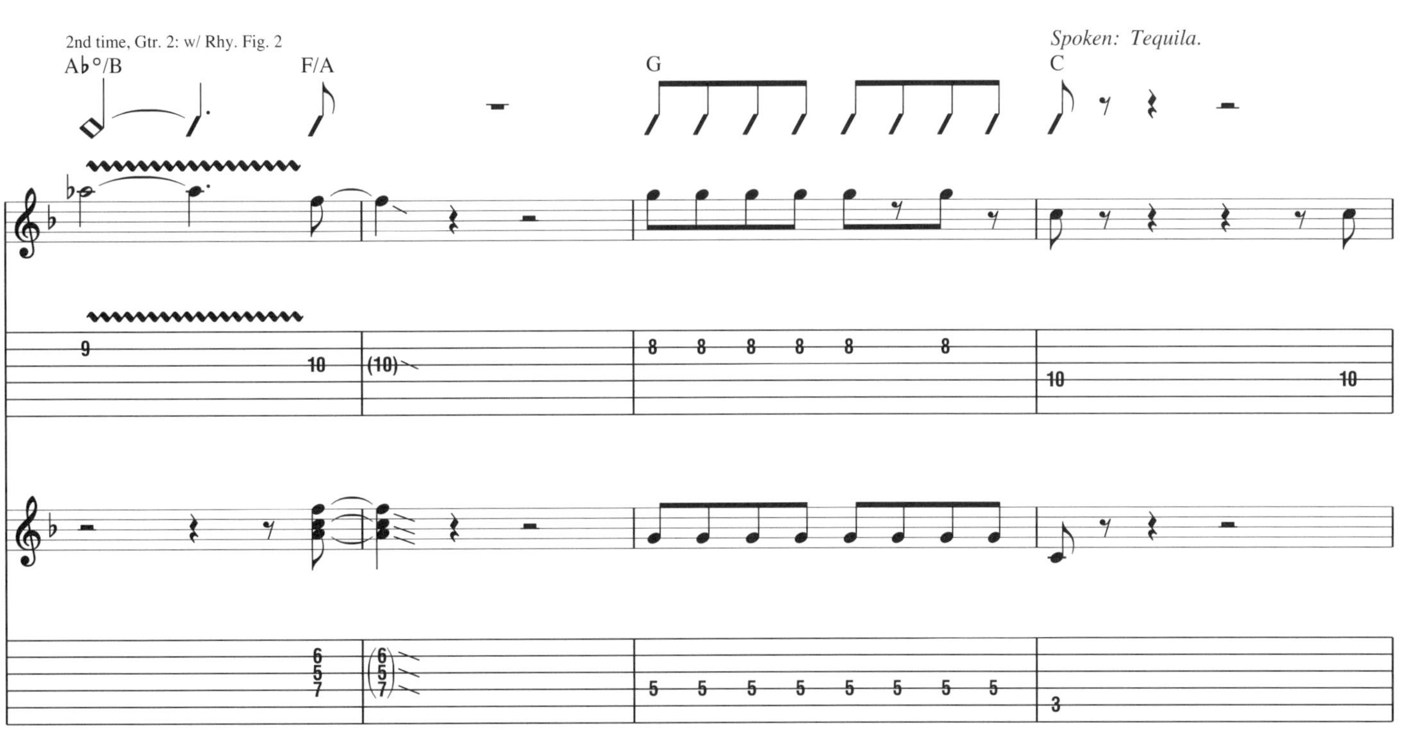
2nd time, Gtr. 2: w/ Rhy. Fig. 2
Ab°/B
F/A
G
Spoken: Tequila.
C

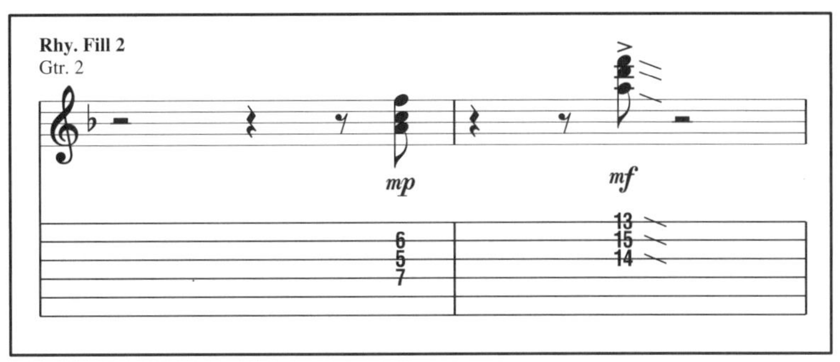
Rhy. Fill 2
Gtr. 2
mp
mf

D
Gtr. 1: w/ Rhy. Fig. 1 (2 times)
Gtr. 2: w/ Riff A
2nd time, Gtr. 2: w/ Riff A (1st 7 meas.)
Gtr. 3
F
Eb/C
To Coda
E
Gtr. 1: w/ Rhy. Fig. 1 (3 3/4 times)
Gtr. 2: w/ Riff A (1 1/2 times)

D.S. al Coda
Gtr. 1: w/ Rhy. Fill 1
F Eb/C F Eb/C F Eb/C F Eb/Bb
Gtr. 3
Gtr. 2
mf
steady gliss.
Coda
F
Gtr. 3 tacet
Gtr. 1: w/ Rhy. Fig. 1 (1 1/4 times)
Gtr. 2 Eb/C F Eb/C F Eb/C F Eb/C F
P.M.
* T = Thumb on 6th string
Eb/C F Eb/C
Gtr. 2 tacet
Gtr. 1 F Eb/C F Eb/C F
Eb/C F Eb/C F Eb/C F Eb/C F
Tequila!
Eb/C F Eb F Eb F Eb F N.C.

Wham

By Lonnie Mack

† Tune Down 1 Step, Capo III:

① = D ④ = C
② = A ⑤ = G
③ = F ⑥ = D

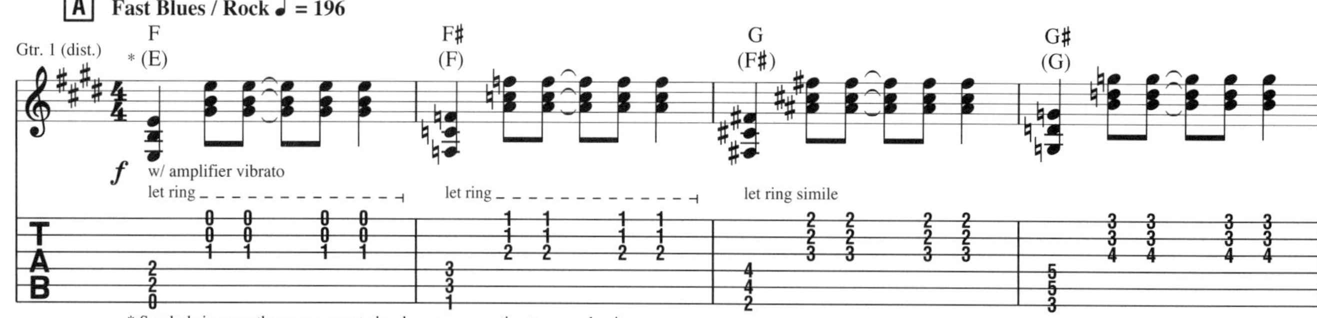

* Symbols in parentheses represent chord names respective to capoed guitar. Symbols above reflect actual sounding chord. Capoed fret is "0" in TAB. Chord symbols reflect basic harmony.

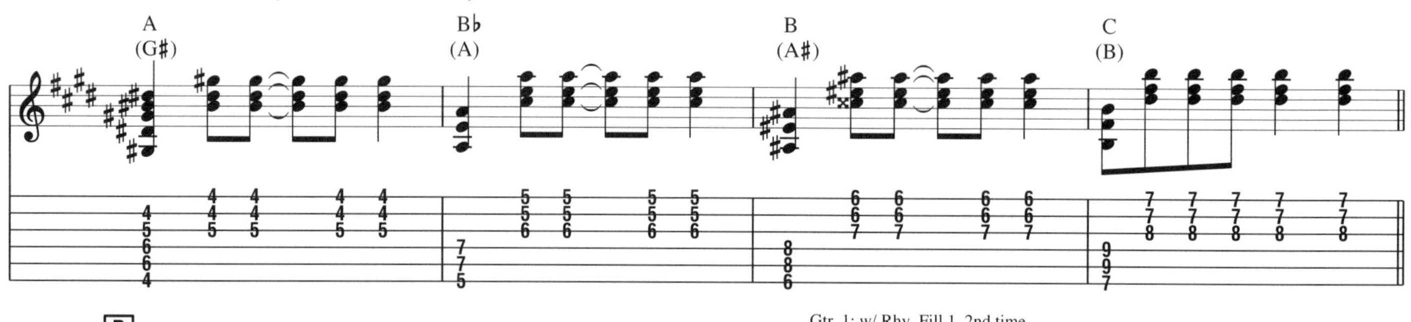

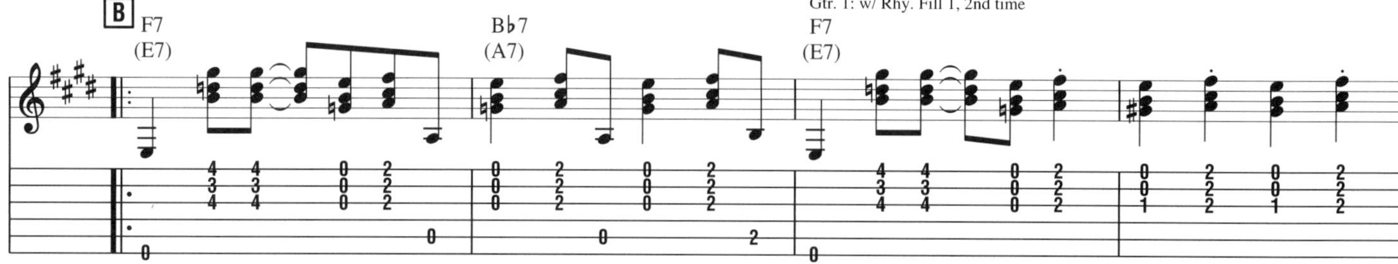

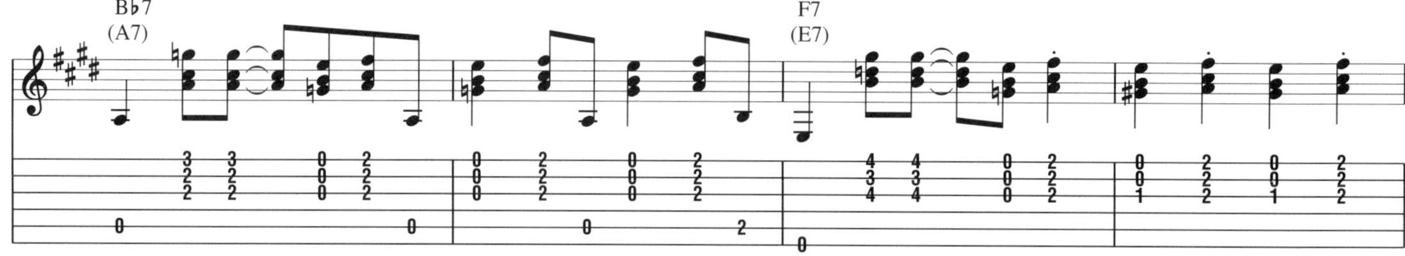

† Editors note: You can accomplish the same result without tuning down a whole step by remaining in standard tuning and capoing at the first fret.

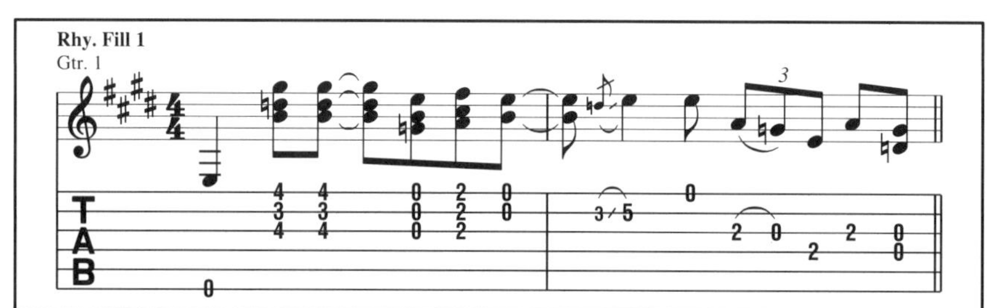

2.
C
F7
(E7)
D
B♭7
(A7)
full
F7
(E7)
C7
(B7)
full
full
full
full
full
full

B♭7
(A7)
F7
(E7)
E
F7
(E7)
B♭7
(A7)
F7
(E7)
C7
(B7)
full
full
B♭7
(A7)
F7
(E7)

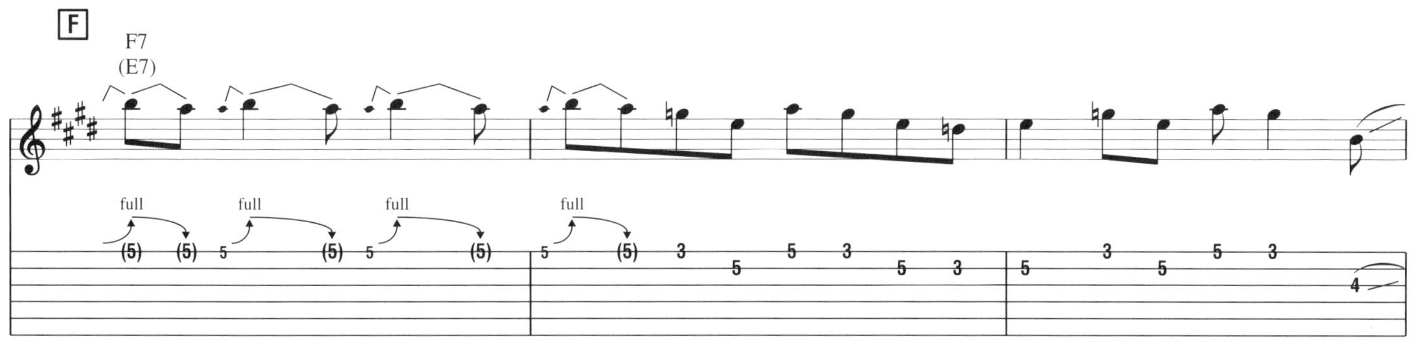

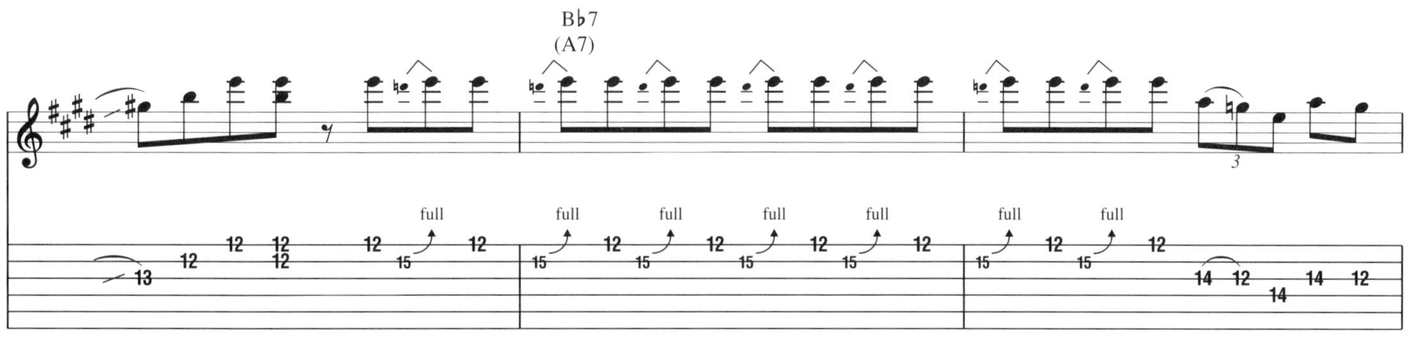

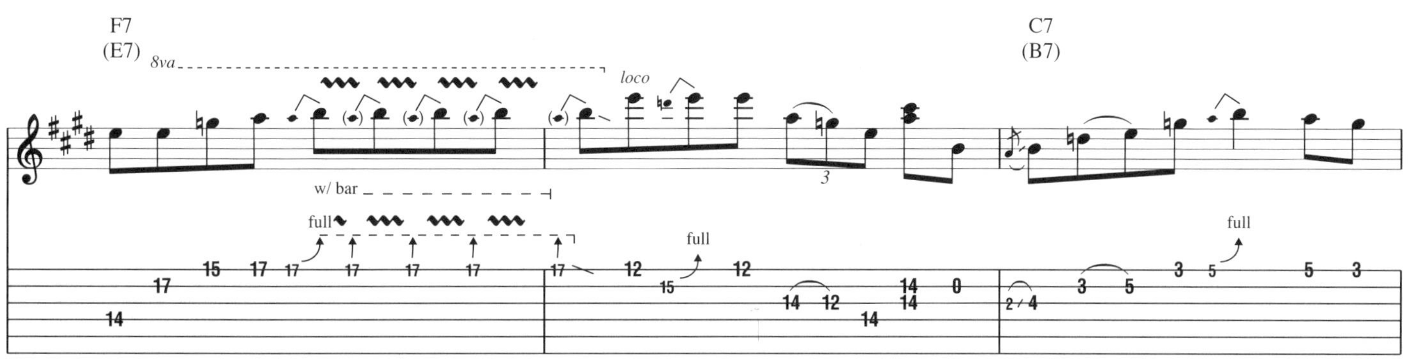

D.C. al Coda
(no repeat)

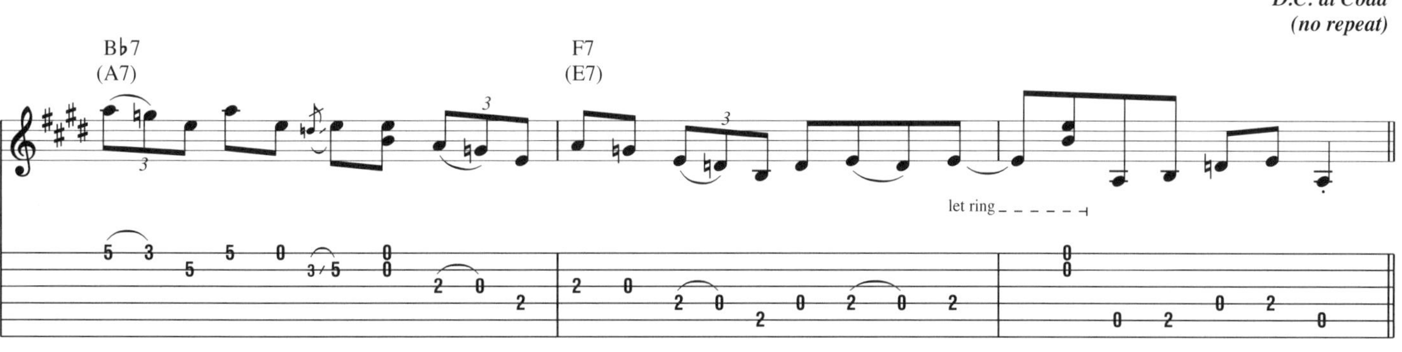

Coda

Free Time

Wipe Out

By The Surfaris

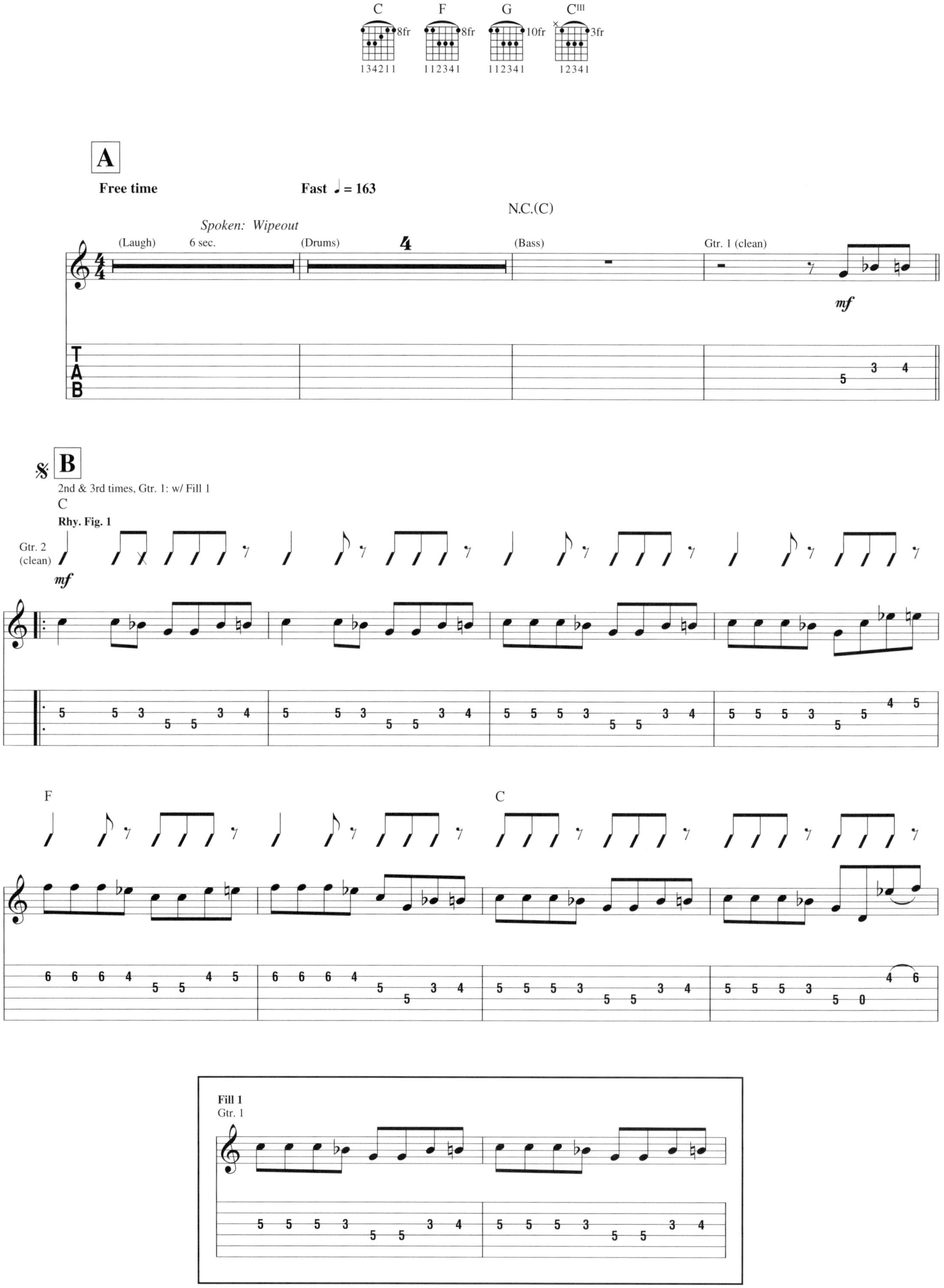

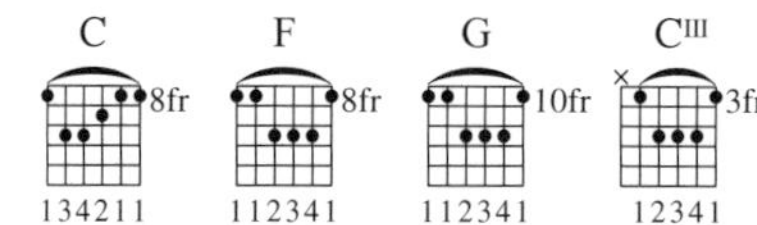

A

Free time

Fast ♩ = 163

N.C.(C)

Spoken: Wipeout

(Laugh) 6 sec.

(Drums) 4

(Bass)

Gtr. 1 (clean)

mf

B

2nd & 3rd times, Gtr. 1: w/ Fill 1

C

Rhy. Fig. 1

Gtr. 2 (clean)

mf

F

C

Fill 1

Gtr. 1

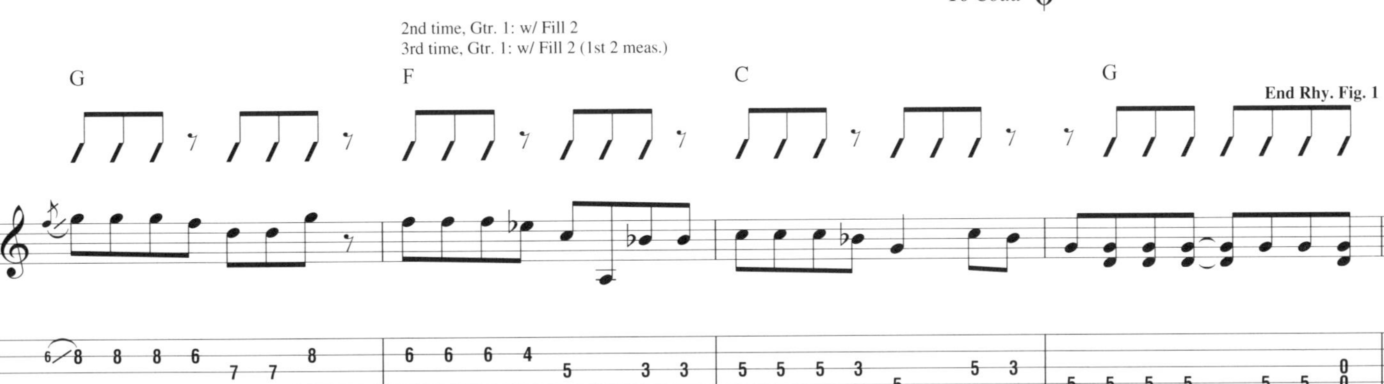
To Coda
2nd time, Gtr. 1: w/ Fill 2
3rd time, Gtr. 1: w/ Fill 2 (1st 2 meas.)
G
F
C
G
End Rhy. Fig. 1

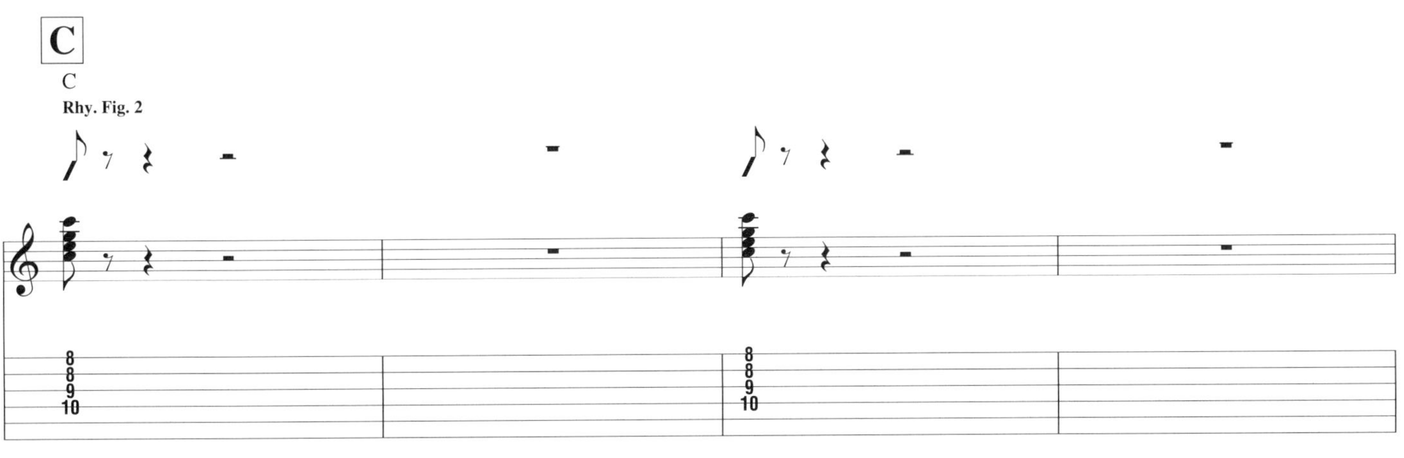
C
C
Rhy. Fig. 2

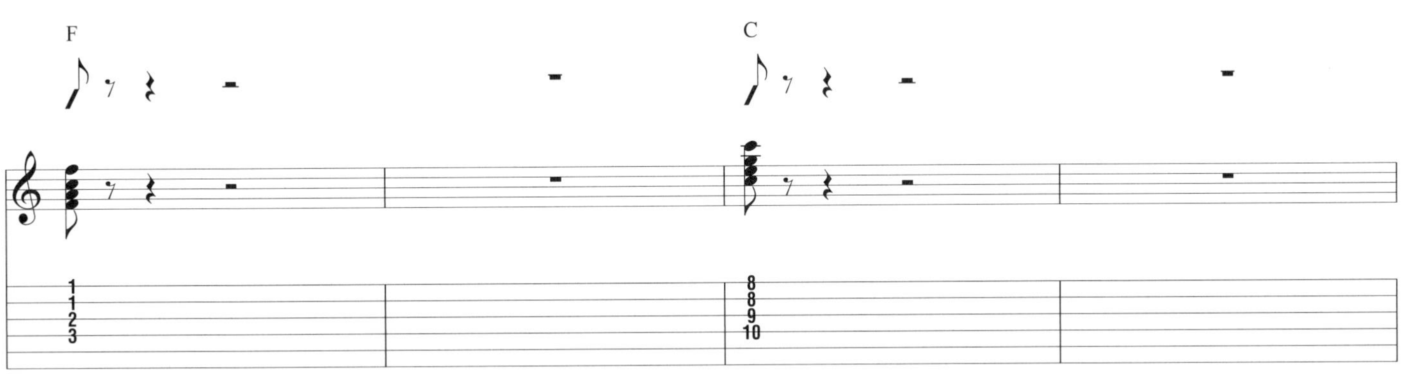
F
C

Fill 2
Gtr. 1

G
F
C
1.
End Rhy. Fig. 2
2.
D
Gtr. 2: w/ Rhy. Fig. 1
C
F
C
G
F
C
G

E
Gtr. 2: w/ Rhy. Fig. 2
C N.C.
C N.C.
F N.C.
C N.C.
G N.C.
F N.C.
C N.C.
D.S. al Coda
Coda
F
Begin fade
G
CIII
F
Fade out

Walk Don't Run

By Johnny Smith

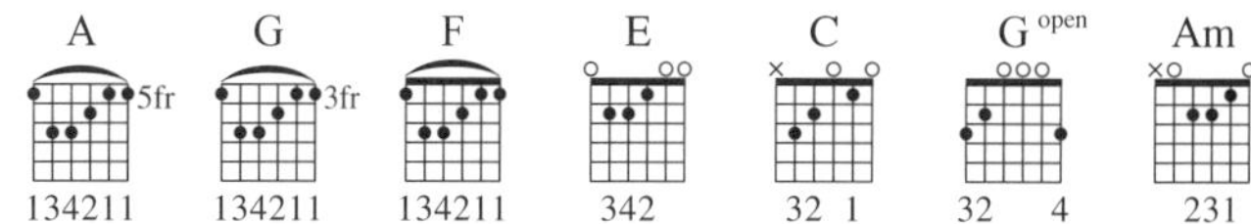

Tune up 1/4 step

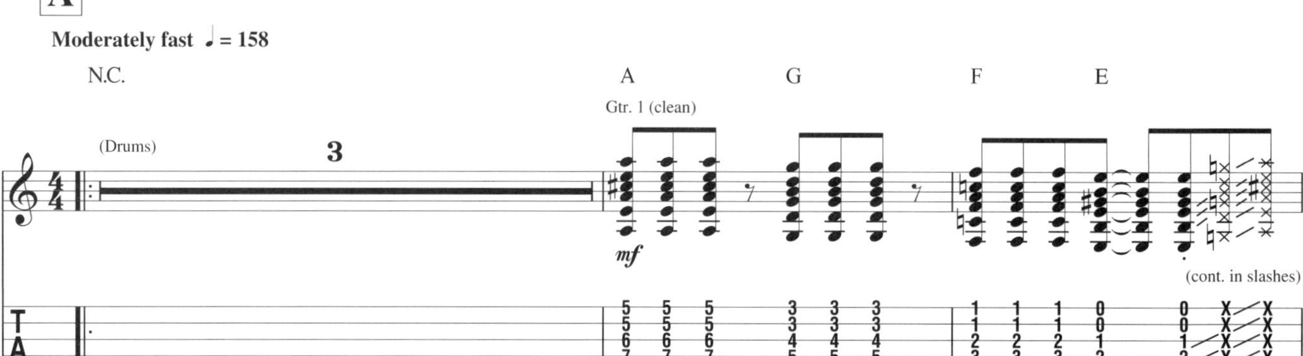

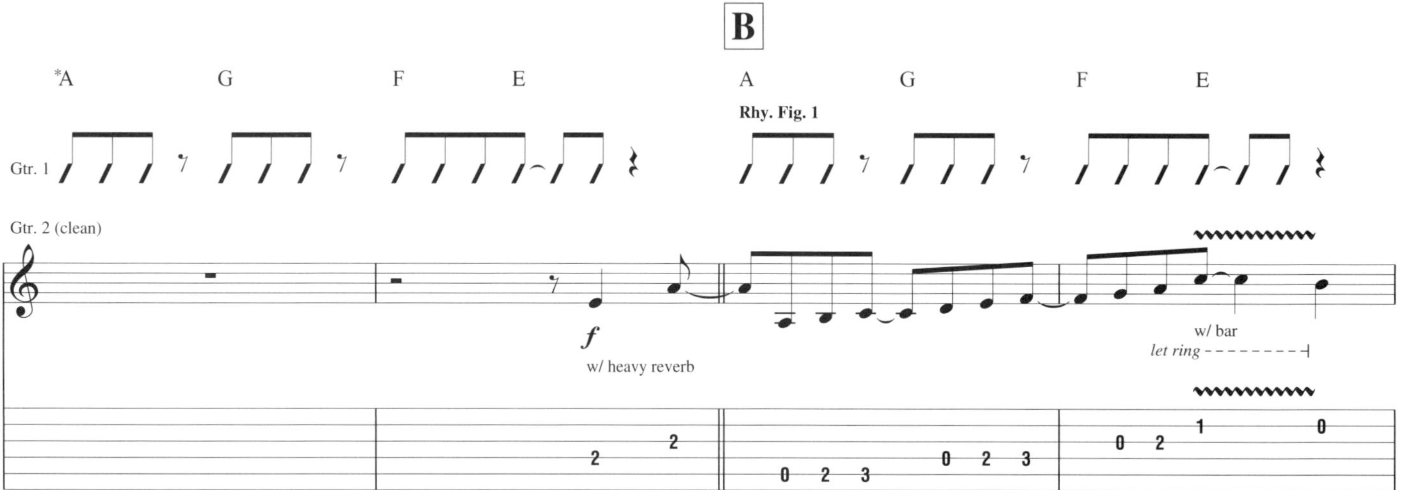

*See top of page for chord diagrams pertaining to rhythm slashes.

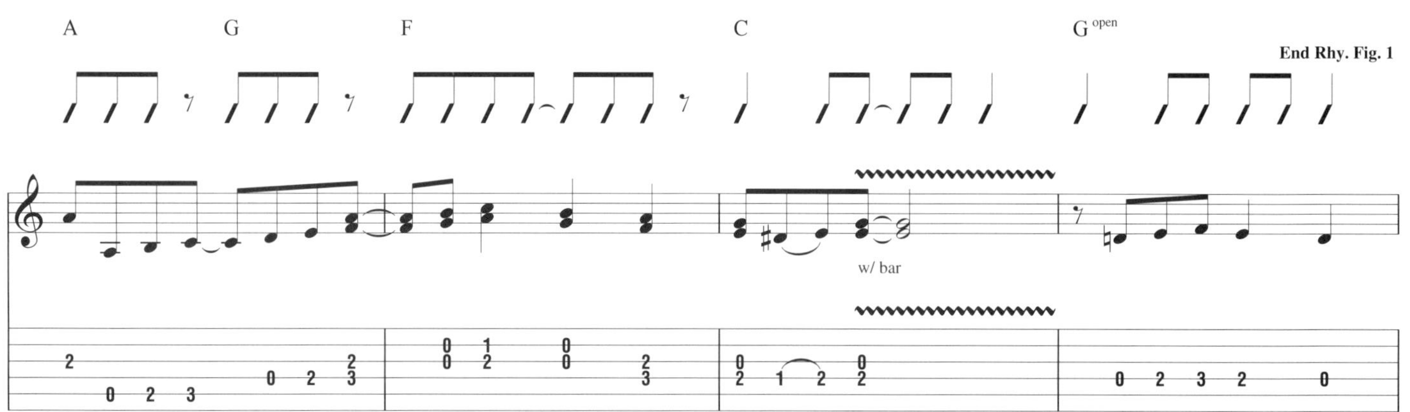

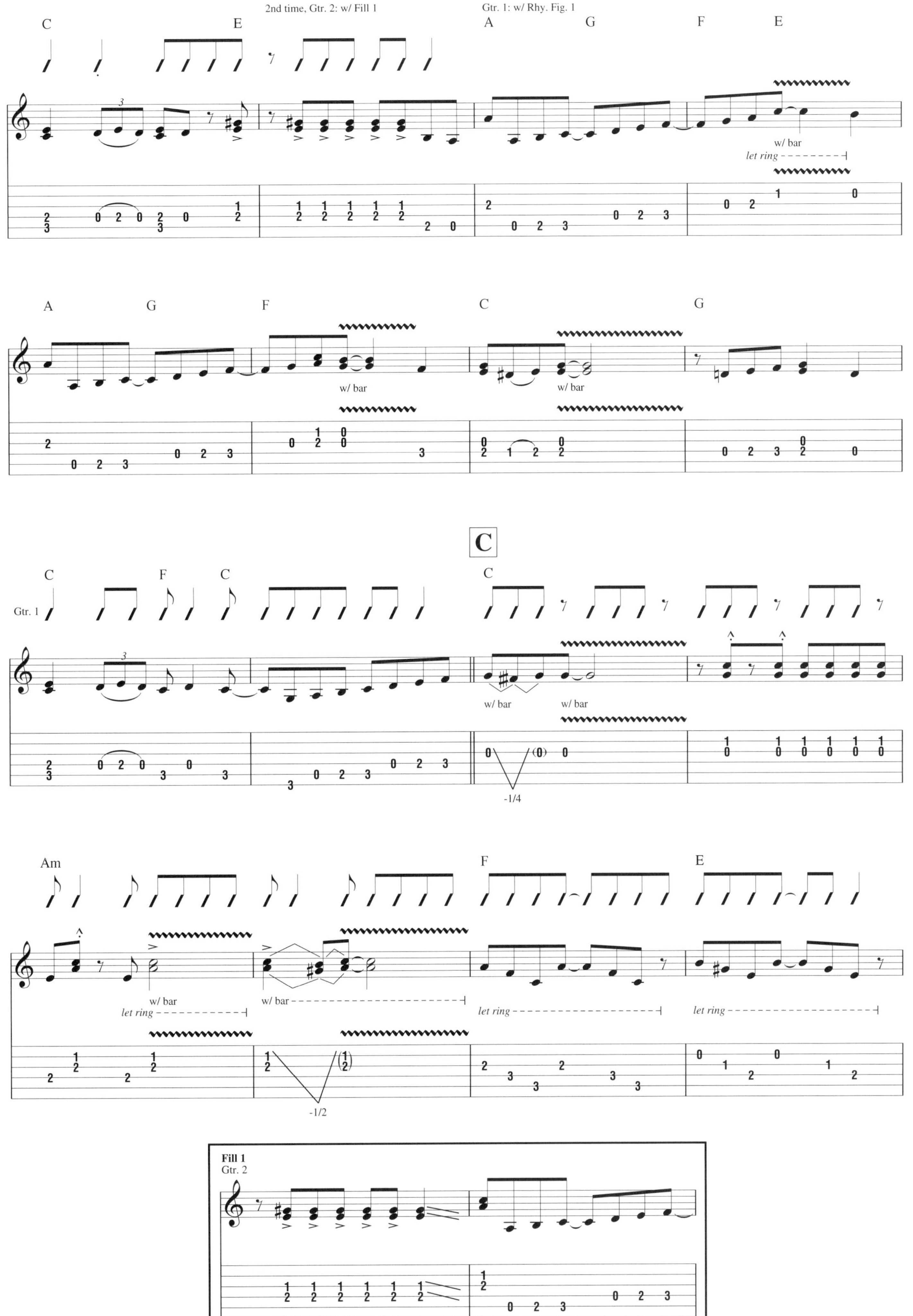
2nd time, Gtr. 2: w/ Fill 1
Gtr. 1: w/ Rhy. Fig. 1
C
E
A
G
F
E
w/ bar
let ring
A
G
F
C
G
w/ bar
w/ bar
C
C
F
C
C
Gtr. 1
w/ bar
w/ bar
-1/4
Am
F
E
w/ bar
let ring
w/ bar
let ring
let ring
-1/2
Fill 1
Gtr. 2

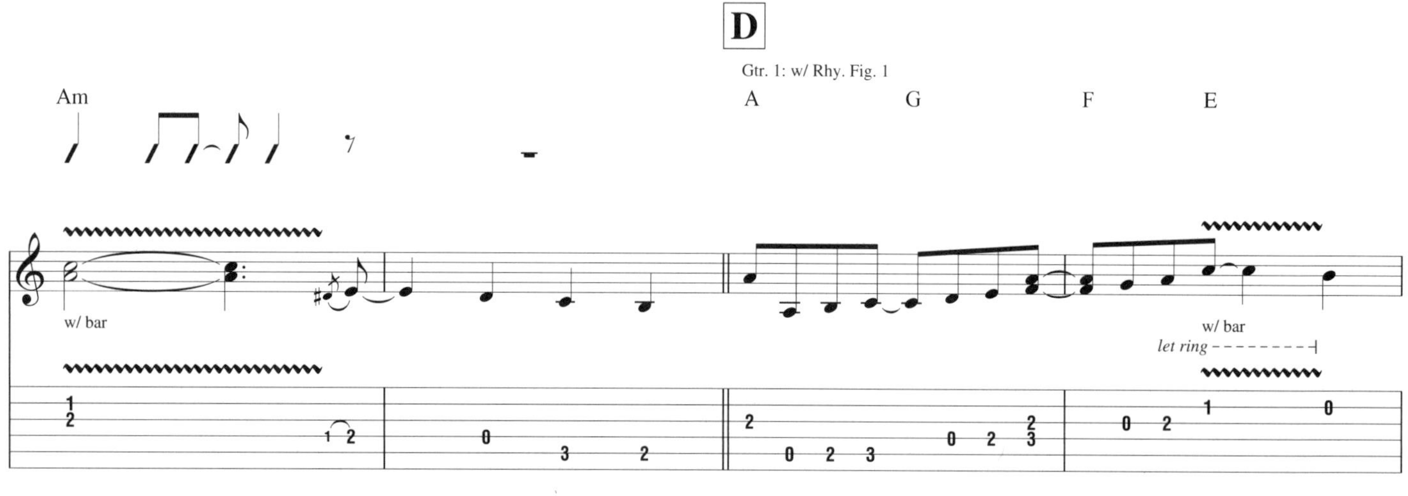
D
Gtr. 1: w/ Rhy. Fig. 1
Am
A
G
F
E
w/ bar
w/ bar
let ring

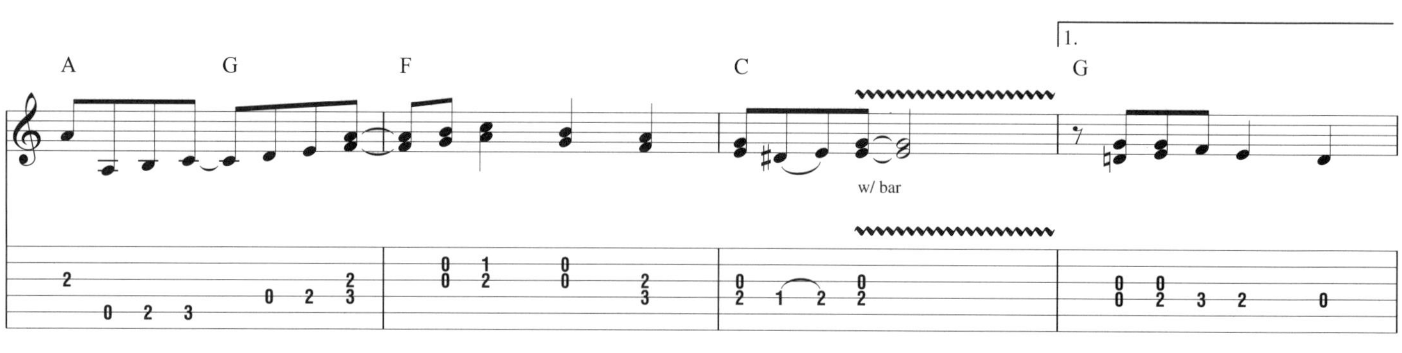
1.
A
G
F
C
G
w/ bar

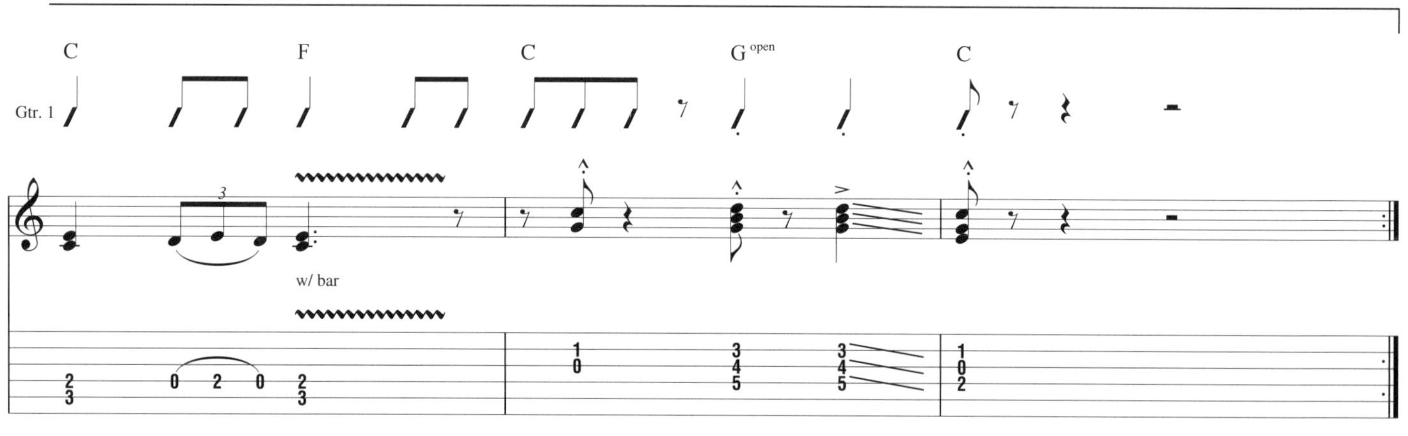
C
F
C
G open
C
Gtr. 1
w/ bar

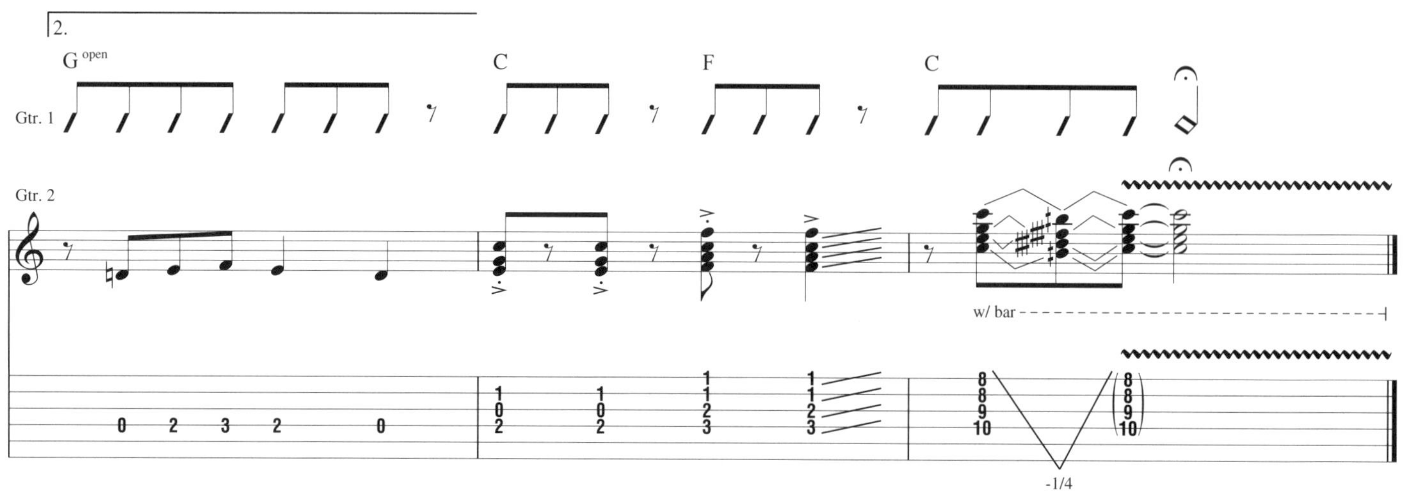
2.
G open
C
F
C
Gtr. 1
Gtr. 2
w/ bar
-1/4

GUITAR NOTATION LEGEND

Guitar music can be notated three different ways: on a *musical staff*, in *tablature*, and in *rhythm slashes.*

RHYTHM SLASHES are written above the staff. Strum chords in the rhythm indicated. Use the chord diagrams found at the top of the first page of the transcription for the appropriate chord voicings. Round noteheads indicate single notes.

THE MUSICAL STAFF shows pitches and rhythms and is divided by bar lines into measures. Pitches are named after the first seven letters of the alphabet.

TABLATURE graphically represents the guitar fingerboard. Each horizontal line represents a string, and each number represents a fret.

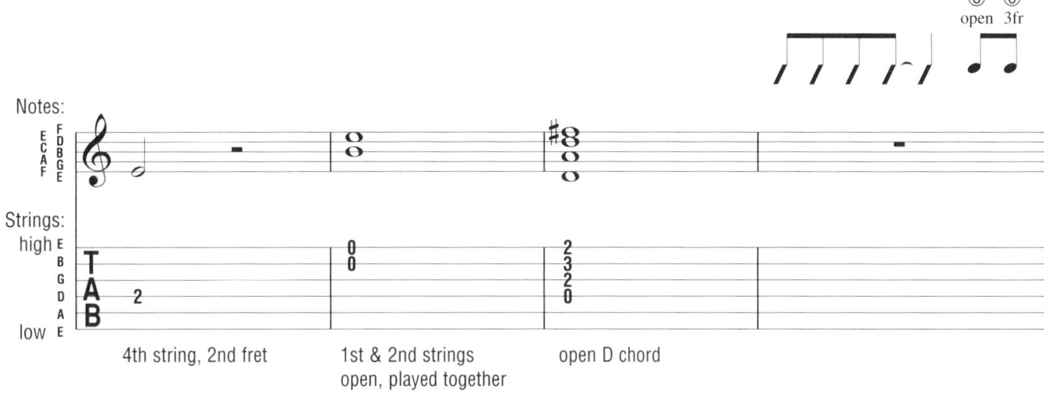

4th string, 2nd fret

1st & 2nd strings open, played together

open D chord

Definitions for Special Guitar Notation

HALF-STEP BEND: Strike the note and bend up 1/2 step.

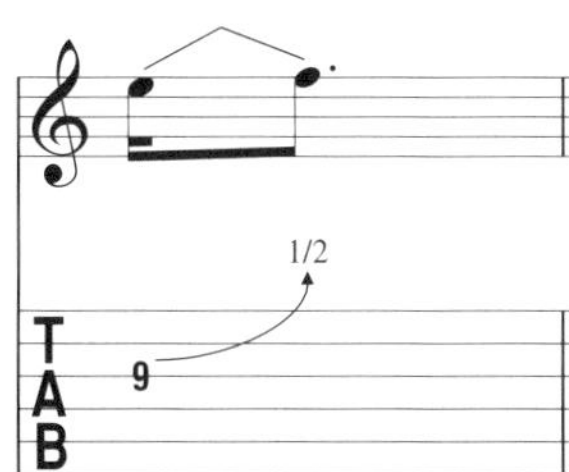
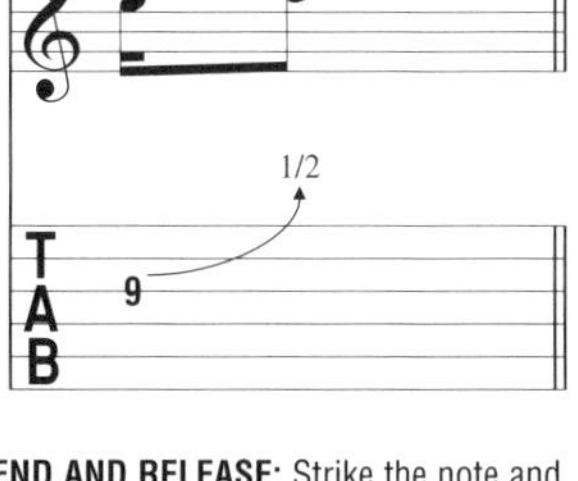

WHOLE-STEP BEND: Strike the note and bend up one step.

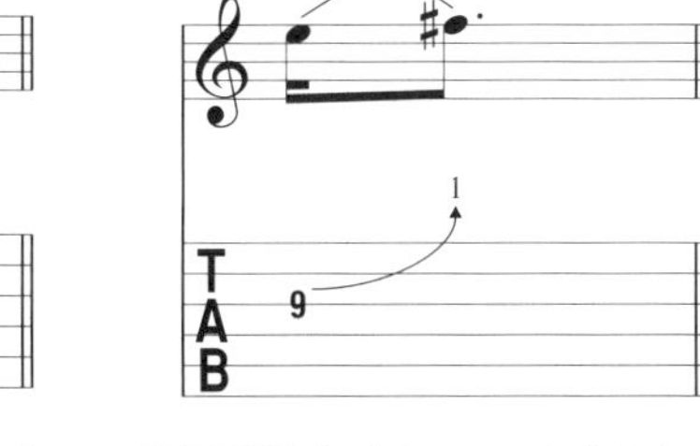

GRACE NOTE BEND: Strike the note and immediately bend up as indicated.

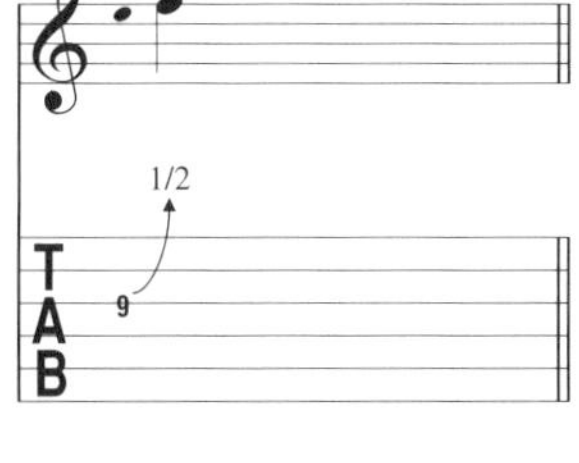

SLIGHT (MICROTONE) BEND: Strike the note and bend up 1/4 step.

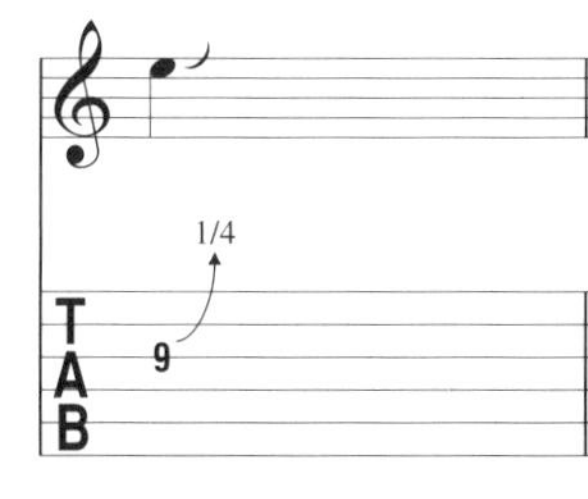

BEND AND RELEASE: Strike the note and bend up as indicated, then release back to the original note. Only the first note is struck.

PRE-BEND: Bend the note as indicated, then strike it.

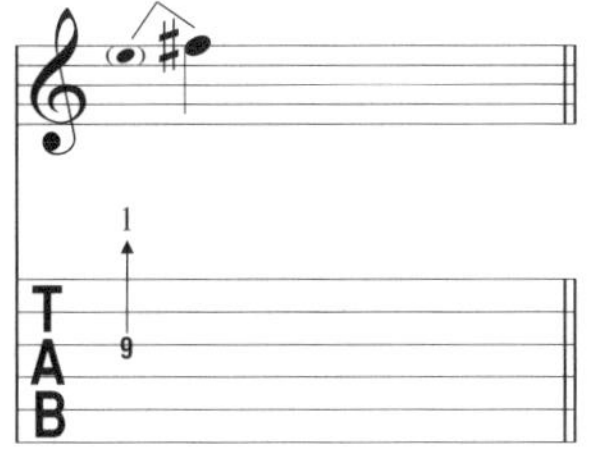

PRE-BEND AND RELEASE: Bend the note as indicated. Strike it and release the bend back to the original note.

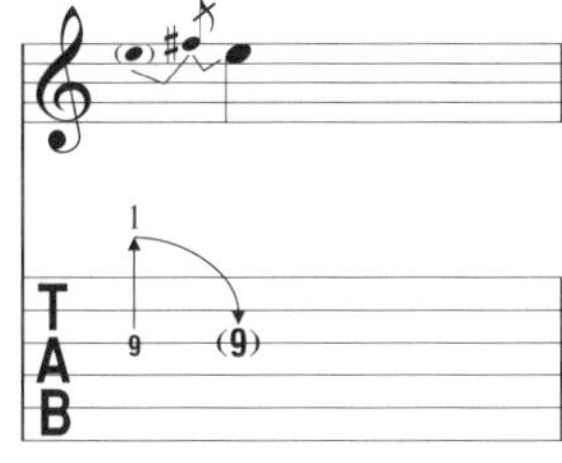

UNISON BEND: Strike the two notes simultaneously and bend the lower note up to the pitch of the higher.

VIBRATO: The string is vibrated by rapidly bending and releasing the note with the fretting hand.

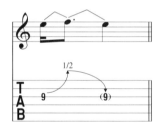

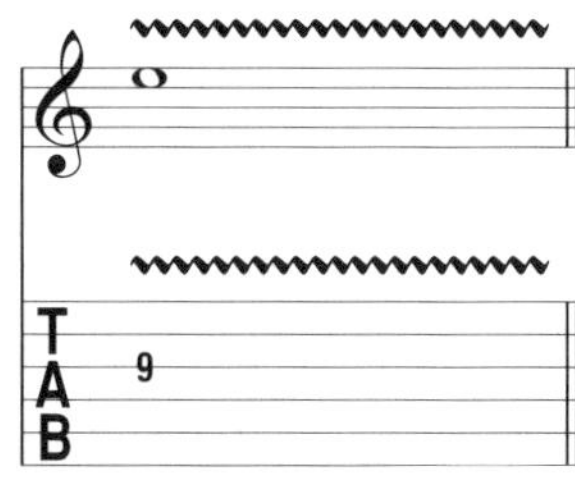

WIDE VIBRATO: The pitch is varied to a greater degree by vibrating with the fretting hand.

HAMMER-ON: Strike the first (lower) note with one finger, then sound the higher note (on the same string) with another finger by fretting it without picking.

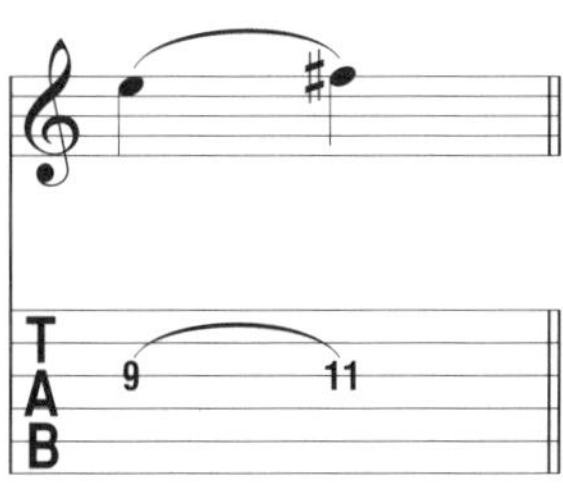

PULL-OFF: Place both fingers on the notes to be sounded. Strike the first note and without picking, pull the finger off to sound the second (lower) note.

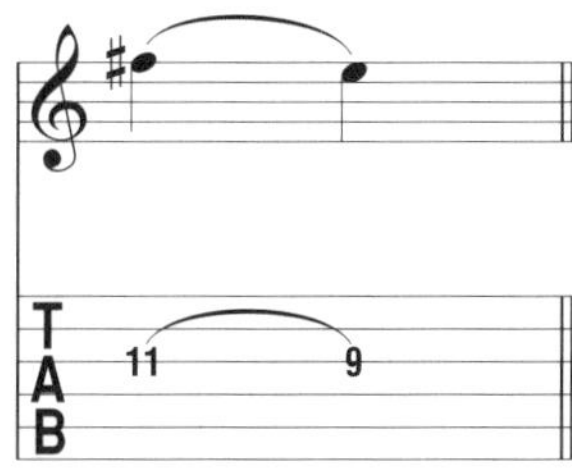

LEGATO SLIDE: Strike the first note and then slide the same fret-hand finger up or down to the second note. The second note is not struck.

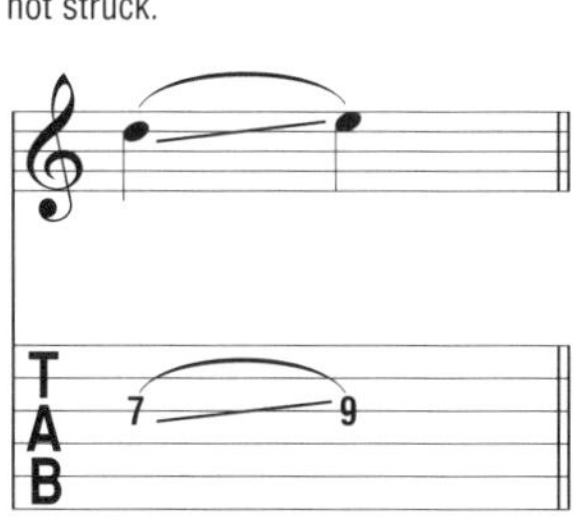

SHIFT SLIDE: Same as legato slide, except the second note is struck.

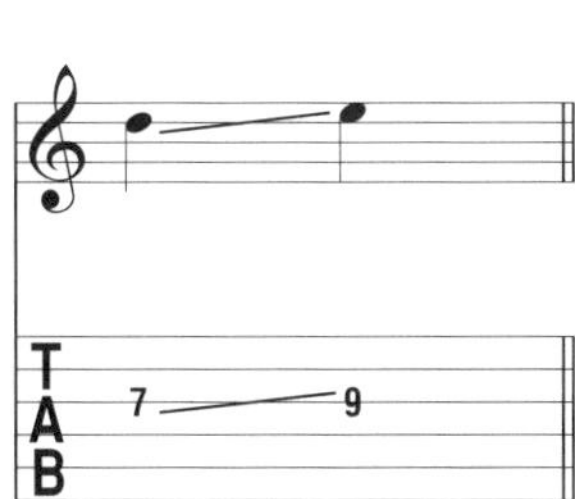

TRILL: Very rapidly alternate between the notes indicated by continuously hammering on and pulling off.

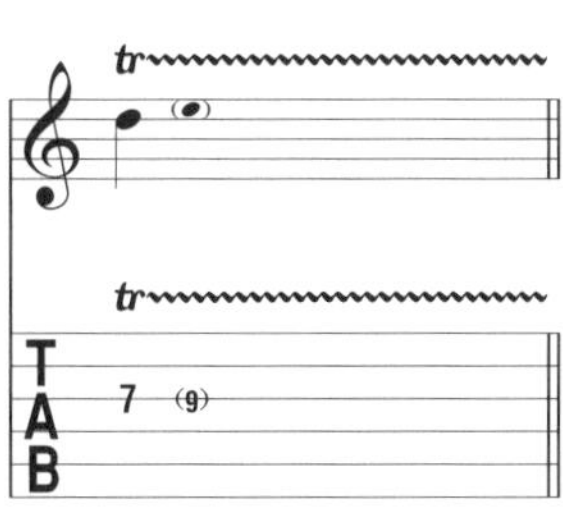

TAPPING: Hammer ("tap") the fret indicated with the pick-hand index or middle finger and pull off to the note fretted by the fret hand.

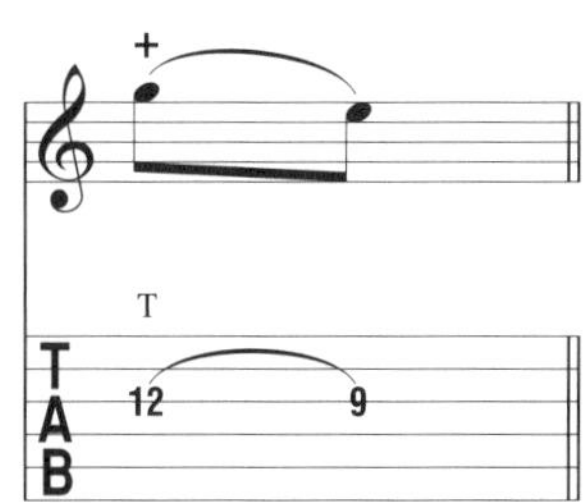

NATURAL HARMONIC: Strike the note while the fret-hand lightly touches the string directly over the fret indicated.

PINCH HARMONIC: The note is fretted normally and a harmonic is produced by adding the edge of the thumb or the tip of the index finger of the pick hand to the normal pick attack.

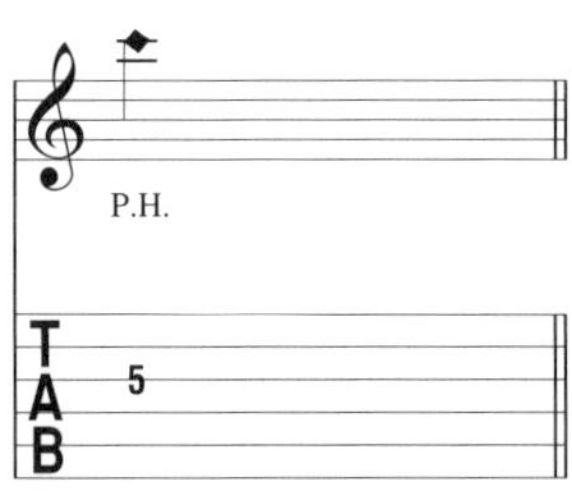

HARP HARMONIC: The note is fretted normally and a harmonic is produced by gently resting the pick hand's index finger directly above the indicated fret (in parentheses) while the pick hand's thumb or pick assists by plucking the appropriate string.

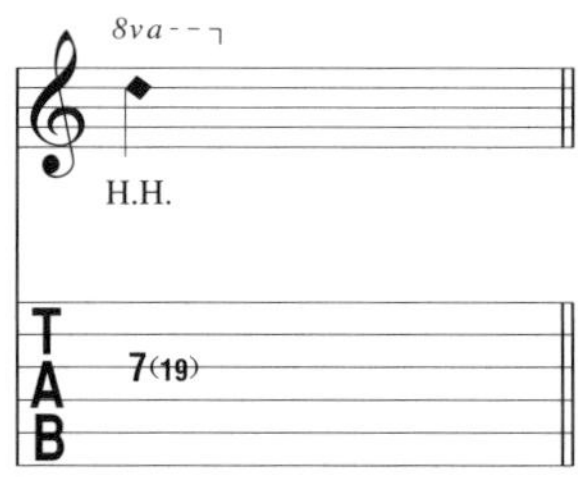

PICK SCRAPE: The edge of the pick is rubbed down (or up) the string, producing a scratchy sound.

MUFFLED STRINGS: A percussive sound is produced by laying the fret hand across the string(s) without depressing, and striking them with the pick hand.

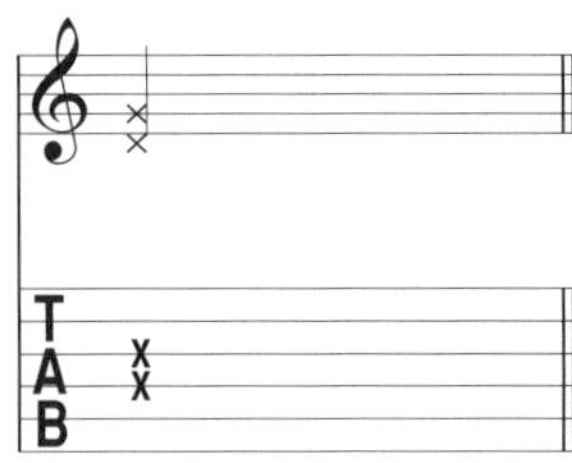

PALM MUTING: The note is partially muted by the pick hand lightly touching the string(s) just before the bridge.

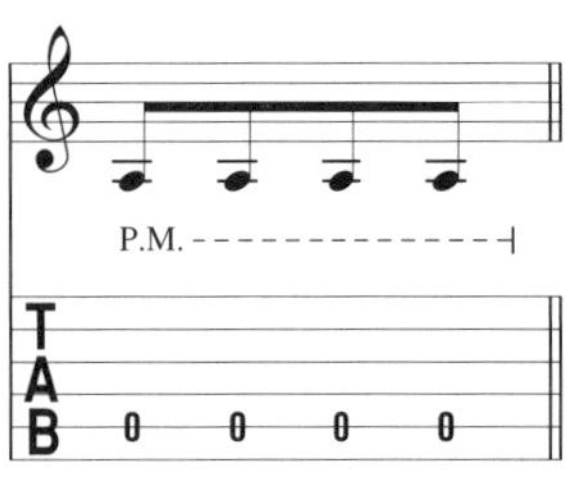

RAKE: Drag the pick across the strings indicated with a single motion.

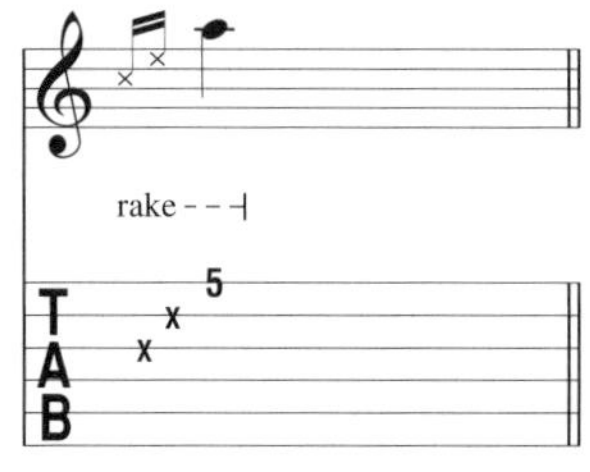

TREMOLO PICKING: The note is picked as rapidly and continuously as possible.

ARPEGGIATE: Play the notes of the chord indicated by quickly rolling them from bottom to top.

VIBRATO BAR DIVE AND RETURN: The pitch of the note or chord is dropped a specified number of steps (in rhythm), then returned to the original pitch.

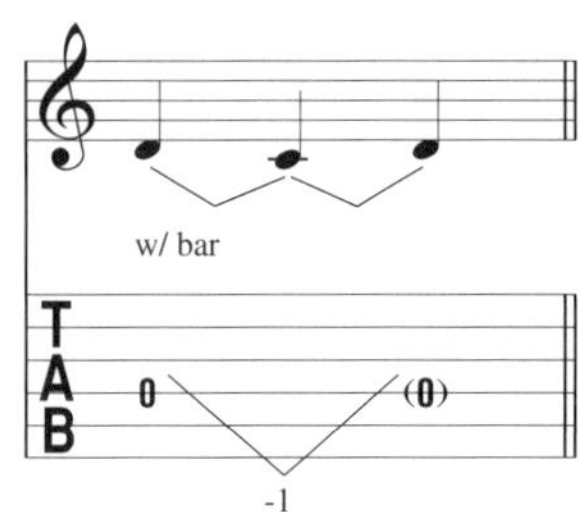

VIBRATO BAR SCOOP: Depress the bar just before striking the note, then quickly release the bar.

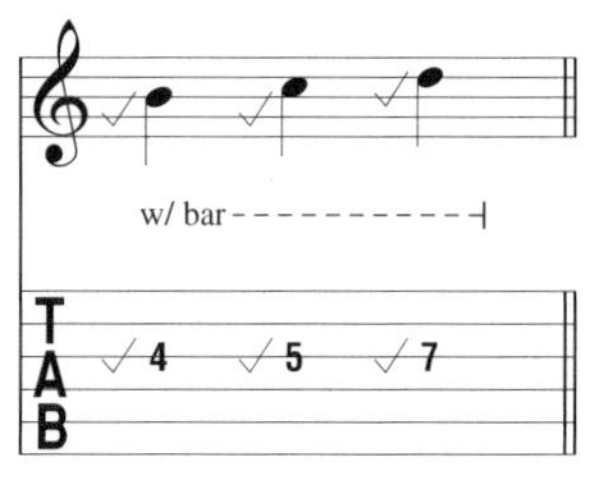

VIBRATO BAR DIP: Strike the note and then immediately drop a specified number of steps, then release back to the original pitch.

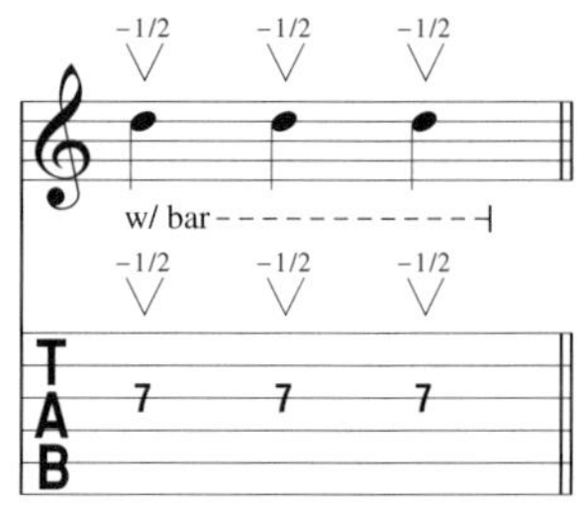

Additional Musical Definitions

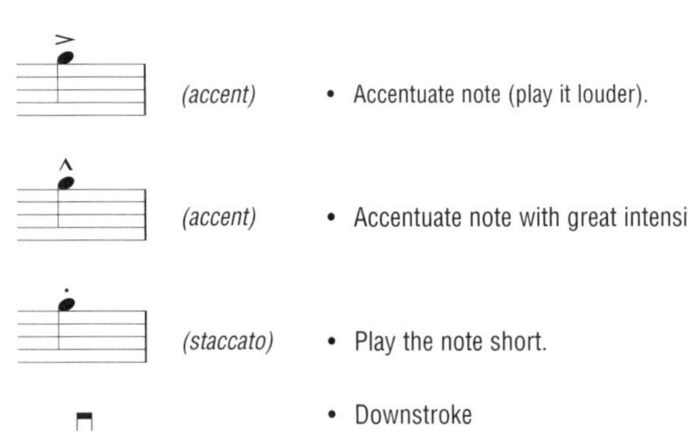

(accent) • Accentuate note (play it louder).

(accent) • Accentuate note with great intensity.

(staccato) • Play the note short.

• Downstroke

V • Upstroke

D.S. al Coda • Go back to the sign (𝄋), then play until the measure marked "***To Coda***," then skip to the section labelled "**Coda**."

D.C. al Fine • Go back to the beginning of the song and play until the measure marked "***Fine***" (end).

Rhy. Fig. • Label used to recall a recurring accompaniment pattern (usually chordal).

Riff • Label used to recall composed, melodic lines (usually single notes) which recur.

Fill • Label used to identify a brief melodic figure which is to be inserted into the arrangement.

Rhy. Fill • A chordal version of a Fill.

tacet • Instrument is silent (drops out).

• Repeat measures between signs.

1. 2. • When a repeated section has different endings, play the first ending only the first time and the second ending only the second time.

NOTE: Tablature numbers in parentheses mean:

1. The note is being sustained over a system (note in standard notation is tied), or
2. The note is sustained, but a new articulation (such as a hammer-on, pull-off, slide or vibrato) begins, or
3. The note is a barely audible "ghost" note (note in standard notation is also in parentheses).

RECORDED VERSIONS®

The Best Note-For-Note Transcriptions Available

RECORDED VERSIONS GUITAR®

ALL BOOKS INCLUDE TABLATURE

14037551 AC/DC – Backtracks $32.99
00692015 Aerosmith – Greatest Hits $22.95
00690178 Alice in Chains – Acoustic $19.95
00694865 Alice in Chains – Dirt $19.95
00690812 All American Rejects – Move Along $19.95
00690958 Duane Allman Guitar Anthology $24.99
00694932 Allman Brothers Band – Volume 1 .... $24.95
00694933 Allman Brothers Band – Volume 2 .... $24.95
00694934 Allman Brothers Band – Volume 3 .... $24.95
00690865 Atreyu – A Deathgrip on Yesterday $19.95
00690609 Audioslave $19.95
00690820 Avenged Sevenfold – City of Evil $24.95
00690366 Bad Company – Original Anthology $19.95
00690503 Beach Boys – Very Best of $19.95
00690489 Beatles – 1 .... $24.99
00694832 Beatles – For Acoustic Guitar $22.99
00691014 Beatles Rock Band $34.99
00690110 Beatles – White Album (Book 1) $19.95
00691043 Jeff Beck – Wired $19.99
00692385 Chuck Berry $19.95
00690835 Billy Talent $19.95
00690901 Best of Black Sabbath $19.95
00690831 blink-182 – Greatest Hits $19.95
00690913 Boston $19.95
00690932 Boston – Don't Look Back $19.99
00690491 David Bowie – Best of $19.95
00690873 Breaking Benjamin – Phobia $19.95
00690451 Jeff Buckley – Collection $24.95
00690957 Bullet for My Valentine – Scream Aim Fire $19.95
00691004 Chickenfoot $22.99
00690590 Eric Clapton – Anthology $29.95
00690415 Clapton Chronicles – Best of Eric Clapton $18.95
00690936 Eric Clapton – Complete Clapton $29.99
00690074 Eric Clapton – The Cream of Clapton $24.95
00694869 Eric Clapton – Unplugged $22.95
00690162 The Clash – Best of $19.95
00690828 Coheed & Cambria – Good Apollo I'm Burning Star, IV, Vol. 1: From Fear Through the Eyes of Madness $19.95
00690593 Coldplay – A Rush of Blood to the Head $19.95
00690962 Coldplay – Viva La Vida $19.95
00690819 Creedence Clearwater Revival – Best of $22.95
00690648 The Very Best of Jim Croce $19.95
00690613 Crosby, Stills & Nash – Best of $22.95
00690967 Death Cab for Cutie – Narrow Stairs $22.99
00690289 Deep Purple – Best of $17.95
00690784 Def Leppard – Best of $19.95
00692240 Bo Diddley $19.99
00690347 The Doors – Anthology $22.95
00690348 The Doors – Essential Guitar Collection $16.95
00690810 Fall Out Boy – From Under the Cork Tree $19.95
00690664 Fleetwood Mac – Best of $19.95
00690870 Flyleaf $19.95
00690931 Foo Fighters – Echoes, Silence, Patience & Grace $19.95
00690808 Foo Fighters – In Your Honor $19.95
00690805 Robben Ford – Best of $19.95
00694920 Free – Best of $19.95
00691050 Glee Guitar Collection $19.99
00690848 Godsmack – IV $19.95
00690943 The Goo Goo Dolls – Greatest Hits Volume 1: The Singles $22.95
00701764 Guitar Tab White Pages – Play-Along $39.99
00694854 Buddy Guy – Damn Right, I've Got the Blues $19.95

00690840 Ben Harper – Both Sides of the Gun $19.95
00694798 George Harrison – Anthology $19.95
00690841 Scott Henderson – Blues Guitar Collection $19.95
00692930 Jimi Hendrix – Are You Experienced? $24.95
00692931 Jimi Hendrix – Axis: Bold As Love $22.95
00692932 Jimi Hendrix – Electric Ladyland $24.95
00690017 Jimi Hendrix – Live at Woodstock $24.95
00690602 Jimi Hendrix – Smash Hits $24.99
00690793 John Lee Hooker Anthology $24.99
00690692 Billy Idol – Very Best of $19.95
00690688 Incubus – A Crow Left of the Murder $19.95
00690544 Incubus – Morningview $19.95
00690790 Iron Maiden Anthology $24.99
00690721 Jet – Get Born $19.95
00690684 Jethro Tull – Aqualung $19.95
00690959 John5 – Requiem $22.95
00690814 John5 – Songs for Sanity $19.95
00690751 John5 – Vertigo $19.95
00690845 Eric Johnson – Bloom $19.95
00690846 Jack Johnson and Friends – Sing-A-Longs and Lullabies for the Film Curious George $19.95
00690271 Robert Johnson – New Transcriptions $24.95
00699131 Janis Joplin – Best of $19.95
00690427 Judas Priest – Best of $22.99
00690742 The Killers – Hot Fuss $19.95
00690975 Kings of Leon – Only by the Night $22.99
00694903 Kiss – Best of $24.95
00690355 Kiss – Destroyer $16.95
00690834 Lamb of God – Ashes of the Wake $19.95
00690875 Lamb of God – Sacrament $19.95
00690823 Ray LaMontagne – Trouble $19.95
00690679 John Lennon – Guitar Collection $19.95
00690781 Linkin Park – Hybrid Theory $22.95
00690743 Los Lonely Boys $19.95
00690720 Lostprophets – Start Something $19.95
00690955 Lynyrd Skynyrd – All-Time Greatest Hits $19.99
00694954 Lynyrd Skynyrd – New Best of $19.95
00690754 Marilyn Manson – Lest We Forget $19.95
00694956 Bob Marley– Legend $19.95
00694945 Bob Marley– Songs of Freedom $24.95
00690657 Maroon5 – Songs About Jane $19.95
00120080 Don McLean – Songbook $19.95
00694951 Megadeth – Rust in Peace $22.95
00690951 Megadeth – United Abominations $22.99
00690505 John Mellencamp – Guitar Collection $19.95
00690646 Pat Metheny – One Quiet Night $19.95
00690558 Pat Metheny – Trio: 99>00 .... $19.95
00690040 Steve Miller Band – Young Hearts $19.95
00694883 Nirvana – Nevermind $19.95
00690026 Nirvana – Unplugged in New York $19.95
00690807 The Offspring – Greatest Hits $19.95
00694847 Ozzy Osbourne – Best of $22.95
00690399 Ozzy Osbourne – Ozzman Cometh $22.99
00690933 Best of Brad Paisley $22.95
00690995 Brad Paisley – Play: The Guitar Album $24.99
00690866 Panic! At the Disco – A Fever You Can't Sweat Out $19.95
00690938 Christopher Parkening – Duets & Concertos $24.99
00694855 Pearl Jam – Ten $19.95
00690439 A Perfect Circle – Mer De Noms $19.95
00690499 Tom Petty – Definitive Guitar Collection $19.95
00690428 Pink Floyd – Dark Side of the Moon $19.95
00690789 Poison – Best of $19.95
00693864 The Police – Best of $19.95

00694975 Queen – Greatest Hits $24.95
00690670 Queensryche – Very Best of $19.95
00690878 The Raconteurs – Broken Boy Soldiers $19.95
00694910 Rage Against the Machine $19.95
00690055 Red Hot Chili Peppers – Blood Sugar Sex Magik $19.95
00690584 Red Hot Chili Peppers – By the Way $19.95
00690852 Red Hot Chili Peppers –Stadium Arcadium $24.95
00690511 Django Reinhardt – Definitive Collection $19.95
00690779 Relient K – MMHMM $19.95
00690631 Rolling Stones – Guitar Anthology $27.95
00694976 Rolling Stones – Some Girls $22.95
00690264 The Rolling Stones – Tattoo You $19.95
00690685 David Lee Roth – Eat 'Em and Smile $19.95
00690942 David Lee Roth and the Songs of Van Halen $19.95
00690031 Santana's Greatest Hits $19.95
00690566 Scorpions – Best of $22.95
00690604 Bob Seger – Guitar Collection $19.95
00690803 Kenny Wayne Shepherd Band – Best of $19.95
00690968 Shinedown – The Sound of Madness $22.99
00690813 Slayer – Guitar Collection $19.95
00690733 Slipknot – Vol. 3 (The Subliminal Verses) $22.99
00120004 Steely Dan – Best of $24.95
00694921 Steppenwolf – Best of $22.95
00690655 Mike Stern – Best of $19.95
00690877 Stone Sour – Come What(ever) May $19.95
00690520 Styx Guitar Collection $19.95
00120081 Sublime $19.95
00120122 Sublime – 40oz. to Freedom $19.95
00690929 Sum 41 – Underclass Hero $19.95
00690767 Switchfoot – The Beautiful Letdown $19.95
00690993 Taylor Swift – Fearless $22.99
00690830 System of a Down – Hypnotize $19.95
00690799 System of a Down – Mezmerize $19.95
00690531 System of a Down – Toxicity $19.95
00694824 James Taylor – Best of $16.95
00690871 Three Days Grace – One-X $19.95
00690737 3 Doors Down – The Better Life $22.95
00690683 Robin Trower – Bridge of Sighs $19.95
00699191 U2 – Best of: 1980-1990 .... $19.95
00690732 U2 – Best of: 1990-2000 .... $19.95
00660137 Steve Vai – Passion & Warfare $24.95
00690116 Stevie Ray Vaughan – Guitar Collection $24.95
00660058 Stevie Ray Vaughan – Lightnin' Blues 1983-1987 .... $24.95
00694835 Stevie Ray Vaughan – The Sky Is Crying $22.95
00690015 Stevie Ray Vaughan – Texas Flood $19.95
00690772 Velvet Revolver – Contraband $22.95
00690071 Weezer (The Blue Album) $19.95
00690966 Weezer – (Red Album) $19.99
00690447 The Who – Best of $24.95
00690916 The Best of Dwight Yoakam $19.95
00690905 Neil Young – Rust Never Sleeps $19.99
00690623 Frank Zappa – Over-Nite Sensation $22.99
00690589 ZZ Top Guitar Anthology $24.95

Prices and availability subject to change without notice. Some products may not be available outside the U.S.A.

0211

This series will help you play your favorite songs quickly and easily. Just follow the tab and listen to the CD to hear how the guitar should sound, and then play along using the separate backing tracks. Mac or PC users can also slow down the tempo without changing pitch by using the CD in their computer. The melody and lyrics are included in the book so that you can sing or simply follow along.

INCLUDES TAB

Volume	Item / Price
VOL. 1 – ROCK	00699570 / $16.99
VOL. 2 – ACOUSTIC	00699569 / $16.95
VOL. 3 – HARD ROCK	00699573 / $16.95
VOL. 4 – POP/ROCK	00699571 / $16.99
VOL. 5 – MODERN ROCK	00699574 / $16.99
VOL. 6 – '90s ROCK	00699572 / $16.99
VOL. 7 – BLUES	00699575 / $16.95
VOL. 8 – ROCK	00699585 / $14.99
VOL. 9 – PUNK ROCK	00699576 / $14.95
VOL. 10 – ACOUSTIC	00699586 / $16.95
VOL. 11 – EARLY ROCK	00699579 / $14.95
VOL. 12 – POP/ROCK	00699587 / $14.95
VOL. 13 – FOLK ROCK	00699581 / $14.95
VOL. 14 – BLUES ROCK	00699582 / $16.95
VOL. 15 – R&B	00699583 / $14.95
VOL. 16 – JAZZ	00699584 / $15.95
VOL. 17 – COUNTRY	00699588 / $15.95
VOL. 18 – ACOUSTIC ROCK	00699577 / $15.95
VOL. 19 – SOUL	00699578 / $14.95
VOL. 20 – ROCKABILLY	00699580 / $14.95
VOL. 21 – YULETIDE	00699602 / $14.95
VOL. 22 – CHRISTMAS	00699600 / $15.95
VOL. 23 – SURF	00699635 / $14.95
VOL. 24 – ERIC CLAPTON	00699649 / $17.99
VOL. 25 – LENNON & McCARTNEY	00699642 / $16.99
VOL. 26 – ELVIS PRESLEY	00699643 / $14.95
VOL. 27 – DAVID LEE ROTH	00699645 / $16.95
VOL. 28 – GREG KOCH	00699646 / $14.95
VOL. 29 – BOB SEGER	00699647 / $14.95
VOL. 30 – KISS	00699644 / $16.99
VOL. 31 – CHRISTMAS HITS	00699652 / $14.95
VOL. 32 – THE OFFSPRING	00699653 / $14.95
VOL. 33 – ACOUSTIC CLASSICS	00699656 / $16.95
VOL. 34 – CLASSIC ROCK	00699658 / $16.95
VOL. 35 – HAIR METAL	00699660 / $16.95
VOL. 36 – SOUTHERN ROCK	00699661 / $16.95
VOL. 37 – ACOUSTIC METAL	00699662 / $16.95
VOL. 38 – BLUES	00699663 / $16.95
VOL. 39 – '80s METAL	00699664 / $16.99
VOL. 40 – INCUBUS	00699668 / $17.95
VOL. 41 – ERIC CLAPTON	00699669 / $16.95
VOL. 42 – 2000s ROCK	00699670 / $16.99
VOL. 43 – LYNYRD SKYNYRD	00699681 / $17.95
VOL. 44 – JAZZ	00699689 / $14.99
VOL. 45 – TV THEMES	00699718 / $14.95
VOL. 46 – MAINSTREAM ROCK	00699722 / $16.95
VOL. 47 – HENDRIX SMASH HITS	00699723 / $19.95
VOL. 48 – AEROSMITH CLASSICS	00699724 / $17.99
VOL. 49 – STEVIE RAY VAUGHAN	00699725 / $17.99
VOL. 50 – 2000s METAL	00699726 / $16.99
VOL. 51 – ALTERNATIVE '90s	00699727 / $12.95
VOL. 52 – FUNK	00699728 / $14.95
VOL. 53 – DISCO	00699729 / $14.99
VOL. 54 – HEAVY METAL	00699730 / $14.95
VOL. 55 – POP METAL	00699731 / $14.95
VOL. 56 – FOO FIGHTERS	00699749 / $14.95
VOL. 57 – SYSTEM OF A DOWN	00699751 / $14.95
VOL. 58 – BLINK-182	00699772 / $14.95
VOL. 60 – 3 DOORS DOWN	00699774 / $14.95
VOL. 61 – SLIPKNOT	00699775 / $14.95
VOL. 62 – CHRISTMAS CAROLS	00699798 / $12.95
VOL. 63 – CREEDENCE CLEARWATER REVIVAL	00699802 / $16.99
VOL. 64 – THE ULTIMATE OZZY OSBOURNE	00699803 / $16.99
VOL. 65 – THE DOORS	00699806 / $16.99
VOL. 66 – THE ROLLING STONES	00699807 / $16.95
VOL. 67 – BLACK SABBATH	00699808 / $16.99
VOL. 68 – PINK FLOYD – DARK SIDE OF THE MOON	00699809 / $16.99
VOL. 69 – ACOUSTIC FAVORITES	00699810 / $14.95
VOL. 70 – OZZY OSBOURNE	00699805 / $16.99
VOL. 71 – CHRISTIAN ROCK	00699824 / $14.95
VOL. 72 – ACOUSTIC '90S	00699827 / $14.95
VOL. 73 – BLUESY ROCK	00699829 / $16.99
VOL. 74 – PAUL BALOCHE	00699831 / $14.95
VOL. 75 – TOM PETTY	00699882 / $16.99
VOL. 76 – COUNTRY HITS	00699884 / $14.95
VOL. 77 – BLUEGRASS	00699910 / $12.99
VOL. 78 – NIRVANA	00700132 / $16.99
VOL. 80 – ACOUSTIC ANTHOLOGY	00700175 / $19.95
VOL. 81 – ROCK ANTHOLOGY	00700176 / $22.99
VOL. 82 – EASY SONGS	00700177 / $12.99
VOL. 83 – THREE CHORD SONGS	00700178 / $16.99
VOL. 84 – STEELY DAN	00700200 / $16.99
VOL. 85 – THE POLICE	00700269 /$16.99
VOL. 86 – BOSTON	00700465 / $16.99
VOL. 87 – ACOUSTIC WOMEN	00700763 / $14.99
VOL. 88 – GRUNGE	00700467 / $16.99
VOL. 91 – BLUES INSTRUMENTALS	00700505 / $14.99
VOL. 92 – EARLY ROCK INSTRUMENTALS	00700506 / $12.99
VOL. 93 – ROCK INSTRUMENTALS	00700507 / $16.99
VOL. 96 – THIRD DAY	00700560 / $14.95
VOL. 97 – ROCK BAND	00700703 / $14.99
VOL. 98 – ROCK BAND	00700704 / $14.95
VOL. 99 – ZZ TOP	00700762 / $16.99
VOL. 100 – B.B. KING	00700466 / $16.99
VOL. 102 – CLASSIC PUNK	00700769 / $14.99
VOL. 103 – SWITCHFOOT	00700773 / $16.99
VOL. 104 – DUANE ALLMAN	00700846 / $16.99
VOL. 106 – WEEZER	00700958 / $14.99
VOL. 107 – CREAM	00701069 / $16.99
VOL. 108 – THE WHO	00701053 / $16.99
VOL. 109 – STEVE MILLER	00701054 / $14.99
VOL. 111 – JOHN MELLENCAMP	00701056 / $14.99
VOL. 113 – JIM CROCE	00701058 / $14.99
VOL. 114 – BON JOVI	00701060 / $14.99
VOL. 115 – JOHNNY CASH	00701070 / $16.99
VOL. 116 – THE VENTURES	00701124 / $14.99
VOL. 119 – AC/DC CLASSICS	00701356 / $17.99
VOL. 120 – PROGRESSIVE ROCK	00701457 / $14.99
VOL. 122 – CROSBY, STILLS & NASH	00701610 / $16.99
VOL. 123 – LENNON & MCCARTNEY ACOUSTIC	00701614 / $16.99
VOL. 124 – MODERN WORSHIP	00701629 / $14.99
VOL. 127 – 1970s ROCK	00701739 / $14.99
VOL. 128 – 1960s ROCK	00701740 / $14.99
VOL. 129 – MEGADETH	00701741 / $14.99
VOL. 130 – IRON MAIDEN	00701742 / $14.99
VOL. 131 – 1990s ROCK	00701743 / $14.99
VOL. 133 – TAYLOR SWIFT	00701894 / $16.99

Complete song lists available online.

Prices, contents, and availability subject to change without notice.

FOR MORE INFORMATION, SEE YOUR LOCAL MUSIC DEALER, OR WRITE TO:

7777 W. BLUEMOUND RD. P.O. BOX 13819 MILWAUKEE, WI 53213

Visit Hal Leonard online at www.halleonard.com

0311